Legal Accounting

Jacqueline Asselin

Sophia Dunkley

Toronto, Canada
2016

Student working papers available at <http://emond.ca/legal-accounting>.

Emond Montgomery Publications Limited
60 Shaftesbury Avenue
Toronto ON M4T 1A3
http://www.emond.ca/highered

Printed in Canada.
Reprinted July 2018.

We acknowledge the financial support of the Government of Canada. *Nous reconnaissons l'appui financier du gouvernement du Canada.* Canada

Vice-president, publishing: Anthony Rezek
Acquisitions editor: Lindsay Sutherland
Managing editor, development: Kelly Dickson
Developmental editor: Ann Macauley
Director, editorial and production: Jim Lyons
Production editor and coordinator: Laura Bast
Copy editor: Francine Geraci
Permissions editor: Monika Schurmann
Proofreader: David Handelsman
Text designer: Shani Sohn
Cover designer: Tara Wells
Indexer: Paula Pike
Cover image: LiliGraphie/Shutterstock.com

Library and Archives Canada Cataloguing in Publication

Asselin, Jacqueline, author
    Legal accounting / Jacqueline Asselin, Sophia Dunkley.

Includes index.
ISBN 978-1-55239-617-9 (paperback)

    1. Lawyers--Ontario--Accounting--Textbooks.   2. Legal assistants--Ontario.   I. Dunkley, Sophia, author   II. Title.

HF5686.L35A88 2016   657'.834   C2015-903867-7

To Allan
—JA

To my family, K.M. and Z.M.
—SD

Contents

4   Posting and Preparing Financial Statements 65

7 Adjusting Accounts for Financial Statements 155

10   Accounting for GST/HST, Payroll, and Income Tax 247

11 Computerized Time and Money Management 271

Preface

The idea of learning legal accounting can be intimidating—all that math! As instructors, we often tell our students that we are not doing math, just some simple arithmetic.

Legal Accounting introduces students and legal professionals to basic accounting concepts so that they will gain an understanding of what bookkeeping and record-keeping are all about. It is important for licensed paralegals to understand the bylaws and requirements of the Law Society of Upper Canada (LSUC) as they relate to record-keeping in a law firm. An understanding of these requirements is also useful for law clerks, who often see the financial dimensions of client files.

The primary goals of this text are:

- to explain the LSUC's bookkeeping and record-keeping requirements as found in the *Law Society Act*, LSUC bylaws, and the *Paralegal Rules of Conduct*;
- to explore the common bookkeeping issues that arise in a legal services firm;
- to demonstrate how to analyze and record transactions, prepare various adjusting entries, and identify the steps in the financial cycle;
- to explain the basics of financial accounting so that students can create, read, and understand simple financial statements;
- to provide insight into the financial, banking, and tax reporting aspects of a legal services firm; and
- to demonstrate how stakeholders use financial statements in decision-making.

The text uses the example of Justin Case, a paralegal who opens his own firm, to show how to create records at the start of the business and maintain them through the accounting cycle. The firm's books are opened with Justin's initial investment in the firm and continue through the accounting cycle to the preparation of financial reports and closing accounts to start the new year. The examples demonstrate how to comply with LSUC bylaws, especially those with respect to accounting for trust funds received from clients.

The text explains the process of double-entry bookkeeping, and how to record debits and credits, so that students will be able to summarize business transactions in a manner acceptable to the Law Society and meet requirements under the *Income Tax Act*.

The text also explores legal accounting software and shows how it can be used to manage client files, record transactions, and prepare reports.

The skills taught in this text are transferable, so students who start their own business, in any area, will know how to record and interpret financial information.

The text provides general advice regarding common bookkeeping issues; it does not cover every possible situation that can arise in a firm. If you have questions about the bylaws, you can call the Law Society Practice Management Helpline at 416-947-3315 or toll-free in Ontario at 1-800-668-7380, ext. 3315. You can also check the Law Society's website at <www.lsuc.on.ca>. If you have specific bookkeeping, accounting, or tax questions, we suggest that you consult an accountant, financial adviser, or lawyer who practises in these areas.

Chapter Features

Learning Outcomes

To guide the learning process, the learning outcomes at the beginning of each chapter identify the concepts being covered in the chapter.

Chapter Summary

The chapter summary explains why the information presented in the chapter is important. It provides examples of how the information can be applied and how pitfalls can be avoided.

Key Terms

Key terms are boldfaced throughout the chapter. Detailed definitions of all key terms are included in the glossary at the end of the text.

Put It into Practice

Case examples featuring Ann Litigate's paralegal practice are used to demonstrate chapter concepts. Through these examples, instructors can generate discussion and ensure that students have grasped the material presented in the chapter.

Practice Exercises

True-or-false questions allow students to test their knowledge of what has been covered in the chapter and help them focus on important concepts. Short-answer questions require students to apply what they have learned. Accounting is best learned by doing; the longer exercises at the end of the chapter give students an opportunity to put theory into practice.

Acknowledgments

We wish to thank Justin Park, accountant, for his thorough review of the contents for accuracy. We also wish to thank the reviewers of the text for their valuable feedback:

Peggy Hinan, Durham College
Patricia Knight, Sheridan College Institute of Technology and Advanced Learning
Trudie E. Robertson, Robertson Paralegal Professional Corporation
Tammy Storring, George Brown College; FMT Law

We would also like to thank the Emond Publishing team—Lindsay Sutherland, Kelly Dickson, Ann Macaulay, Laura Bast, and the team members behind the scenes—for their full support at all stages of the project.

Jacqueline Asselin, B Admin, LLB, thanks her husband, Allan, for his patience and support, and her co-author, for the practical experience she brought to the project. Jacqueline also thanks her students, in particular Micheline Plante, who used the pre-publication version of the text and offered suggestions for improvement.

Sophia Dunkley, BA (Hons), LLB, thanks her family, K.M. and Z.M., for their support and encouragement, and her co-author for her productive and inspiring collaboration.

1 Role of the Law Society of Upper Canada

After reading this chapter, you should be able to:

- describe the Law Society of Upper Canada's rules of conduct for lawyers and paralegals
- explain the requirements in bylaw 9 of the Law Society dealing with financial transactions and records
- define various forms of business organization
- describe the ethical and professional responsibilities of paralegals as they pertain to maintenance of books and records in the management of a legal services firm

The Law Society of Upper Canada (LSUC) regulates the Ontario legal profession to ensure that legal professionals conduct themselves in a competent and ethical manner pursuant to the *Law Society Act*[1] and regulations made under the Act. **Licensees**—paralegals and lawyers who are licensed to practise by the Law Society—must meet the professional and ethical obligations imposed by the Law Society. Infractions can result in disciplinary action, including but not limited to suspension of the licensee's privileges.

Requirement for Books and Records in Legal Firms

The LSUC requires licensees to keep books and records that reflect the financial activities carried out by them. Licensees have the added duty to maintain accurate records of all their financial activities because of the duty owed by them to their clients.

The LSUC's record-keeping requirements are set out in part V of its bylaw 9.[2] Every licensee is required to maintain financial records to track all money and other property received and disbursed in connection with the licensee's professional business. The goal of this course is to assist paralegals in understanding the type of financial records required to meet their obligations and to learn how to keep the necessary records. The focus is on a small practice; examples of transactions a licensee is likely to encounter will be used for demonstration purposes. Law clerks who perform their duties under the supervision of a lawyer should also be aware of record-keeping requirements to assist the lawyer or law firm in meeting the LSUC's obligations.

A paralegal who is not confident of being able to do his or her own accounting will want to hire a **bookkeeper** to maintain the firm's books and records. Bookkeepers record day-to-day transactions in the appropriate journals. Samples of these tasks include entering bills from vendors, paying bills, processing payroll data, preparing invoices to clients, and recording receipts and payments from clients. The bookkeeper records entries in the proper journals and summarizes the entries using general and trust ledgers. A bookkeeper will usually bring the books to the trial balance stage of the accounting process.

Chartered professional **accountants**, who have a university degree, take over where the bookkeeper leaves off. They prepare adjusting entries to correct the balances in accounts to reflect items such as prepaid expenses and depreciation. Once the adjusting entries are completed, the accountant prepares the firm's financial statements, which include the income statement, statement of owner's equity, and balance sheet. These statements are required for income tax purposes, and the accountant is usually asked to complete the tax returns for the firm. An accountant will ensure that the firm's financial records reflect professional standards.

---

1 *Law Society Act*, RSO 1990, c L.8.

2 Made under s 62(0.1), para 6 of the *Law Society Act, ibid.*

Why do you need to learn **bookkeeping** if bookkeepers and accountants are able to do the job for you? Ultimately, you are the one responsible to ensure that the persons you hire maintain the records in an acceptable manner. This course will introduce you to the essentials of legal accounting and explain why and how you need to keep books and records that conform to the requirements of the Law Society of Upper Canada.

Other reasons to know basic bookkeeping and accounting principles:

- As a business owner, it is in your best interest to be able to analyze financial information for the purpose of making financial decisions in your own practice.
- As a paralegal, you might have to understand a client's financial records in the course of litigation when financial statements are relevant to the case.
- As a community volunteer, you may become a member of a board of directors and be presented with financial statements for review and approval by the board.

The following organizations require that you maintain proper records:

- The Canada Revenue Agency (CRA) requires the filing of income tax, payroll, and GST/HST remittances.
- The Law Society of Upper Canada requires the filing of annual reports and performs audits to ensure that records are correct and, in particular, that all trust funds are properly accounted for.
- The **Law Foundation of Ontario** requires the filing of an annual report.

Forms of Business Organization in Legal Services Firms

Bylaw 7 of the LSUC sets out several ways lawyers and paralegals in Ontario may carry on the practice of law and provision of legal services, respectively. The form of business organization used is often determined by income tax implications as well as bookkeeping issues.

Basic forms of business organization include sole proprietorships, partnerships, limited liability partnerships, multi-discipline practices or affiliations, and professional corporations. The various modes of practice are set out in more detail on the LSUC's website[3] and should be referred to as needed.

Sole Proprietorship

A **sole proprietorship** is a business carried on by an individual who is the owner. The sole proprietor usually makes all management decisions and is personally responsible for all the debts of the business. Many small firms are sole proprietorships. The owner pays personal income taxes on the profit made by the firm. When net profits reach higher levels, there may be tax advantages in switching to a corporate form of ownership.

Partnership

A **partnership** is a business carried on by one or more individuals as owners. Two or more persons may find it worthwhile to combine their talents and money to form a partnership. They may own the business in equal or unequal shares, and their shares of the profits or losses in the business are usually proportionate to their capital investment in the business. All the partners

---

3   Law Society of Upper Canada, *Business Structures*, online: <http://www.lsuc.on.ca/For-Lawyers/Manage-Your-Practice/Practice-Arrangements/Business-Structures>.

are equally liable for all the debts of the business. General partnerships have unlimited personal liability for business debts. The net income or loss of the business is allocated to the members of the partnership, who then pay personal income taxes on their share of the profits.

Limited Liability Partnership

A **limited liability partnership** is one in which partners have limited personal liability for the debts of the business, and no partner is responsible or liable for other partners' misconduct or negligence. The name of the limited liability partnership must be registered under the *Business Names Act*,[4] and the name must include the words "limited liability partnership" or "société à responsabilité limitée," or the abbreviations "LLP," "L.L.P.," or "s.r.l." as the last words or letters of the firm's name.

Multi-Discipline Practice/Affiliation

In a **multi-discipline practice (MDP)** or **affiliation**, lawyers and licensed paralegals work with other professionals—such as accountants, tax consultants, trademark and patent agents, or others—who support or supplement their practice of law or provision of legal services. When a licensee and another professional enter into a formal partnership agreement, it is considered a multi-discipline partnership, which must be approved by the Law Society by application. Licensees are responsible for the actions of professional partners and must maintain professional liability insurance for all professional partners.

Professional Corporation

In a **professional corporation**, lawyers or licensed paralegals carry on the practice of law or the provision of legal services through an incorporated entity. Corporations operate under a government charter and are owned by shareholders. All the shareholders of a professional corporation must be lawyers or licensed paralegals who are entitled to practise law in Ontario. Incorporation does not affect the professional liability of the shareholders, and they are jointly and severally liable with the corporation for all professional liability claims against the company.

Lawyers and licensed paralegals may not practise law or provide legal services through a professional corporation until the company has received a certificate of authorization from the LSUC. Certain tax advantages can be gained by incorporating because the corporation is taxed separately on its profits at corporate taxation rates, which are lower than the personal tax rate after a certain level of income is achieved.

TAX TIP

Taxation Legislation

Canada first collected federal income tax in 1917, at which time it was supposed to be a temporary tax to fund the First World War. This temporary measure evolved into the Canada Revenue Agency in 1927 and has become the largest form of income available to the Canadian government. The CRA administers the tax laws for the government of Canada, including the administration and enforcement of the *Income Tax Act*,[5] and for most provinces and territories. Income tax is collected from individuals and businesses by the CRA for the federal government and the provinces and territories. The Canadian tax system is also based

---

4 *Business Names Act*, RSO 1990, c B.17.
5 *Income Tax Act*, RSC 1985, c 1 (5th Supp), as amended.

on self-assessment, which places the responsibility on Canadian residents to ensure they have paid their taxes according to the requirements of the *Income Tax Act*.

Unincorporated Practices

Sole Proprietorships

The income or loss of a sole proprietorship must be included on the personal tax return of the sole proprietor for the year in which the income was earned. The net profit is taxed at the same rates that apply to individuals. These rates are progressive and increase with income. Sole proprietors are also required to make Canada Pension Plan (CPP) payments on self-employed earnings when their personal income tax return is filed each year. Any person claiming an income tax refund, an HST credit, or the Canada child tax benefit must file a return. Provincial tax credits may also be available. A sole proprietor may be required by the CRA to pay income tax by installments. Financial statements for the licensee's practice must be included with the personal tax return.

Partnerships

The income or loss of the business carried on in partnership is determined at the partnership level and then allocated to the partners in accordance with their share, usually based on the terms of a partnership agreement. A partnership by itself does not pay income tax on its operating results and does not file an annual income tax return. Instead, each partner includes a share of the partnership income (or loss) on his or her personal tax return. The share of the income earned is taxed whether or not it has actually been received from the partnership's capital account. Each partner must file a copy of the financial statements of the partnership with his or her return. The partnership may also be required to register for and collect GST/HST.

Expenditures, capital cost allowance, and other deductions are subtracted from the income of the partnership to determine whether the business has a net income or loss. The resulting income or loss is divided among the partners, prorated to each partner's contribution or as otherwise stipulated in the partnership agreement. Each partner's share of the income or loss is then included in the calculation of that partner's individual income from all sources for tax purposes.

If the partner is an individual, he or she is taxed at the rate applicable to individuals under the *Income Tax Act*, as is a sole proprietor. Like the sole proprietor, a partner must aggregate his or her share of net income or loss with income or losses from all other sources.

Incorporated Practices

A professional corporation is a separate legal entity that is separately taxed on its profits at corporate taxation rates and can select its fiscal year-end for tax planning purposes.

A corporation may have some of the following features:

- It has a perpetual existence.
- It can generally raise larger amounts of capital more easily than a sole proprietorship or partnership.
- The shareholders cannot personally claim any loss the corporation sustains.

When forming a corporation, the owners transfer money, property, or services to the corporation in exchange for shares. The owners are referred to as shareholders. Shares can be bought and sold without affecting the corporation's existence. A corporation continues to exist unless it winds up, amalgamates, or surrenders its charter for reasons such as bankruptcy. Because a corporation has a separate legal existence, it must pay tax on its income, and therefore must file its own income tax return. The corporation may also be required to register for and collect GST/HST.

A corporation must file a corporation income tax return (T2) within six months of the end of every tax year, even if it does not owe taxes. It also has to attach complete financial statements and the necessary schedules to the T2 return. A corporation usually pays its taxes in monthly or quarterly installments.

A licensee who incorporates will receive a salary or take dividends from the corporation as payment for his or her services. These payments will be included on the licensee's individual tax return. An accountant should be consulted to determine whether there is an advantage to incorporating to take advantage of the lower corporate tax rates.

Insurance Requirements

Licensees who provide legal services to the public must carry professional liability insurance in accordance with the Law Society's bylaw 6, part II, section 12. A policy limit for each single claim of not less than $1 million and an aggregate policy limit for all claims of not less than $2 million per year are required. In the case of a limited liability partnership, coverage must be maintained for each partner in the amount required for individual licensees. Some exemptions are allowed, such as when a paralegal is working under the supervision of a lawyer who has professional liability insurance through the LSUC and the paralegal is covered under the lawyer's policy. Licensees must provide written proof of compliance with their insurance requirements before they begin providing legal services and annually thereafter.

Importance of Maintaining Proper Records

In addition to keeping books and records that reflect their financial activities, lawyers and paralegals have an added obligation to maintain accurate records because they hold funds in trust for their clients. The Law Society regulates the Ontario legal profession to ensure that paralegals and lawyers conduct themselves in a competent and ethical manner pursuant to the *Law Society Act* and regulations made under the Act. The LSUC has the role of protecting the public. One way the Law Society fulfills this responsibility is by auditing the records kept by law firms. Licensees who fail to meet the professional and ethical obligations imposed by the LSUC are subject to its complaints process, which can result in disciplinary action including suspension of their privileges.

Failure to maintain proper records can result in errors and an inability to meet financial obligations as they come due. For example:

- Failure to record accounts payable as bills are received results in an overstatement of your income and may result in an inability to pay bills when they are due.
- Failure to stay on top of accounts receivable may result in insufficient funds in your general bank account, resulting in an inability to pay your operating expenses.
- Failure to track trust receipts and disbursements in the correct client ledger could result in errors, with a trust account getting overdrawn for a particular client.
- Failure to maintain trust records can result in an inability to meet obligations incurred on a client's behalf and to account to clients for any funds received on their behalf.
- Failure to track income and expenses and properly report to the Canada Revenue Agency may result in assessments and/or audits, with severe penalties and interest being charged if taxes were not properly remitted.
- Inability to know where the firm stands financially impairs good management decision-making regarding day-to-day operations, expansion, addition of staff, and other such matters.
- Failure to maintain financial statements may result in lenders refusing your applications for loans or lines of credit because lenders require financial statements in order to assess interest rates imposed on loans and qualification for loans.
- The LSUC conducts regular audits of licensees. Failure to maintain up-to-date trust records can result in suspension or other action by the Law Society.

Retainers

A **retainer** is an agreement between a client and a legal services provider for the engagement of legal services. The form of retainer can vary and be customized for each situation. Because clients can believe that they have retained the legal services provider based on an oral conversation, it is important to observe client identification protocols and to document any conversation in writing.

It is a good practice to get monetary retainers from clients to ensure that you will not have difficulty getting paid once work has started or a task is completed. The cash flow in an office is important, and having to worry about paying bills can interfere with your ability to focus on providing excellent service to clients.

Firms usually require that clients provide a **monetary retainer** when the paralegal–client relationship is entered into. This is usually obtained when the client signs a retainer agreement, with the firm setting out the scope of the work to be performed and the hourly rate that will be charged by the paralegal primarily responsible for the file, as well as the rate charged by other persons who will work on it. The retainer agreement should also set out the firm's billing policies.

The money received from the client must be deposited into the firm's mixed trust account (described below) by the end of the next banking day after funds are received. Money includes by definition cash, cheques, drafts, credit card sales slips, post office orders, and express and bank money orders.

A **general monetary retainer**, which is described in section 8(2)1 of the LSUC's bylaw 9, does not need to be deposited into the trust account. This is money received for which the paralegal is not required either to account to the client or to provide services. A general retainer should be evidenced by a written agreement with the client. As an example, it might be used when a paralegal is asked to do all collections for a client at a fixed monthly rate and the firm agrees to do all the collections and will be paid whether or not the client submits any claims in a particular period. This type of retainer is not common in small practices and is carefully scrutinized by the Law Society.

Bank Accounts in a Legal Services Firm

At the very least, most law firms have one general bank account and one mixed trust account. It is important to understand which transactions require use of the trust bank account and which the use of the general bank account. You are not allowed to mix trust funds, which are funds that belong to the client, with general firm funds, which are funds that belong to the firm.

General Bank Account

Just as individuals have a bank account that they use for their day-to-day deposits and cheque writing, a business must have a **general bank account** for making deposits and for payment of bills. The general bank account will be opened in the name of the firm. If the firm is a sole proprietorship, the bank account will be in the name of the owner. Corporations will open such accounts in the name of the corporation. The types of funds that will be deposited into the general bank account include

- funds that belong to the firm and not to clients,
- funds invested into the firm by the owner,
- funds received by the firm for payment on bills sent to the client, and
- other receipts, such as interest income and miscellaneous income.

Regardless of the accounting system being used, care must be taken to ensure that the correct bank account is used when making deposits and writing cheques. Firms usually use cheques of a different colour for their general and trust bank accounts so there is a visual cue for the person writing a cheque.

Mixed or Pooled Trust Bank Account

A **mixed** or **pooled trust bank account** is a bank account into which money received from clients for certain purposes is deposited. This account is called "mixed" or "pooled" because the firm opens one bank account into which money for many clients will be deposited. The funds must be deposited into the mixed trust account because the money does not belong to the firm. It belongs to the client and is to be used for specific purposes (for example, to pay court fees on behalf of the client or to be applied to a bill sent to the client). How will you know what amount belongs to which client? A separate client ledger must be kept for each client, so you always know how much money you have in the trust account for each one.

EXAMPLE

The table in Figure 1.1 illustrates a list of funds in the trust account that are pooled. Why a record is required for the amount held for each client is explained below.

Justin Case is a paralegal who has three clients. He has received a retainer from each client and has made payments out of the mixed trust account for some clients. The bank balance for the mixed trust account is $5,950. Justin needs to know that he has $250 left in trust for Client A, $700 for Client B, and $5,000 for Client C. The best way to track this information is to have a separate client trust ledger sheet for each individual client that shows all the transactions for each client with a running balance at all times.[6]

If Justin did not have proper records and wrote another cheque in the amount of $300 from the trust account to pay for a disbursement on behalf of Client A, the trust ledger account for Client A would be overdrawn by $50 ($250 less $300). However, the cheque would still go through the bank because there was $5,950 in the pooled account before the $300 cheque was written. Errors like this must be reported to the Law Society when submitting the annual report with an explanation as to why the error occurred.

The financial records required to be maintained for trust accounts must be entered in the account journal and **posted** in each client's ledger so as to be current at all times.

The LSUC's *Rules of Professional Conduct*[7] dictate that trust accounts are to be used only for clients' money. If you do not receive retainers from clients, you may not need to open a trust account. Trust accounts can never be used for the personal or office use of the business owner.

Justin knew he would have to send a cheque to the CRA every quarter to remit the HST he collected. So he deposited money in the trust account to cover the potential HST he would have to pay. However, LSUC rules dictate that this action is not allowed for the purpose of remitting HST at the end of each quarter. HST funds must be accumulated in the firm's general bank account.

Client	Receipts	Payments	Balance
Client A	300	50	250
Client B	800	100	700
Client C	5,000	0	5,000
Totals	6,100	150	5,950

FIGURE 1.1 Summary of clients and balance held in trust

Overdraft in Trust Account

It is a good practice to place a hold on trust funds received from clients (unless paid in cash, money order, or other certified instrument) to make sure the funds clear the client's bank

---

6   Bylaw 9, s 22(1).

7   Law Society of Upper Canada, *Rules of Professional Conduct*, online: <http://www.lsuc.on.ca/lawyer-conduct-rules>.

account. You should confirm with your financial institution how many days it takes a cheque to clear. If a cheque from a client is returned by the bank for insufficient funds (NSF), and the licensee has written a cheque against that amount, the trust ledger for that client will be overdrawn. In addition, bank charges may be taken out of the trust account because of the NSF transaction. You should direct your bank to charge any service fees against the trust account to the firm's general account instead.

Paralegals are personally responsible to ensure that any overdraft in a client's trust account is corrected as soon as an error is discovered. This can be done by having the client bring in funds to deposit into the account, or by the paralegal personally putting funds into the trust bank account to make up for the deficiency.

With experience, you will develop an instinct for knowing which funds should go into the mixed trust account and which funds should go into the general bank account. If you are unsure, refer to bylaw 9 to determine whether or not the funds belong in the trust account. The table in Figure 1.2 shows which bank account must be used for different types of deposits.

Mixed Trust Account	General Account
Funds that must be deposited to the trust account:	Funds that must be deposited to the general account:
• money received on behalf of the client • money received for future disbursements • money received for future or unbilled legal services • an overpayment of billed services—the excess payment must be either returned to the client or held in the trust account if the client instructs you to do so	• money paid on account of a bill previously sent to the client • reimbursement for proper expenses paid on behalf of the client • lawyer/paralegal's or firm's money • general money retainer

FIGURE 1.2   Accounts for depositing funds

Separate Interest-Bearing Trust Account

Another type of trust account can be set up to hold funds for only one client. This may be done on the client's written instructions when a large amount is to be held in trust for an extended period of time. For example, if a client deposits $20,000 with a firm to hold until a case settles, and it is anticipated that the case may go on for an extended period, the client may want the interest on the account to accrue to herself. If a client wants interest on the trust funds that you hold for her, you must obtain her written instructions to deposit such funds into a **separate interest-bearing trust account**—for example, a GIC, term deposit, or passbook account—in your firm's name in trust for that client.[8]

Opening a separate interest-bearing account for a client requires additional paperwork and bookkeeping for the paralegal and is not usually done unless the return on investment is significant. Bank charges on this account would be charged to the account and noted as a disbursement to the client.

Separate interest-bearing trust accounts must be reconciled and included in the monthly trust comparison.[9] If a client instructs you to put his funds in an interest-bearing account, you may require some additional information from him, such as his social insurance number or corporate number, if applicable, as well as how the interest is to be allocated for income tax purposes. This is especially important when the funds being held are in dispute.

8   Bylaw 9, s 8(1).

9   Bylaw 9, s 18(8).

Financial Institutions for Mixed Trust Accounts

The following institutions are approved for opening a mixed trust account for all client funds, or a separate account for one client:

- Chartered bank
- Provincial savings office
- Credit union
- A league to which the *Credit Unions and Caisses Populaires Act, 1994*[10] applies
- Registered trust corporation

The institution in which the account is opened must have an agreement with the Law Foundation of Ontario for the payment of interest on mixed trust accounts. The institution must also provide monthly bank statements and the original or copies of the front and back of returned cheques, including certified cheques. Any time a mixed trust account is opened, the Law Foundation of Ontario must be notified by sending a letter to the Foundation (Form 2: Report on Opening a Mixed Trust Account, available on the Law Foundation of Ontario's website).

TAX TIP

Registering for GST/HST

If you are just starting a business, you will probably be a **small supplier**, exempt from collecting GST/HST. You are deemed to be a small supplier if your total annual revenues from taxable supplies (before expenses) from all of your businesses are $30,000 or less. Once your annual revenues exceed the $30,000 threshold, you must register and start collecting GST/HST.

You can register voluntarily before you have reached the $30,000 threshold, and may want to do so in order to recover the GST/HST you pay when starting up your business. Once you have registered, you will be required to charge, collect, and remit GST/HST on all invoices sent to clients and to file returns. You have to stay registered for at least one year before you can ask to cancel your registration. If you are a small business and choose not to register voluntarily, you cannot collect GST/HST from your clients and cannot claim back the income tax credits you pay on your business purchases.

Obtaining a Business Number

Before you can register for GST/HST, you will need to obtain a **business number (BN)** from the Canada Revenue Agency if you do not already have one. You can register for a business number online at the CRA website. This number conveniently identifies you to the government for all business purposes, including remittances of GST/HST, corporate income tax remittances, and payroll remittances.

Informing Your Clients

You must let your clients know if GST/HST is being charged on your fees. The invoice sent to the client should show the total amount charged for fees and disbursements and the rate and amount charged for GST/HST. Your GST/HST registration number must also appear on the invoice. The amount collected from clients will be recorded as GST/HST payable in your journals and ledgers.

Interest on Trust Accounts

Section 57 of the *Law Society Act* states that interest earned on a mixed trust account must be remitted to the Law Foundation of Ontario by the financial institution in which the account is located.[11] This is done by signing a letter of direction regarding interest on a mixed trust

---

10 *Credit Unions and Caisses Populaires Act, 1994*, SO 1994, c 11.

11 *Law Society Act, supra* note 1, s 57(1).

account, which directs the financial institution to forward interest on the account to the Law Foundation (see Figure 1.3).

It is your responsibility to ensure that the financial institution where you wish to open a mixed trust account pays interest at a rate approved by the trustees of the Law Foundation. Most financial institutions have an agreement with the Law Foundation and are accustomed to remitting the interest as required. The Law Foundation uses these funds to carry out its mandate, which is to promote access to justice.

An annual report must be sent to the Law Society of Upper Canada and to the Law Foundation of Ontario by March 31 each year.

FIGURE 1.3   Letter of direction

To:	The Manager
Name of Bank:	[Name of chartered bank, provincial savings office, registered trust company, credit union, or caisse populaire]
Branch:	_____
Address:	_____
Re:	The Law Foundation of Ontario and Account No.

The above account is in: _____ my name

_____ the name of the firm with which I am associated

In accordance with Section 57 of the *Law Society Act*, I direct you, until further notice, to compute the amount earned by applying to the balance in the above account the rate of interest approved from time to time by the Trustees of The Law Foundation of Ontario. Please pay into an account held in your main office in Ontario in the name of The Law Foundation of Ontario amounts so calculated and give written notice to me at the address shown on the above account and to The Law Foundation of Ontario, 20 Queen Street West, Suite 3002, Box #19, Toronto, Ontario, M5H 3R3, when each such payment is made. This notice should show, as applicable as per the terms of the interest agreement between the LFO and your financial institution, the amount of the payment, the amounts of the daily/monthly balances, and the rates of interest used in computing the payment.

Dated: the day of   _____ , _____ , 20_____

Signature

Firm Name: _____

Address: _____

Source: Law Foundation of Ontario. Used with permission.

CHAPTER SUMMARY

Whether you decide on a career as a paralegal working alone or in association with other licensees, you need to have an understanding of record-keeping. Although you may not be directly involved in preparing bookkeeping entries and financial statements, you will be accountable to clients and must protect their interests. It is your responsibility to ensure that the firm you work with acts ethically and with integrity. Even when working in association with other paralegals, a licensee often maintains his or her own trust account and is required to account for funds received in trust.

You will be required to submit annual reports to the Law Society of Upper Canada, the Law Foundation of Ontario, and the Canada Revenue Agency. Having proper systems in place makes it easier to comply with all these obligations.

KEY TERMS

accountants, 2
bookkeeper, 2
bookkeeping, 3
business number (BN), 10
general bank account, 7
general monetary retainer, 7
Law Foundation of Ontario, 3
licensees, 2
limited liability partnership, 4
mixed or pooled trust bank account, 8
monetary retainer, 7
multi-discipline practice (MDP) or affiliation, 4
partnership, 3
posted, 8
professional corporation, 4
retainer, 6
separate interest-bearing trust account, 9
small supplier, 10
sole proprietorship, 3

FURTHER READING

Law Foundation of Ontario, "Reporting Mixed Trust Accounts," online: <http://www
.lawfoundation.on.ca/our-revenue-sources/interest-on-mixed-trust-accounts>.
Law Society of Upper Canada, *The Bookkeeping Guide for Paralegals* (Toronto: LSUC, February
2014), online: <http://www.lsuc.on.ca/uploadedFiles/PDC/Practice_Review/Paralegal%20
Bookkeeping%20Guide%20-%20February%202014.pdf>.

PUT IT INTO PRACTICE

Case Example: LSUC Rules

Ann Litigate is currently operating her legal services firm under the business name "Ann Litigate Paralegal Services." If Ann is interested in transitioning her legal services practice from a sole proprietorship to a corporation, what steps will she need to take? What are the advantages and disadvantages of Ann's establishing her legal services practice as a corporation? Discuss.

REVIEW QUESTIONS

True or False

[handwritten: Can operate w/o it. So long as you don't hold onto client money.]

[handwritten: Individuals partnership is individuals]

__F__ 1. A separate interest-bearing trust account should be opened for each client.

__T__ 2. A general monetary retainer does not need to be deposited into the trust account.

__F__ 3. It is a mandatory requirement for a legal professional (e.g., a lawyer or paralegal) to open and maintain a trust account.

__T__ 4. Lawyers and paralegals may operate a legal practice with unlicensed professionals who provide other non-legal services.

__F__ 5. Bylaw 9 of the Law Society of Upper Canada deals with the form of business organization.

__F__ 6. Income taxes payable to the Canada Revenue Agency (CRA) in a partnership are paid by the partnership itself.

__F__ 7. Understanding basic bookkeeping and accounting principles is useful only for the legal professional's reporting requirements to the Law Society.

__T__ 8. Moneys received from a client for services not yet rendered should be deposited into the trust bank account.

__F__ 9. A cheque received from a supplier as a refund for goods returned would be deposited in trust. *[handwritten: like ink, paint etc.]*

Fill in the Blanks

1. Refer to *Law Society of Upper Canada v Sam*, 2014 ONLSTH 140, and then fill in the blanks in the following quotation from the case: "[T]he Respondent ... b) failed to immediately deposit those funds into a trust account, contrary to By-Law 9, section ___*7.1*___ , or alternatively, contrary to By-Law 9, section ___*8.2*___ ."

2. Refer to bylaw 9 of the LSUC and fill in the blanks: Section ___*18*___ of bylaw 9 requires licensees to maintain financial records to record all money and other property *[handwritten: (reciept) — recieved]* and *[handwritten: dispersed]* in connection with the licensee's professional business and, at a minimum, the _____ described in sections _____ to _____ .

3. A retainer is considered a ___*monetary*___ retainer when it is deposited in a trust account and when there is an agreement between the paralegal/lawyer and the client regarding legal services.

Short Answer

Give a full answer for each question.

1. What is the difference between the role played by a bookkeeper and that played by an accountant? *(handwritten: filing taxes, year end, giving info, Proff. (C.P.A))*

2. What business structure is most likely to be used by a paralegal opening an office who plans to work from home? *(handwritten: Sole Proprietorship.)*

3. Assume a firm has two bank accounts—a general bank account and a mixed trust account. Indicate whether the following transactions would involve a deposit or cheque, and the bank account that would be used.

Transaction	General Bank Account	Trust Bank Account
Paralegal pays rent for the month	(General) Cheque	
Paralegal receives a retainer in the amount of $1,000 from a new client, Jane Phillips		✓
Paralegal invests $5,000 into the firm	✓	
Paralegal pays court filing fees of $150 on the Jane Phillips file		✓
Paralegal pays telephone bill	✓	
Paralegal withdraws money for personal expenses	✓	
Paralegal prepares an invoice on the Jane Phillips file and writes a cheque in payment of invoice	✓	

(handwritten note below table: money from trust to general)

4. What happens to interest earned on a mixed trust account? *(handwritten: → Law Foundation.)*

5. In what circumstances should a paralegal maintain a separate interest-bearing trust for a client? *(handwritten: If the client asks for one.)*

6. Look up the Law Foundation of Ontario online. What is its mandate?

(handwritten at top of page: - day to day)

2 Introduction to Bookkeeping

After reading this chapter, you should be able to:

- understand the basic terminology used in accounting
- identify the generally accepted accounting principles (GAAP) and understand the accounting standards for private enterprises
- define the categories of accounts—assets, liabilities, owner's equity, income, and expenses—and classify accounts by category
- create an opening balance sheet for a firm
- demonstrate an understanding of the accounting equation

You probably have some experience with basic bookkeeping if you keep track of the balance in your personal chequing account. However, using such a simple method in a business would be inadequate because it does not provide the information needed for making business decisions. Your business records must show where money came from and how it was spent in much more detail. Throw into the mix a trust account with money that belongs to your clients, and you will quickly see the importance of a good system of record-keeping. With the increased popularity of electronic banking and the use of debit cards, it is easy to lose track of funds received and funds paid out.

As a legal professional, you do not want to have cheques returned by your bank for insufficient funds. You always need to know what is going into and coming out of your bank accounts on a regular basis. Remember that the bank balance you view online might not accurately reflect how much money you have in the bank, because some cheques may not yet have cleared. Keeping accurate records will not only help track your actual bank balance, but also help you plan your spending over the next period.

What Is Accounting?

Accounting is the language of business. You may wish to communicate financial information about your business to various **stakeholders**, each of whom has a different interest:

- **Internal users** are interested in managerial accounting. People working in the business need to have financial information for making management decisions. Is the business profitable? Can the business afford to expand? The user wants information that is as accurate as possible to help make appropriate decisions.
- **External users** are interested in financial accounting. People who lend money to the business will want to review its financial statements to assess the risks associated with a loan. Usually, the owner wants external users to think the business is doing very well and is profitable. The Law Society of Upper Canada uses the information generated by the firm to complete audits and to ensure that its bylaws are being followed.
- **Government users** are interested in tax accounting, and businesses are required to submit income tax returns annually. The owner usually wants to present less profit on its financial statement in order to minimize tax liability.

Business owners communicate information using financial statements prepared in keeping with generally accepted accounting principles, described in the next section.

Accounting Standards for Private Enterprises

Effective January 1, 2012, accounting has been restructured to move away from a single financial reporting framework, formerly known as generally accepted accounting principles, to implement a variety of rules for different types of organizations. For example, Canada adopted the **International Financial Reporting Standards (IFRS)**, which is a set of international accounting rules imposed on corporations whose shares are listed on a stock exchange. In the case of not-for-profit organizations, the standards for these entities are set out in part III of the *CPA Canada Handbook: Accounting*.

Paralegals are concerned with the standards set out in part II of the handbook regarding **accounting standards for private enterprises (ASPE)**. Financial statements must present fairly and in accordance with Canadian **generally accepted accounting principles (GAAP)** the financial position, results of operations, and cash flows of an entity.

These standards apply to sole proprietorships and small private enterprises with a view to ensuring that bookkeeping records and financial statements are prepared using acceptable accounting practices. The standards ensure that everyone prepares and interprets financial reports the same way. Such consistency enables users of the information—including paralegals, lawyers, lenders, auditors, and regulators such as the Canada Revenue Agency and the Law Society—to rely on the financial statements and information presented.

Some examples of common accounting standards that paralegals should adhere to include the following principles.

- *Business entity principle.* Every business should be treated as a separate unit for the purpose of keeping accounting records. You should not mix personal and business transactions. Separate bank accounts should be used for personal and business activities. Personal expenses should not be recorded as expenses in the records of the business and vice versa. It is good practice to have separate credit cards for your business and for personal expenses for record-keeping purposes. For example, it would be a breach of this principle to take a spouse out to a movie and charge it to the business credit card and claim it as a business expense.
- *Conservatism principle.* A business should report moderate and realistic financial information to prevent overvaluation.
- *Consistency principle.* The same accounting methods must be used period after period.
- *Going concern principle.* A business is presumed to continue its operations for the foreseeable future.
- *Cost principle.* Assets purchased are recorded at their actual cost. Even though you may have paid $10 for a painting at a yard sale that you believe to be worth $1,000, the business records should show the painting's value at the amount that was actually paid.
- *Revenue recognition principle.* Revenue is recorded when it is earned, regardless of whether or not payment has been received; expenses are recorded when incurred. This method of accounting is referred to as the **accrual basis of accounting** and is the one used by paralegals as required under the *Income Tax Act*.[1] The **cash basis of accounting**

---

1 *Income Tax Act*, RSC 1985, c 1 (5th Supp), as amended.

recognizes revenue only when the revenue is actually received, and expenses only when payment has actually been made.

In the event that a client does not pay for fees billed, the firm would have to write the invoice off as a bad debt if it had already been included in income. Income recorded in the firm's records is taxed when it is earned, not when the client pays the bill.

- *Matching principle.* Expenses must be reported in the same period as the revenues that were earned as a result of the expenses.

TAX TIP

Work in Progress

Lawyers and accountants receive special treatment when dealing with work in progress (WIP) under the *Income Tax Act*.[2] When lawyers file their first tax return, an election can be filed with the Canada Revenue Agency to report WIP only after it has been billed; then work that is in progress at the end of the fiscal period cannot be included in income. When this election is made, revenue is considered to have been earned when the bill is sent to the client and not before. The value of work done on a file is not included for tax purposes.

At the time of this printing, the *Income Tax Act* had not been amended to permit paralegals to file this election. The Act requires paralegals to include the value of WIP, even if the time spent on a file has not yet been billed to the client at the end of the fiscal period.

Categories of Accounts

The books of a business are set up using three main categories of accounts: assets, liabilities, and owner's equity. Two further categories are revenue (or income) and expenses. Each category will have individual accounts listed under it.

The **chart of accounts** is a numbered list of all the business accounts used in a particular firm. A typical chart of accounts is printed on the inside cover of this textbook and shows the sample account names used in the book. You will notice that the five categories of accounts are broken down into account names. Individual accounts are given an account name and an account number.

Note that the account categories each have a number range. The table in Figure 2.1 shows how numbers might be assigned to each category and the **normal balance** for each.

Account Name	Account Number (Range)	Normal Balance
Assets	100–199	Debit
Liabilities	200–299	Credit
Owner's equity	300–399	Credit
Revenue (income)	400–499	Credit
Expenses	500–599	Debit

FIGURE 2.1　Categories of accounts

The accounts are numbered to make it easier to locate each account quickly. In other words, when you see an account numbered 300 you will know that it is listed under owner's equity. If the number is 500 you will know that it is an expense account. You should also note

---

2　*Ibid*, s 34.

that the list may skip over some numbers. This allows the addition of additional accounts if the bookkeeper decides in the future that a new account is needed.

Transactions are recorded in a **general journal** and then are summarized in the individual accounts listed in the chart of accounts in the form of a general ledger. The accounts are listed in the general ledger, and the totals from the general ledger are used to prepare financial statements. There are individual accounts for each of the subdivisions of the accounting equation (described below)—asset accounts, liability accounts, owner's equity accounts, income accounts, and expense accounts. These accounts are used to record increases and decreases in each category.

Assets are items of value that are owned by a business or a person. Assets are often broken down into current assets and fixed or capital assets. **Current assets** are cash, or assets that will be converted into cash or used up within one year. Examples are cash in bank accounts, accounts receivable, or prepaid insurance. **Fixed or capital assets** are assets that have a long life. Examples are land, buildings, equipment, and vehicles. Assets are not always purchased with cash. They often are purchased on credit.

Liabilities are debts owed to others by a business or a person. Examples of liabilities are personal or bank loans and accounts payable (if supplies or assets are purchased on credit). In a firm, the money held in trust for clients is also shown as a liability. Should the owner decide to close the business, liabilities would have to be paid off before the owner could receive a return on investment from the firm. Companies that are owed money are referred to as creditors.

Owner's equity represents the value of assets remaining after all liabilities have been deducted. The owner's net worth is represented by owner's equity. The amount of the investment by an owner in a firm is often referred to as capital. The equity account in an incorporated company is identified as **shareholder's equity**. Capital does not always mean cash; it may refer to the value of assets other than cash that have been invested in the firm by an owner.

Income is a subcategory of owner's equity and is revenue earned by the firm. Examples of income accounts are fees, income, interest income, and expense recovery.

Expenses are also a subcategory of owner's equity and represents the costs incurred of doing business. The Canada Revenue Agency allows the deduction of any reasonable current expense paid or an expense that will have to be paid for the purpose of earning business income.

The Accounting Equation

The financial position of a business is stated in the form of the **accounting equation**. All transactions are analyzed using this basic accounting equation. You will encounter the terms *debit* and *credit* as you learn about the accounting equation. *Debit* refers to the left side of the equation; *credit* refers to the right side of the equation. More about the terms *debit* and *credit* will be covered in Chapters 3 and 4 of this book. To keep things simple, get used to thinking of these terms as meaning "left side" and "right side," and nothing more.

$$Assets = Liabilities + Owner's\ Equity$$

An essential component of the accounting system is **double-entry bookkeeping**. This system of **internal controls** requires that there be a check and a balance of the debits and the credits. There must be at least two entries for every transaction—one entry must be a debit entry and the other a credit entry.

We will introduce the application of the accounting equation by using the paralegal firm of Justin Case.

EXAMPLE

Justin Case has decided to open his own paralegal practice as a sole proprietor. He plans to start the business by investing the following:

Cash that he received as a graduation present	$1,000
Money borrowed from his father	4,000
Total cash he has to deposit in the bank	$5,000
His credit card debt (used to purchase assets)	$500
Computer and printer that he bought for school; now valued at	$900
Desk and office chair valued at	$150

STEP 1

To apply the accounting equation to Justin's situation, list his assets in the accounts for cash, computer equipment, and office furniture.

Assets	
General Bank Account (cash)	$5,000
Computer Equipment	900
Office Furniture	150
Total Assets	$6,050

STEP 2

Calculate Justin's total liabilities by listing the accounts for the personal loan and credit card debt.

Liabilities	
James Case (father), Loan	$4,000
Credit Card Debt	500
Total Liabilities	$4,500

Calculating Owner's Equity

STEP 3

Calculate owner's equity by deducting the total liabilities or debts owed to creditors from the total assets. As you can see, the calculation yields an answer of $1,550 for owner's equity.

$$\text{Assets} - \text{Liabilities} = \text{Owner's Equity}$$
$$6,050 - 4,500 = ?$$

STEP 4

Check to ensure that the accounting equation is balanced.

Justin's assets are worth $6,050 and are equal to his liabilities plus owner's equity, which also equal $6,050.

We have included the cash borrowed from Justin's father in the listing of cash assets. Realistically, Justin has the cash; he also has a corresponding debt that is owed to his father and a credit card debt. Because he has total debts of $4,500, his equity in the firm is only $1,550.

In the event that Justin were to sell all his assets at the value shown in his books and he were to pay off all his debts, he would be left with $1,550.

Depending on which variable you are trying to calculate, the accounting equation can be stated in three ways:

$$\text{Assets} - \text{Liabilities} = \text{Owner's Equity}$$
$$6,050 - 4,500 = 1,550$$

$$\text{Assets} = \text{Liabilities} + \text{Owner's Equity}$$
$$6,050 = 4,500 + 1,550$$

$$6,050 = 6,050$$

$$\text{Assets} = \text{Liabilities} + \text{Owner's Equity}$$

$$\text{Assets} - \text{Liabilities} = \text{Owner's Equity}$$

$$\text{Assets} - \text{Owner's Equity} = \text{Liabilities}$$

Accounting Software

Accounting software also uses the double-entry system of bookkeeping. All the principles that apply to manual record-keeping apply when using computer software.

Even though most accounting software is designed to detect errors, this does not mean that every transaction is always correct. Understanding accounting basics will help you locate errors regardless of what system you use.

Preparing an Opening Balance Sheet

The **opening balance** is the total balance for each account at the beginning of each accounting period. The total is taken from the ending or **closing balance** of that account from the last period.

			Justin Case, Paralegal	
			Opening Balance Sheet	
			Oct. 1, 20**	
Assets			Liabilities	
General Bank Account (cash)	$5,000		Personal Loan	$4,000
Computer Equipment	900		Credit Card Debt	500
Office Furniture	150		Total Liabilities	$4,500
			Owner's Equity	
			Justin Case, Capital	1,550
Total Assets	$6,050		Total Liabilities and Owner's Equity	$6,050

FIGURE 2.2   Opening balance sheet

Capital account (here called Justin Case, Capital) refers to the investment by the owner in the business. Capital is not always cash; it can be assets that the owner chooses to invest in the business. The capital account includes the owner's beginning investment plus or minus the profits or losses earned by the firm. Any withdrawals by the owner will also reduce the amount in Justin Case's capital account.

Expanded Accounting Equation

The **expanded accounting equation** takes into account three categories of accounts, in addition to assets, liabilities, and owner's equity:

1. **Withdrawals** refers to amounts taken out of the business for the personal use of the owner.
2. Income, as previously defined, refers to all earnings for the firm. In a paralegal firm, the main source of income is fees billed to clients. When clients are billed for services rendered, the amount of fees billed is entered immediately as income, regardless of whether or not the client has actually paid the bill. A firm could have other sources of income, such as interest income or expense recovery (such as charges for photocopies).
3. Expenses, as previously defined, are costs incurred by the business for the purpose of earning income. These include operating costs, such as advertising expense, dues and licences, interest, motor vehicle expenses, rent, telephone, and wages.

Net income is calculated by totalling the income of the firm minus expenses. This is often referred to as **profit** (when income exceeds expenses) or **loss** (when expenses exceed income). If revenues are lower than expenses, the firm will have a **net loss** (the calculation in which expenses exceed income, which causes a decrease in equity). If there is net income or profit from operations, the amount is added to the capital account with a resulting increase in the capital account. If there is a loss, it will be deducted from the capital account with a resulting reduction of the capital account. The capital account is the investment by the owner in the business.

The expanded accounting equation is stated as follows and is illustrated in Figure 2.3.

Assets = Liabilities + Capital – Withdrawals + (Income – Expenses)

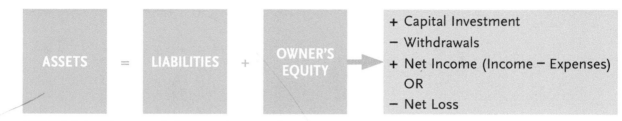

FIGURE 2.3   The expanded accounting equation

Owner's equity typically is increased or decreased depending on the following conditions:

- *Investments made by the owner, such as cash, computer equipment, and office furniture, increase owner's equity* (this is also referred to as capital contribution).
- *Income from operation of the business increases owner's equity.* When profits are earned, they can be retained within the business to increase the owner's investment in the firm. For example, when profits are used to pay off a loan, the funds are being used to reduce the firm's liabilities and this results in an increase in owner's equity. If Justin in our example uses the profit from operations to pay off the loan to his father, his debt will decrease and his investment (capital) in the firm will increase.
- *Expenses from operation of the business will decrease owner's equity.* When the expenses are higher than revenues, a net loss results and the owner's equity is decreased.
- *Withdrawals by the owner will decrease owner's equity.* A sole proprietor does not receive a salary from the business. Instead, when the owner writes a cheque to himself for personal use, the amount withdrawn from the bank account results in a reduction of the amount of money in the general bank account as well as a reduction in the capital account of the owner. If the proprietor removes an asset other than cash from the firm, the transaction is recorded as a withdrawal and will reduce owner's equity in the firm.

Figure 2.4 shows how Justin's transactions and the expanded equation work together.

Classifying Expenses

It can sometimes be difficult to decide whether something purchased is an asset or an expense. For example, Justin may go out and purchase office supplies at a cost of $1,000, including such items as pens, paper, and ink for printers. Should these items be recorded as assets (something of value owned by the business), or should they be recorded as expenses (something that will be used up within the fiscal period)?

Transaction	ASSETS: General Bank Account	Accounts Receivable	Computer Equipment	Office Furniture	=	LIABILITIES: Personal Loan	Credit Card Debt	Accounts Payable	+	OWNER'S EQUITY: J. Case Capital	-	Withdrawals	+	Fees Earned	-	Expenses
1	5,000		900	150	=	4,000	500		+	1,550	-		+		-	
BAL	5,000		900	150	=	4,000	500		+	1,550	-		+		-	
2	-600		600		=				+		-		+		-	
BAL	4,400		1,500	150	=	4,000	500		+	1,550	-		+		-	
3				200	=			200	+		-		+		-	
BAL	4,400		1,500	350	=	4,000	500	200	+	1,550	-		+		-	
4	-1,000				=				+		-	1,000	+		-	
BAL	3,400		1,500	350	=	4,000	500	200	+	1,550	-	1,000	+		-	
5	800				=				+		-		+	800	-	
BAL	4,200		1,500	350	=	4,000	500	200	+	1,550	-	1,000	+	800	-	
6		1,200			=				+		-		+	1,200	-	
BAL	4,200	1,200	1,500	350	=	4,000	500	200	+	1,550	-	1,000	+	2,000	-	
7	-300				=				+		-		+		-	300
END BAL	3,900	1,200	1,500	350	=	4,000	500	200	+	1,550	-	1,000	+	2,000	-	300

TOTAL ASSETS 6,950 = TOTAL LIABILITIES 4,700 + TOTAL OWNER'S EQUITY

CAPITAL				PROFIT		
1,550	-	1,000	+	2,000	-	300
		550	+			1,700

2,250

6,950 = 4,700 + 2,250

TRANSACTIONS

1	Balances from the opening balance sheet were entered.
2	A shift in assets occurred. Computer equipment costing $600 was purchased and paid for using cash. Because cash was used to pay for the equipment, cash or the General Bank Account balance has been reduced, and there is an addition to the account for computer equipment.
3	Justin purchased $200 worth of office furniture from a furniture store on credit. Justin has not used cash to pay for the item, but he now owes the store $200, which is recorded under Accounts Payable. Justin has increased what he owes to creditors.
4	Justin needed money to pay for personal expenses, so he withdrew $1,000 from the firm's bank account. This withdrawal results in a reduction in the General Bank Account and is shown in Owner's Equity under Withdrawals.
5	Legal fees of $800 were invoiced to a client and the client paid the bill. The transaction provided an inward flow of cash in the General Bank Account and an increase in income as a result of legal fees charged.
6	Legal fees of $1,200 were invoiced to a client and the client has not paid the bill. These fees billed are an asset for the firm called Accounts Receivable and an increase in legal fees.
7	Justin paid one month's rent in the amount of $300. This is an expense (rent expense), which reduces Owner's Equity as well as the General Bank Account balance.

FIGURE 2.4   Demonstration of expanded accounting equation

There are different ways to handle such an entry. Justin may want to show the supplies as an asset (which Justin has numbered account 130) and at the end of the period do an inventory and record what has been used up. He would expense only the amount that was used, leaving the balance in the asset portion of the balance sheet. If the amount purchased is small, it will be easier for Justin to simply record the purchase as office supplies expense (numbered as account 535).

Recording the Opening Balance Sheet in the Firm's Records

The numbers from the opening balance sheet are recorded in the firm's general journal when the firm's books are first set up. These entries are then posted to the firm's general ledger accounts as opening entries.

Justin Case, Paralegal General Journal					GJ1
Date 20**		Description	PR	Debit	Credit
Oct.	1	General Bank Account	100	5,000	
		Computer Equipment	155	900	
		Office Furniture and Equipment	158	150	
		Personal Loan	205		4,000
		Credit Card Debt	210		500
		Justin Case, Capital	300		1,550
		To record opening balance sheet			
		Totals		6,050	6,050

FIGURE 2.5 **Opening entries**

1. The balances from the opening balance sheet are recorded in the general journal. This is referred to as the "book of original entry" because transactions are always recorded first in a general journal. The heading indicates that the page number is 1 (GJ1), which is the first page of the general journal.
2. The month and year are placed in the first column for the first entry. We did not repeat the month for entries that follow because the date did not change.
3. Note that the debit entries in the Description column are placed at the margin and the credit entries are indented three spaces.
4. The post reference (PR) column (which will be explained in more detail in later chapters) shows the number of the general ledger account to which the amount was posted. The account number is entered only after the number has been recorded in the firm's general ledger.
5. "To record opening balance sheet" is the description of the general journal entries above.

Recording Transactions Using the Basic Accounting Equation

The **T-accounts** shown below illustrate how posting the opening entries affects the individual ledger accounts. The total debits equal the total credits once all posting is completed.

General Bank Account

Dr.	Cr.
5,000	

Computer Equipment

Dr.	Cr.
900	

Office Furn. & Equip.

Dr.	Cr.
150	

Personal Loan

Dr.	Cr.
	4,000

Credit Card Debt

Dr.	Cr.
	500

Justin Case, Capital

Dr.	Cr.
	1,550

Total Debits = 6,050   Total Credits = 6,050

FIGURE 2.6   T-accounts showing ledger balances after posting

CHAPTER SUMMARY

One of the first challenges a paralegal starting a firm might encounter is obtaining financing for the business. This involves preparing a business plan that presents the investment being made and forecasts the anticipated income and expenses. Knowing the language of accounting will help you to communicate your plans and needs to an investor, whether a financial institution or an individual. You want to understand the general principles applied in maintaining records and be able to present a financial plan in a professional manner when asked to do so. Many situations may require you to be conversant with the language and principles that apply to record-keeping.

Understanding debits and credits takes time, and the aim of this chapter is merely to introduce you briefly to some transactions. You have seen the categories of accounts and know why you need to have a chart of accounts. The intricacies of debit and credit will be explored in more detail in the chapters that follow.

KEY TERMS

accounting equation, 21
accounting standards for private
    enterprises (ASPE), 19
accrual basis of accounting, 19
assets, 21
capital account, 23
cash basis of accounting, 19
chart of accounts, 20
closing balance, 23
current assets, 21
double-entry bookkeeping, 21
expanded accounting equation, 23

expenses, 21
external users, 18
fixed or capital assets, 21
general journal, 21
generally accepted accounting
    principles (GAAP), 19
government users, 18
income, 21
internal controls, 21
internal users, 18
International Financial Reporting
    Standards (IFRS), 19

liabilities, 21
loss, 24
net income, 24
net loss, 24
normal balance, 20
opening balance, 23
owner's equity, 21
profit, 24
shareholder's equity, 21
stakeholders, 18
T-accounts, 27
withdrawals, 23

FURTHER READING

CPA Canada Handbook: Accounting (Toronto: Chartered Professional Accountants of Canada, 2015), online: <http://www.cpacanada.ca>.

Nortel Networks Corporation
    <http://www.nortel.canada.com>.
    In re Nortel Networks Corp Securities Litigation, Master File No 04 Civ 2115 (LAP) (10 September 2004 and 16 September 2005).
    Nortel Networks Corporation (Re) (2009), 55 CBR (5th) 229, 2009 CanLII 39492 (Ont Sup Ct).
    Ontario Public Service Employees Union Pension Trust Fund v Clark (2005), 77 OR (3rd) 38, 2005 CanLII 51027 (Sup Ct).
    Re Nortel Networks Corporation (2006), 29 OSC Bull 8608.

PUT IT INTO PRACTICE

Case Example: Accounting Standards

Nortel Networks

The *Nortel Networks* case is an infamous and well-documented example of the lack of oversight and compliance with accounting standards in the corporate context.

Since as early as 2001, various class-action proceedings and other lawsuits were commenced against Nortel Networks Corporation, a telecommunications company, and its directors and officers for discrepancies in the company's financial reporting. The affected stakeholders were internal, external, and international in nature. For example, the government securities regulator in Canada and the United States brought charges against the company; current and former employees joined in a class action to protect themselves from losses on their pension plans as well as employment interruptions as a result of Nortel's financial losses; and shareholders and investors were defrauded and misinformed about the company's financial health. In 2009, Nortel filed for bankruptcy protection under the *Companies' Creditors Arrangement Act* (CCAA) in Ontario. Appeals and motions against the company are still before the courts, and the fallout from Nortel's decisions since 2000 continues.

Some of the charges laid against the company include these from the class-action suit[3] brought by David Lucescu, individually, and on behalf of other shareholders against Nortel:

- Statements made by the company about its financial position were materially false and misleading (para 28).
- The financial results made by the company were materially overstated (para 28).
- "The [defendants] lacked a reasonable basis for their positive statements about the Company, its business, operations, earning and prospects" (para 28).
- The defendants "materially misled the investing public, thereby inflating the price of Nortel common stock, by publicly issuing false and misleading statements and omitting to disclose material facts necessary to make Defendant's statements, as set forth herein, not false and misleading. Said statements and omissions were materially false and misleading in that they failed to disclose material adverse information and misrepresented the truth about the Company, its business and operations, as alleged herein" (para 36).

See the Further Reading section above for this case and related cases.

Use the table below to identify and discuss the accounting standards and generally accepted accounting principles (GAAP) that Nortel violated based on the charges identified in the class action against Nortel Networks.

	Action taken by/charge laid against Nortel	Accounting principle/standard violated
1.	The company made materially false and misleading statements about its financial position	• Reliability • Going concern • Relevance principle
2.	The financial results were materially overstated	
3.	There was no reasonable basis for the company's positive outlook	
4.	The company materially misled the investing public	
5.	The company's stock value was overinflated	
6.	The company failed to disclose adverse material facts	
7.	The company misrepresented the truth about the company, its business, and its operations	

---

3   See <http://securities.stanford.edu/filings-documents/1043/NTL09_01/2009518_f01c_0904691.pdf>.

REVIEW QUESTIONS

True or False

1. Cash and capital are equivalent terms that can be used interchangeably.
2. Going concern is one of the principles of accounting.
3. In accrual accounting, cash must be received before the transaction is recognized on the financial statement.
4. For every transaction reported on a financial statement, there are at least two entries.
5. A chart of accounts is a standardized list of accounts that is only created using accounting software.
6. Businesses are concerned only about external stakeholders in their financial reporting.
7. Paying down a bank loan or other forms of credit will decrease equity.
8. Purchasing or selling assets will increase equity.
9. The balance sheet and the statement of financial position mean the same thing.
10. The general journal is an example of a book of original entry.
11. Business owners take money out of their business by way of a salary.
12. The equity account for a corporation is typically identified as shareholder's equity.

Short Answer

Give a full answer for each question:

1. What are the steps involved in entering transactions in the general journal?
2. What does it mean to understand the financial position of your business (or even your personal finances)?
3. Which accounts have an impact on owner's equity?

PRACTICE EXERCISES

Practice Exercise 2.1

Using the definitions explained in this chapter, determine the classification (assets, liabilities, owner's equity, income, and expenses) of each of the following account names. If necessary, refer to the chart of accounts on the inside front cover of this textbook.

	Account name	Category
1	Cash	Asset
2	Motor Vehicle	
3	Telephone Expense	
4	Salaries and Wages	
5	Professional Fees	
6	Capital	
7	Computer Equipment	
8	Accounts Receivable	
9	Advertising Expense	
10	Interest Earned	
11	Prepaid Rent	
12	General Bank Account	
13	Office Equipment	
14	Withdrawals	

Practice Exercise 2.2

Balance the accounting equation on each line by calculating the value of the missing number represented by a question mark.

	Assets	=	Liabilities	+	Owner's Equity
Example:	35,000	=	15,000	+	?
	Answer: 35,000 − 15,000 = 20,000				
1	40,000	=	10,000	+	?
2	80,000	=	?	+	60,000
3	?	=	24,000	+	10,000
4	?	=	5,000	+	10,000
5	20,000	=	?	+	6,000
6	31,000 + ?	=	24,000	+	10,000
7	58,500	=	2,500	+	80,000 − ?
8	1,700 + 5,000	=	?	+	700
9	?	=	10,000	+	30,000
10	20,000 − 5,000	=	5,400 + ?	+	8,000

Practice Exercise 2.3

In the following list of accounts, complete the table as follows:

a. Indicate the category of account: asset, liability, capital, withdrawal, income, or expense.

b. Indicate the normal balance for that category of account.

c. Indicate whether the balance in the account increases or decreases when an entry is made on the side indicated.

	Account name	Category	Normal balance	Side	Increases/ decreases
1	Accounting and Bookkeeping Expense	Expense	Debit	Dr.	Increases
2	Accounts Payable/General			Dr.	
3	Auto Expense			Cr.	
4	Credit Card Debt			Cr.	
5	Fees Earned			Cr.	
6	General Bank Account			Dr.	
7	Insurance—Prof. Liability			Dr.	
8	Interest Income			Cr.	
9	Accounts Payable/General			Dr.	
10	Office Furniture			Dr.	
11	Owner, Capital			Cr.	
12	Owner, Drawings			Cr.	
13	Photocopy Expense			Dr.	
14	Prepaid Insurance			Dr.	
15	Prepaid Rent			Cr.	
16	Salaries			Dr.	
17	Utilities			Cr.	
18	Vacation Accrual Payable			Cr.	
19	General Bank Account			Cr.	

Practice Exercise 2.4

Using the worksheet provided, complete the expanded accounting equation by recording the following transactions.

1	Balances from the opening balance sheet were entered by Ann Litigate. She had invested $8,000 in her firm.
2	Office equipment costing $800 was purchased and paid for using cash.
3	Ann purchased $900 worth of office furniture from a furniture store on credit.
4	Ann paid for personal expenses from the firm's bank account in the amount of $1,500.
5	Legal fees of $1,600 were invoiced to a client and the client paid the bill.
6	Legal fees of $800 were invoiced to a client and the client has not paid the bill.
7	Ann paid one month's salaries expense in the amount of $2,000.

	ASSETS			=	LIABILITIES	+	OWNER'S EQUITY						
Transaction	General Bank Account	Accounts Receivable	Office Furniture and Equipment	=	Accounts Payable	+	A. Litigate Capital	−	Withdrawals	+	Fees Earned	−	Expenses
1	8,000						8,000						
BAL	8,000	0	0	=	0	+	8,000	−	0	+	0	−	0
2													
BAL				=		+		−		+		−	
3													
BAL				=		+		−		+		−	
4													
BAL				=		+		−		+		−	
5													
BAL				=		+		−		+		−	
6													
BAL				=		+		−		+		−	
7													
END BAL				=		+		−		+		−	

TOTAL ASSETS			=	TOTAL LIABILITIES	+	TOTAL OWNER'S EQUITY				
						CAPITAL		+	PROFIT	
							−	+		−
								+		
			=		+					
			=							

Practice Exercise 2.5

For each of the following transactions, (a) identify the two account names and the account type using the chart of accounts printed on the inside cover of this textbook and (b) identify the appropriate financial statement: balance sheet, statement of owner's equity, or income statement. Hint: Don't forget the double-entry accounting principle.

Transaction	Account Name/Type	Financial Statement
1. Paralegal contributed $10,000 to the legal services firm from personal funds.		
2. Paralegal took a draw ($1,200) against the legal services firm's equity for personal use.		
3. Paralegal purchased a new all-in-one printer for the office ($350) with cash.		
4. Paralegal paid bookkeeper for bookkeeping services ($1,000) with cash.		
5. Paralegal paid office rent, which included utilities and telephone ($1,500), with cash.		
6. Paralegal billed a client for professional fees and received payment from the client ($1,700).		
7. Paralegal paid Law Society dues ($1,100).		
8. Paralegal paid principal and interest on her bank loan ($500 principal; $100 interest).		

Practice Exercise 2.6

Using the transactions from Practice Exercise 2.5, complete the following accounting equations.

Assume that the opening balances are as follows: Assets: $5,000; Liabilities: $2,500; and Owner's Equity: $2,500 (Capital). List each transaction entry under the appropriate heading of the expanded accounting equation. Hint: Decreases in the debit or credit record should be expressed as a negative using brackets ( ).

					OWNER'S EQUITY								
TRANSACTION	ASSETS		LIABILITIES										
		=		+	Capital	−	Withdrawals	+	Revenue	−	Expenses		
Opening	5,000	=	2,500	+	2,500	−		+		−			
1		=		+		−		+		−			
2		=		+		−		+		−			
3		=		+		−		+		−			
4		=		+		−		+		−			
5		=		+		−		+		−			
6		=		+		−		+		−			
7		=		+		−		+		−			
8		=		+		−		+		−			
Ending Balance		=		+		−		+		−			
PROOF		=											

Ann Litigate Paralegal Services
May 1 – May 30

Practice Exercise 2.7

Complete the T-account chart based on the opening balances provided for each account and the transactions listed. Calculate the ending balance for each account. Opening balances are shown in green.

1	Withdrew $5,000 from legal practice for personal use.
2	Billed and received payment for legal services rendered, $2,300 (Client A).
3	Received payment for legal services rendered, $1,800 (Client B). This client was billed previously and an account receivable for the amount of the account had been recorded at that time.
4	Paid supplier for legal texts, $400.
5	Paid process server for filing court documents, $130.
6	Paid for Internet and business email services, $105.
7	Obtained business line of credit, $15,000.
8	Paid interest on bank loan, $85.

General Bank Account

Dr.	Cr.
8,000	

Accounts Receivable

Dr.	Cr.
3,000	

Liabilities

Dr.	Cr.
	2,000

Owner's Equity

Dr.	Cr.
	9,000

Professional Fees Earned

Dr.	Cr.

Expenses

Dr.	Cr.

3 Keeping Books and Records

After reading this chapter, you should be able to:

- understand the concept of a fiscal year
- understand the accounting cycle
- demonstrate an understanding of debits and credits
- complete an analysis of transactions using double-entry bookkeeping
- record transactions in a general journal

Accounting Period

Accounting records are prepared, and procedures are performed, over the course of the **accounting period**. The process that begins with analyzing and recording business transactions into journals, and ends with the completion of a post-closing trial balance, is referred to as the **accounting cycle**. The steps in the accounting cycle are described in the next section.

Accounting periods of equal length, called **fiscal periods**, are used to measure the financial progress of a business over time. Periods may be defined as monthly, quarterly, or annual. The accounting or fiscal period refers to the period of time for which an income statement is prepared. The length of each accounting period will vary depending on the type and size of business being conducted. If you wish to compare results from one period to the next, you must examine the results over consistent periods of time. It is not helpful to compare the results for six months with results for a 12-month period. When you file tax returns, the results you report to the Canada Revenue Agency will have to cover a 12-month period. When the period covers 12 months it is called the **fiscal year**. The fiscal year-end is the date upon which the financial year finishes. The fiscal year-end does not have to be December 31.

Selecting a year-end for a business depends on various concerns the owner may have, such as the following:

- Are tax benefits available if the business does not use December 31 (the calendar year) as the year-end?
- What additional records will be required if the business does not use the calendar year?
- Is the business seasonal, and does the owner prefer to have a fiscal period that corresponds to a quiet time of the year?

Once you have selected your fiscal year-end for tax purposes, the Canada Revenue Agency will not allow you to change it without its consent, as this would create inconsistencies in the financial reports. Having a year-end that does not finish on December 31 complicates the bookkeeping because many expenses—such as Law Society dues, remittances of employees' tax deductions, and Canada Pension Plan and Employment Insurance premiums—must be calculated on a calendar-year basis. T4 slips issued to employees must cover salary over the calendar year. The additional record-keeping required when selecting a year-end other than December 31 is often a deterrent.

The Accounting Cycle

The accounting cycle is the process of analyzing and recording business transactions and producing financial statements from the information. This cycle takes place over a fiscal period covered by the income statement. You may wish to complete the cycle once every month, every quarter, or once a year. Many paralegals use a one-year accounting period but may produce interim reports each month.

The order in which the steps in the accounting cycle are completed is as follows:

1. After a business transaction occurs, journalize the transaction using a general journal, trust journal, and/or specialized journal.
2. Post the journal entry to the general ledger and/or trust ledger.
3. Prepare the trial balance.
4. Prepare the worksheet.
5. Prepare the adjusted trial balance.
6. Prepare the financial statements.
7. Record adjusting and closing entries.
8. Calculate the **post-closing trial balance**.

Figure 3.1 illustrates the steps of the accounting cycle.

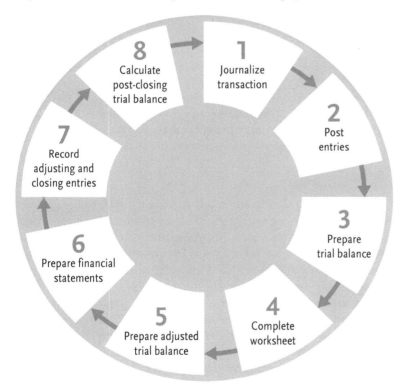

FIGURE 3.1   Steps of the accounting cycle. Note that the post-closing trial balance in step 8 is carried forward as the opening balance for the next period.

The Transaction

The process starts when the business owner enters into a financial transaction. The transaction might be for cash or for credit. As an example, the paralegal may purchase a piece of equipment, pay rent, or charge fees to a client. All financial activities involving the business are transactions. An additional consideration for paralegals is that the transaction may involve the trust account and trust records.

Journal Entries

The basic general journal usually has two columns—a debit column and a credit column. It is called the "book of original entry" because this is where transactions are first recorded in chronological order. The **journal entries** involve a double-entry system in which there is at least one debit entry and one credit entry for each transaction. The basic trust journals, which are also books of original entry, will be used to record funds received in the trust account and disbursements made from the trust account.

Posting

Once the entries have been recorded in the general journal, they are summarized using **general ledgers**. The ledger posts the journal entries by category in the order shown on the chart of accounts. The set of books will have one general ledger sheet for each of the accounts used in the business. Each general journal entry is posted to the account affected by the transaction. **Posting** also will be done from the trust journal to the individual client trust ledger sheets so that the funds held in the mixed trust account are properly accounted for.

Trial Balance

When the accounting period is at an end (month, quarter, or year), a list of the totals in all the ledger accounts is prepared. This is called a **trial balance** and it is calculated to ensure that debits are equal to credits. If they are not equal, this indicates that an error occurred in one or more journal entries. Errors must be corrected before proceeding to the next step.

Worksheet

If **adjustments** need to be made to the balances in any accounts after the trial balance is prepared, the worksheet is used to make the changes desired. The worksheet is an internal document used to track the changes made to various accounts. Adjustments can also be made at the end of a period to allocate expenses to the correct accounts. For example, the paralegal may have paid motor vehicle insurance premiums and entered the amount as an asset under the account called "prepaid insurance." However, at the end of the period, part of the premiums will have been used up, and the amount used must be moved from the assets portion of the balance sheet to the expense portion. An adjusting entry would be made reducing the amount in the asset account (prepaid insurance) and increasing the insurance expense amount in the books to show how much insurance was expended. Once the adjustments for the period are done, another trial balance is prepared to ensure that the debits and credits are still equal. This is called the adjusted trial balance.

Adjusting Journal Entries

The worksheet is an internal document that does not form part of the office records of the company. The adjustments made on the worksheet must be entered into the general journal in order to update and bring the entries from the worksheet into the official records of the firm.

Financial Statements

The **financial statements**—an income statement showing the revenue and expenses of the business, a statement of owner's equity, and a balance sheet—are prepared once the adjusting entries have been entered in the ledgers, and an adjusted trial balance has been prepared.

Closing the Books

The owner will want to start a new accounting cycle each fiscal year, so the revenue and expense accounts in the ledgers (referred to as temporary accounts) must be closed. This is called **closing the books**, the final step of the accounting cycle after adjusting and closing entries are recorded. The balance sheet accounts (permanent accounts) are not closed at the end of the cycle because the amounts in those accounts are carried forward from period to period.

Basic Rules of Debit and Credit

You will recall that in Chapter 2 we created journal entries to record the opening balance sheet of Justin Case's firm as of October 1, 20**. When making the entries in the general journal, we had at least two entries for each transaction—an entry on the left side, referred to as a **debit (Dr.)**, and an entry on the right side, called a **credit (Cr.)**. The total debits were equal to the total credits.

As a rule, the assets side of the balance sheet is the debit side (left side). The liabilities and owner's equity side is the credit side (right side). Do not give any other meaning to the words debit and credit.

$$\begin{aligned} \text{Debits (Dr.)} &= \text{Credits (Cr.)} \\ \text{Left Side} &= \text{Right Side} \end{aligned}$$

This double-entry method of accounting requires that two entries be made for each transaction: a debit entry in one account is always offset by an equal credit entry in another account. In order for the books to be balanced, the total debits entered must equal the total credits.

Debits and Credits

Points to keep in mind about the terms *debit* and *credit*:

- Assets are shown on the left side of the accounting equation and normally have a debit balance (**normal debit balance**).
- Liabilities and owner's equity are shown on the right side of the accounting equation and normally have a credit balance (**normal credit balance**).
- Every transaction you record will have at least one debit and one credit. The total amount of the debits and credits must be equal when you are finished creating the entry.
- You may have a transaction, called a **compound entry**, that affects three or more accounts. At the end of the entry, the total debits must still equal the total credits.
- A debit entry might increase the balance in some accounts (for example, asset accounts), and a debit entry might decrease the balance in other accounts (for example, liability accounts).
- The account balance is the difference between the debit entries and credit entries, which either increases or decreases the value of an account.
- A credit entry can increase the balance in some accounts (for example, liabilities), and a credit entry can decrease the balance in some accounts (for example, assets).

Loan Payable (Liability Account)		General Bank Account (Asset Account)	
Dr.	Cr.	Dr.	Cr.
Entry on this side *decreases* balance	Entry on this side *increases* balance	Entry on this side *increases* balance	Entry on this side *decreases* balance

- Although your personal bank statement may show deposits as a credit, a credit in your cash or general bank account in your books does not result in an increase in your bank balance; it actually represents a *decrease* in your bank account balance. When you receive a statement from your bank, the bank shows a deposit you make as a credit because the deposit is actually a liability for the bank—the bank owes you the money you have deposited in the bank account. Bank statements are done from the perspective of the bank and what it owes to its customers.
- Making an entry on the debit side (left side) or credit side (right side) is simply a system used to increase or decrease the balance in an account—nothing more.
- All asset accounts, such as cash, equipment, or office furniture, normally have a debit balance. Therefore, to increase the balance in an asset account, you need to debit the account. For example, if $1,000 in cash is deposited into the bank account, you will show the deposit in your books as a "general bank account" debit.

General Bank Account

Dr.	Cr.
Increase	Decrease
1,000	

- If a cheque for $50 is written against your bank account, you need to credit the general bank account by that amount because you are decreasing the balance in the asset (general bank account) by $50 (credit), leaving a balance of $950.

General Bank Account

Dr.	Cr.
Increase	Decrease
1,000	
	50
Bal. 950	

- Liability accounts (such as loans payable or credit card debt) are shown on the right side of the accounting equation and have a normal credit balance. To increase the balance in a liability account, the account is credited. For example, if a charge of $120 is made to the credit card, you will credit the credit card debt account because the debt is increasing.

Credit Card Debt

Dr.	Cr.
Decrease	Increase
	120

- If a payment is made on the credit card debt, you are decreasing the amount of the debt, which is a liability, and you will make the entry on the debit side. If $100 was paid on the credit card you would show it as a debit, leaving a balance of $20 owing on the credit card.

Credit Card Debt

Dr.	Cr.
Decrease	Increase
	120
100	
	Bal. 20

- Owner's equity is on the right side of the accounting equation. The capital account, which shows the investment made by the owner in the business, has a normal credit balance. If the owner invests $1,000 into the business, the capital account must be credited to show an increase in the balance.

Justin Case, Capital	
Dr.	Cr.
Decrease	Increase
	1,000

- When a business owner takes $800 out of the business for personal use, it is called a withdrawal. The drawings account (which has a normal debit balance) is debited when a withdrawal is made because the owner's capital (which has a normal credit balance) is being decreased.

Justin Case, Withdrawal	
Dr.	Cr.
Increase	Decrease
800	

- Revenues are entered as a credit because when income is earned, this ultimately results in an increase in the owner's capital (which has a normal credit balance). Fees earned of $2,000 would be shown on the credit side in the fees earned account (which has a normal credit balance).

Fees Earned	
Dr.	Cr.
Decrease	Increase
	2,000

- Expenses are entered as a debit because they ultimately reduce the owner's capital. For example, telephone expense of $180 would be recorded as a debit.

Telephone Expense	
Dr.	Cr.
Increase	Decrease
180	

Proving the Business Transaction

When a business transaction occurs, evidence of that transaction must be retained. This may be a bill sent online or in the mail, or a receipt or voucher from a purchase made at a store.

Receipts

When accounting to the Canada Revenue Agency, you must keep all receipts to prove the nature of your business transactions. A charge as shown on a credit card or bank statement, or even a cancelled cheque, is not considered a valid receipt for tax purposes. The original voucher from a vendor must be available for the purpose of auditing. The reason is that although the charge shown on your bank statement or credit card indicates that something was purchased at an office supply store, it does not specify what was bought—were the purchases really office supplies for the business, or school supplies for the owner's children? The original receipt from the store explains what the expense was for, not just the fact that money was spent at a particular place of business.

The receipt obtained must be kept and entered into the firm's books. A system for filing receipts must be established. Some people like to file bills by order of date; others prefer to have separate file folders with the names from the chart of accounts so that the receipts for a particular account are kept in one folder. This enables you to look at the file and see all the bills charged to that account. For example, you may wish to have a file folder named Telephone Expense and place all bills related to telephone expenses for the office in that file. If a question arises, you need to look through only one folder rather than through the bills for all the items the firm may have purchased over a particular period of time.

If a bill shows a charge for GST or HST, the registration number of the business must be included on the bill. If the registration number is not shown, the tax department may refuse to allow a credit for the tax paid.

Analyzing the Transaction

Business transactions must be recorded in the firm's books. As previously mentioned, the general journal is the "book of original entry." When you make a general journal entry, you must analyze the transaction to determine which accounts in your firm's chart of accounts are affected. The following questions will help your analysis:

- Which accounts are affected by the transaction? Look at the chart of accounts and identify which accounts will be used to record the transaction.
- Determine the category of account that is affected. Is it an asset, liability, capital, income, or expense account?
- Does the balance in the account increase or decrease because of the transaction?
- Which account will be debited and which account will be credited?
- Is the entry balanced—are your debts and credits equal after you have finished making the entry?

The biggest challenge for people learning double-entry bookkeeping is knowing which account to use and when to debit or credit an account. One simple memory device to help you distinguish debits from credits is the acronym **DEAD CLIC** (Figure 3.2).

FIGURE 3.2 **The acronym DEAD CLIC will help you distinguish debits from credits.**

DEAD stands for the categories of accounts that have a normal debit balance, that is, you debit expenses, assets, and drawings to increase their balance. If you want to decrease the balance in any of these accounts, you will need to credit the account.

CLIC stands for the categories of accounts that have a normal credit balance, that is, liabilities, income, and capital. If you want to increase the balance in any of these accounts, you must credit the account. If you want to decrease the balance, you will need to debit the account.

Your first step in using DEAD CLIC is to learn to recognize the category of account with which you are dealing.

In a double-entry bookkeeping system, two or more accounts will be affected by any transaction. Remember that the total debits and credits must be equal after each entry is made in the general journal.

In order to analyze a transaction, ask yourself the following questions:

- What did the firm give and what did the firm receive in this transaction?
- Which account is used for the item received and which account is used for the item given?
- What is the normal balance of the account—debit (DEAD) or credit (CLIC)?
- Will the account increase or decrease because of the transaction?
- Will the account be debited or credited? By what amount?
- Is the entry balanced?

Other Types of Entries

Sometimes you may run into an entry that involves more than two accounts or a shift in assets.

Compound Entries

A compound entry requires more than one debit or more than one credit. For example, if office furniture is purchased for $2,000, and $500 is paid by cheque and $1,500 is purchased on credit, you will have three entries.

	Debit	Credit
Office Furniture	2,000	
General Bank Account		500
Accounts Payable/General Liabilities		1,500
To record purchase of office furniture		

FIGURE 3.3   **Recording a compound entry**

Shift in Assets

A shift in assets occurs when two asset accounts are affected by a transaction. For example, suppose computer equipment is purchased that costs $1,000 and it is paid for with cash (a cheque drawn on the general bank account). You will have an increase in the computer equipment account and your general bank account will decrease. The total value of your assets has not changed; however, the value of the computer equipment account has increased and the value of the general bank account has decreased, reflecting a shift in assets. This entry would be shown by debiting the computer equipment account and crediting the general bank account.

	Debit	Credit
Computer Equipment	1,000	
General Bank Account		1,000
To record purchase of computer equipment		

FIGURE 3.4   Recording a shift in assets

Examples of Transactions

The following examples illustrate the application of debits and credits in double-entry book-keeping and recording transactions in a general journal.

EXAMPLE 1

On October 5, Justin Case wrote a cheque for $300 to Bell Canada to pay the telephone bill for his office.

Analysis of Transaction		Result
Step 1:	What did the firm give and what did the firm receive in this transaction?	• The firm received a phone bill. • The firm gave money (a cheque) as payment.
Step 2:	Which account is used for the item received and which account is used for the item given?	• Telephone Expense is used to record telephone bills received. • General Bank Account is used to record payment.
Step 3:	What category of account is it?	• Telephone Expense is an expense account. • General Bank Account is an asset account.
Step 4:	Will the account increase or decrease because of the transaction?	• Telephone Expense will increase. • General Bank Account will decrease.
Step 5:	Will the account be debited (DEAD) or credited (CLIC)? By what amount?	• Telephone Expense will be debited for $300. • General Bank Account will be credited for $300.
Step 6:	Is the entry balanced?	• Yes, there is a debit of $300 and a credit of $300.

General Journal					GJ2
Date 20**		Description	PR	Debit	Credit
Oct.	5	Telephone Expense		300	
		General Bank Account (Cash)			300
		Paid telephone expense for Oct.			

EXAMPLE 2

Compound entry: On October 5, Justin Case purchased office furniture from IKEA for $2,000. He paid $500 by cheque and $1,500 was put on his credit card. This compound entry will involve three different accounts.

Analysis of Transaction	Result
Step 1: What did the firm give and what did the firm receive in this transaction?	• The firm received office furniture. • The firm gave money (a cheque) as partial payment. • The firm also gave the credit card as partial payment.
Step 2: Which account is used for the item received and which account is used for the item given?	• Office Furniture and Equipment Fixtures is the account used for furniture received. • General Bank Account is used to record payment for the furniture. • Credit Card Debt is used to record the liability incurred on the card.
Step 3: What category of account is it?	• Office Furniture and Equipment is an asset account. • General Bank Account is an asset account. • Credit Card Debt is a liability account.
Step 4: Will the account increase or decrease because of the transaction?	• Office Furniture and Equipment will increase. • General Bank Account will decrease. • Credit Card Debt will increase.
Step 5: Will the account be debited (DEAD) or credited (CLIC)? By what amount?	• Office Furniture and Equipment will be debited $2,000. • General Bank Account will be credited $500. • Credit Card Debt will be credited $1,500.
Step 6: Is the entry balanced?	• Yes, there is a debit of $2,000 and a credit of $500 plus $1,500.

General Journal					GJ2
Date 20**		Description	PR	Debit	Credit
Oct.	5	Telephone Expense		300	
		General Bank Account (Cash)			300
		Paid telephone expense for Oct.			
	5	Office Furniture and Equipment		2,000	
		General Bank Account (Cash)			500
		Credit Card Debt			1,500
		To record furniture purchased from IKEA			

EXAMPLE 3

On October 8, Justin Case received $500 by way of a scholarship for having obtained the highest marks in his class. Justin wishes to invest this amount in his firm.

Analysis of Transaction		Result
Step 1:	What did the firm receive and what did the firm give in this transaction?	• The firm received money from Justin. • The firm gave equity in the firm to Justin.
Step 2:	Which account is used for the item received and which account is used for the item given?	• General Bank Account is used to record cash received. • Justin Case, Capital is used to record an increase in investment by the owner.
Step 3:	What category of account is it?	• General Bank Account is an asset. • Justin Case, Capital is an owner's equity account.
Step 4:	Will the account increase or decrease because of the transaction?	• General Bank Account will increase. • Justin Case, Capital will increase.
Step 5:	Will the account be debited (DEAD) or credited (CLIC)? By what amount?	• General Bank Account will be debited for $500. • Justin Case, Capital will be credited for $500.
Step 6:	Is the entry balanced?	• Yes, there is a debit of $500 and a credit of $500.

General Journal					GJ2
Date 20**		Description	PR	Debit	Credit
_ _ _ _ _	_ _	_ _ _ _ _ _ _ _ _ _ _ _ _ _ _ _ _ _ _ _	_ _	_ _ _	_ _ _¹
Oct.	5	Office Furniture and Equipment		2,000	
		General Bank Account (Cash)			500
		Credit Card Debt			1,500
		To record furniture purchased from IKEA			
	8	General Bank Account		500	
		Justin Case, Capital			500
		To record investment of scholarship			

---

1 The broken lines here and in the tables that follow indicate that the page has been split, so that the whole general journal need not be shown each time.

EXAMPLE 4

On October 10, Justin opened an account with a legal stationer, Legal Supplies Inc., and purchased office supplies from them worth $580. Terms for payment on account are net 30 days, after which interest will be charged.

Analysis of Transaction		Result
Step 1:	What did the firm give and what did the firm receive in this transaction?	• The firm received office supplies. • The firm gave a promise to pay within 30 days.
Step 2:	Which account is used for the item received and which account is used for the item given?	• Office Supplies/General Expense is used because the supplies will be used up within the year. • Accounts Payable/General Liabilities is used to record the promise to pay Legal Supplies Inc. for the purchase on credit.
Step 3:	What category of account is it?	• Office Supplies/General Expense is an expense account. • Accounts Payable/General Liabilities is a liability account.
Step 4:	Will the account increase or decrease because of the transaction?	• Office Supplies/General Expense will increase. • Accounts Payable/General Liabilities will increase.
Step 5:	Will the account be debited (DEAD) or credited (CLIC)? By what amount?	• Office Supplies/General Expense will be debited by $580. • Accounts Payable/General Liabilities will be credited by $580.
Step 6:	Is the entry balanced?	• Yes, there is a debit of $580 and a credit of $580.

General Journal					GJ2
Date 20**		Description	PR	Debit	Credit
- - - -	- - -	- -	- - -	- - -	- - -
Oct.	8	General Bank Account		500	
		Justin Case, Capital			500
		To record investment of scholarship			
	10	Office Supplies/General Expense		580	
		Accounts Payable/General Liabilities			580
		To record purchase from Legal Supplies Inc.			

EXAMPLE 5

Shift in assets: On October 15, Justin purchased a second-hand filing cabinet at Office Equipment Inc., a used office equipment store. He paid $100 by cheque.

Analysis of Transaction		Result
Step 1:	What did the firm give and what did the firm receive in this transaction?	• The firm received a filing cabinet. • The firm gave cash (a cheque) to pay for the cabinet.
Step 2:	Which account is used for the item received and which account is used for the item given?	• Office Furniture and Equipment is used for the item received. • General Bank Account is used for the item given.
Step 3:	What category of account is it?	• Office Furniture and Equipment is an asset account. • General Bank Account is also an asset account.
Step 4:	Will the account increase or decrease because of the transaction?	• Office Furniture and Equipment will increase. • General Bank Account will decrease.
Step 5:	Will the account be debited (DEAD) or credited (CLIC)? By what amount?	• Office Furniture and Equipment will be debited $100. • General Bank Account will be credited for $100.
Step 6:	Is the entry balanced?	• Yes, there is a debit of $100 and a credit of $100.

General Journal					GJ2
Date 20**		Description	PR	Debit	Credit
- - - -	- - - -	- -	- - - -	- - - -	- - - -
Oct.	10	Office Supplies/General Expense		580	
		Accounts Payable/General Liabilities			580
		To record purchase from Legal Supplies Inc.			
	15	Office Furniture and Equipment		100	
		General Bank Account			100
		Purchased filing cabinet from Office Equipment Inc.			

EXAMPLE 6

Payment for services rendered: On October 20, Justin gave a bill to his first client, Judith Sabourin, in the amount of $3,000 and she paid him with a cheque.

Analysis of Transaction	Result
Step 1: What did the firm give and what did the firm receive in this transaction?	• The firm provided services to a client. • The firm received a cheque payment for the services rendered.
Step 2: Which account is used for the item received and which account is used for the item given?	• General Bank Account is used to record the payment received. • Fees Earned is used to record the bill given to the client for the services rendered.
Step 3: What category of account is it?	• General Bank Account is an asset account. • Fees Earned is an income account.
Step 4: Will the account increase or decrease because of the transaction?	• General Bank Account will increase. • Fees Earned will increase.
Step 5: Will the account be debited (DEAD) or credited (CLIC)? By what amount?	• General Bank Account will be debited for $3,000. • Fees Earned will be credited for $3,000.
Step 6: Is the entry balanced?	• Yes, there is a debit of $3,000 and a credit of $3,000.

	General Journal				GJ2
Date 20**		Description	PR	Debit	Credit
		- -			
Oct.	15	Office Furniture and Equipment		100	
		General Bank Account			100
		Purchased filing cabinet from Office Equipment Inc.			
	20	General Bank Account		3,000	
		Fees Earned			3,000
		To record fees billed to Sabourin and paid			

EXAMPLE 7

Expenses: On October 30, Justin Case paid rent of $500 for one month. Use the same process to record this expense as was used in example 1 to record an expense.

Analysis of Transaction	Result
Step 1: What did the firm give and what did the firm receive in this transaction?	• The firm paid money (a cheque) in exchange for one month's rent (for the use of the office).
Step 2: Which account is used for the item received and which account is used for the item given?	• Rent Expense is used to record rent charged. • General Bank Account is used to record payment given.
Step 3: What category of account is it?	• Rent Expense is an expense account. • General Bank Account is an asset account.
Step 4: Will the account increase or decrease because of the transaction?	• Rent Expense will increase. • General Bank Account will decrease.
Step 5: Will the account be debited (DEAD) or credited (CLIC)? By what amount?	• Rent Expense will be debited for $500. • General Bank Account will be credited for $500.
Step 6: Is the entry balanced?	• Yes, there is a debit of $500 and a credit of $500.

General Journal					GJ2
Date 20**		Description	PR	Debit	Credit
- - - -	- - - -	- - - - - - - - - - - - - - - - - - - -	- - - -	- - - -	- - - -
Oct.	20	General Bank Account		3,000	
		Fees Earned			3,000
		To record fees billed to Sabourin and paid			
	30	Rent Expense		500	
		General Bank Account			500
		To record rent paid for one month			

Figure 3.5 shows the general journal after all October transactions (examples 1 through 7) have been entered and totalled.

General Journal					GJ2
Date 20**		Description	PR	Debit	Credit
Oct.	5	Telephone Expense		300	
		General Bank Account (Cash)			300
		Paid telephone expense for Oct.			
	5	Office Furniture and Equipment		2,000	
		General Bank Account (Cash)			500
		Credit Card Debt			1,500
		To record furniture purchased from IKEA			
	8	General Bank Account		500	
		Justin Case, Capital			500
		To record investment of scholarship			
	10	Office Supplies/General Expense		580	
		Accounts Payable/General Liabilities			580
		To record purchase from Legal Supplies Inc.			
	15	Office Furniture and Equipment		100	
		General Bank Account			100
		Purchased filing cabinet from Office Equipment Inc.			
	20	General Bank Account		3,000	
		Fees Earned			3,000
		To record fees billed to Sabourin and paid			
	30	Rent Expense		500	
		General Bank Account			500
		To record rent paid for one month			
		Totals		6,980	6,980

FIGURE 3.5   General journal after all October transactions have been entered and totalled

The General Journal

As each transaction in examples 1 through 7 was analyzed, it was recorded in the general journal on page 2 (GJ2). All the information regarding each transaction is captured in this journal—the date the transaction occurred, the names of the accounts affected, the amounts debited and credited, and an explanation of what the entry was for.

There are a number of conventions regarding journal entries that you should keep in mind:

- Enter the year on the first line at the top of the first column.
- Enter the month on the first line of the journal entry. You do not need to enter the month again unless you start a new page or the month changes.
- Enter the day of the transaction in the second column on the first line of each entry. Transactions are entered in chronological order (by order of date).
- Enter the name of the account to be debited on the first line of the entry. Note that debits are always entered first. Use the name of the account as it is shown on the chart of accounts being used by the firm. The debit entry should be aligned at the margin. Enter the amount to be debited in the debit column on the same line. Dollar signs are not usually used in journals and ledgers.
- Enter the name of the account to be credited on the next line of the entry. Use the name of the account as it is shown on the chart of accounts being used by the firm. The credit entry should be indented by about three spaces (or 1 cm). This provides a visual clue that the entry is a credit entry.
- Enter the credit amount in the credit column.
- Enter a brief explanation of what the entry is for. This entry is usually indented by about four spaces (or 1.2 cm) and italicized to distinguish it from the credit entries. When providing the explanation for the transaction, you may want to indicate the name of who was paid, or what month the bill was for.
- Skip one line between each new entry.
- Total the general journal columns to ensure that your debits are equal to your credits. The line with totals should have a single line above and a double border below the totals.

Post Reference Column

The post reference (PR) column, sometimes referred to as the "folio" in the general journal, is left blank when a transaction is initially recorded. Individual account numbers will be entered into the PR column when entries are posted to the general ledger.

CHAPTER SUMMARY

The accounting cycle has been briefly described in this chapter. You have learned about the practical factors to consider in selecting a fiscal year. The concepts of debit and credit have been explained, and you should understand how to analyze transactions using the chart of accounts. You should be starting to understand the theory about the accounting equation and the rules of debit and credit.

Analyzing business transactions and entering them into a journal are only the first two steps in the accounting cycle, but getting them right at this stage will make completion of the other steps in the cycle much easier. The accuracy of entries in the general journal and other journals is the key to smooth sailing for completion of the other steps.

KEY TERMS

accounting cycle, 38
accounting period, 38
adjustments, 40
closing the books, 41
compound entry, 41
credit (Cr.), 41
DEAD CLIC, 44
debit (Dr.), 41
financial statements, 40
fiscal periods, 38
fiscal year, 38
general ledgers, 40
journal entries, 40
normal credit balance, 41
normal debit balance, 41
post-closing trial balance, 39
posting, 40
trial balance, 40

FURTHER READING

Canadian Tax & Your Business (New York: About.com, 2015), online: <http://sbinfocanada.about.com/od/taxinfo/u/Canadian-Tax-And-Your-Business.htm>.
Law Society of Upper Canada, *The Bookkeeping Guide for Paralegals* (Toronto: LSUC, February 2014), online: <http://www.lsuc.on.ca/uploadedFiles/PDC/Practice_Review/Paralegal%20Bookkeeping%20Guide%20-%20February%202014.pdf>.

PUT IT INTO PRACTICE

Case Example: Analysis of Transactions

Ann Litigate is updating her bookkeeping records in preparation for the monthly meeting with her accountant. She has the following transactions to enter in the general journal but she is not sure how to analyze the transactions in order to complete the entries. Use the chart of accounts on the inside front cover of this textbook and provide your analysis of the transactions listed below:

1. Ann invoiced her client on January 1 ($3,000), but the account is now more than 40 days past due. What is the entry? What options are available to Ann?
2. Ann earned $1,200 for legal services rendered on another client file. She received a partial payment ($700) by cheque, but there is an outstanding balance of $500. What is the entry?

REVIEW QUESTIONS

True or False

F __ 1. Debit entries always cause an increase in an account.

F __ 2. Adjustments made on a worksheet should be transferred directly to the appropriate financial statement.

T __ 3. Credit entries are found on the right side of the accounting equation or T-account.

F __ 4. The accounting period is established by the tax regulator (e.g., the Canada Revenue Agency).

T __ 5. Accounting periods or fiscal periods may be calculated monthly, quarterly, or annually.

F __ 6. The normal balance for expense accounts is a debit entry.

F __ 7. The normal balance for asset accounts is a credit entry.

T __ 8. Selling office furniture or equipment will result in a credit on the right side of the balance sheet.

T __ 9. A trial balance is balanced when all the debits equal all the credits.

F __ 10. General ledger entries are ordered chronologically.

T __ 11. Each transaction must have a minimum of one debit record entry and one credit record entry.

T __ 12. A review of the journal entries and general ledger for mathematical or recording errors will help correct trial balance errors.

Short Answer

1. What are the pros and the cons of electing a December 31 fiscal year-end?

2. Briefly describe the information that the following financial statements can provide to a business owner and interested third parties or stakeholders:

   a. balance sheet

   b. income statement

   c. statement of owner's equity

3. What does it mean to close the books?

PRACTICE EXERCISES

Practice Exercise 3.1

Using the examples in the box below as a guide, show the increase and decrease that occurs for each of the transactions in the following T-accounts. Identify and insert the name of the account affected in each transaction and place the amount on the debit or credit side depending on whether the account is increasing or decreasing.

Example of T-account form:

Accounting Equation: Assets (left) = Liabilities + Owner's Equity (right)

Example, balance sheet:

Assets (100)	
Debit	Credit
(+) Increase	(−) Decrease

Liabilities (200)	
Debit	Credit
(−) Decrease	(+) Increase

Owner's Equity (300)	
Debit	Credit
(−) Decrease	(+) Increase

Owner, Drawings (350)	
Debit	Credit
(+) Increase	(−) Decrease

Example, income statement:

Income (400)	
Debit	Credit
(−) Decrease	(+) Increase

Expenses (500)	
Debit	Credit
(+) Increase	(−) Decrease

Transactions

a. A paralegal invests capital ($10,000) in a legal services firm.

Capital

Dr.	Cr.
—	+

Gen.

Dr.	Cr.
+	—

b. A paralegal receives a cheque as payment from a client ($5,000) on an outstanding account for legal services.

Gen

Dr.	Cr.
+	—

Acc. Rec.

Dr.	Cr.
—	+

c. A paralegal pays an invoice for professional liability insurance with cash ($1,100).

Insurance

Dr.	Cr.
+	—

Liability

Dr.	Cr.
—	+

Practice Exercise 3.2

Using the examples in the box below as a guide, analyze each transaction that follows and record the appropriate entries in general journal format.

Example: On October 1, Judy Roth wrote a cheque for $300 to Minitel in payment of the phone bill.

Which two accounts are affected?	
General Bank Account	Telephone Expense

To what category do the affected accounts belong?	
Assets	Expenses

Is the affected account increasing or decreasing?	
Decreasing	Increasing

Will the account be debited or credited?	
Credit	Debit

What amount will be debited or credited to each account?	
300	300

Record the journal entry for this transaction:

Date 20**		Description	Dr.	Cr.
Oct.	1	Telephone Expense	300	
		General Bank Account		300
		Payment of September telephone bill		

Transactions

    a. On October 1, Judy Roth invested $2,000 in her firm.

    b. On October 1, Judy Roth purchased computer equipment on account (i.e., on credit) for $800.

    c. On October 5, Judy Roth invoiced a client for professional fees of $2,500.

    d. On October 10, Judy Roth received partial payment of $1,500 from a client for the invoice sent in transaction (c), above.

    e. On October 15, Judy Roth paid $600 cash for office furniture.

Use general journal format to illustrate the transactions in Practice Exercises 3.3 through 3.8.

Practice Exercise 3.3

Paying Office Expenses

a. May 1:   Ann Litigate wrote a general cheque #25 for $200 to pay her telephone bill.

b. May 1:   Ann Litigate wrote a general cheque #26 for $25 to pay Staples for office supplies expense.

Practice Exercise 3.4

Compound Entries

a. May 1:   Ann Litigate purchased a computer for $1,000 from Computers R Us. She paid for the computer using a credit card and a general cheque. The cheque (#27) was written for $300 and she put $700 on the credit card.

b. May 1:   Ann Litigate paid three months' rent with a general cheque #28 in the amount of $3,000 ($1,000 per month). Of that amount, $1,000 was rent expense for the current month and $2,000 was prepaid rent for the next two months' rent.

Practice Exercise 3.5

Recording and Paying Accounts Payable

a. May 15: Ann Litigate purchased a photocopier on account (on credit) from Sharpie Copiers. The cost of the copier is $5,000 and payments are to be made at the rate of $300 per month until the amount is paid in full. Her first payment is due on June 15.

b. June 15: Ann Litigate made a payment to Sharpie Copiers against the amount owed to them for the copier in the amount of $300 (cheque #29).

Practice Exercise 3.6

Recording a Shift in Assets

a. May 15: Ann Litigate purchased a fax machine from FaxMe and paid $150 with a general cheque #30.

Practice Exercise 3.7

Recording Invoices Sent to a Client and
Recording Payment on Account by a Client

a. May 1:   Ann Litigate prepared invoice #10 for fees earned and mailed it to her client Barbara Short for $1,500.

b. May 30: Barbara Short sent a cheque for $1,000 to the firm in partial payment of invoice #10.

Practice Exercise 3.8

Recording Investment by Owner and Withdrawal by Owner

a. May 1: Ann Litigate deposited $10,000 of her personal funds as an investment in her firm.

b. May 15: Ann Litigate withdrew $800 from the firm for her own personal living expenses (cheque #31).

Practice Exercise 3.9

Ann Litigate opened her paralegal service practice, Ann Litigate Paralegal Services, in January 20**. For each of the following transactions, analyze the transaction and prepare the appropriate general journal entry.

January 1–31, 20**:

1 Initial capital investment, $10,000

1 Professional liability insurance expense paid in full for the next 12 months with cash, $1,100

1 Law Society membership dues paid for one month with cash, $125

2 Paid monthly business insurance with cash, $50

3 Purchased office furniture with cash, $500

4 Paid for computer software by credit card, $250

5 Paid for cellphone bill by credit card, $75

5 Paid for telephone and Internet service by credit card, $145

10 Paid for court filing fees by credit card (for client, R. Scott), $200

15 Invoiced client (L. Bailey, invoice #101) for initial consultation, $175

15 Paid biweekly salary for secretary with cash, $1,000

18 Paid installment payment for leased photocopier (equipment) with cash, $240

23 Invoiced client (R. Smythe, invoice #102) for provincial offences file, $300

25 Paid process server for service of court documents and court filing by credit card for client (R. Scott), $108

26 Purchased legal accounting publication, Law Practice, Billing & Accounting, by credit card, $100

27 Retained bookkeeper based on a one-year contract and paid in advance with cash, $2,000

30 Withdrew cash from the business for personal use, $800

30 Paid biweekly salary for secretary with cash, $1,000

30 Paid bank account charges with cash (direct bank payment), $35

Ann Litigate Paralegal Services General Journal				GJ1
Date 20**	Description	PR	Debit	Credit

Practice Exercise 3.10

a. Complete the T-accounts based on the transactions in Practice Exercise 3.9 and provide the balance for each balance sheet account. *Note: Each account starts with $0 opening balance for the purpose of this exercise.*

T-Accounts (Assets)

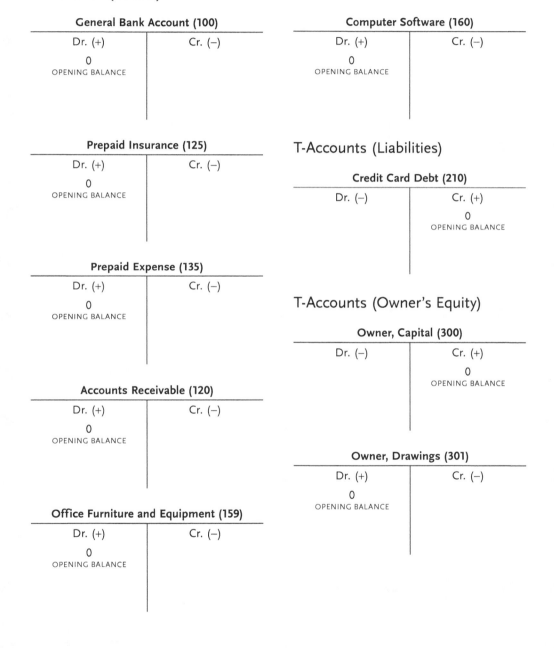

General Bank Account (100)

Dr. (+)	Cr. (−)
0	
OPENING BALANCE	

Computer Software (160)

Dr. (+)	Cr. (−)
0	
OPENING BALANCE	

Prepaid Insurance (125)

Dr. (+)	Cr. (−)
0	
OPENING BALANCE	

T-Accounts (Liabilities)

Credit Card Debt (210)

Dr. (−)	Cr. (+)
	0
	OPENING BALANCE

Prepaid Expense (135)

Dr. (+)	Cr. (−)
0	
OPENING BALANCE	

T-Accounts (Owner's Equity)

Owner, Capital (300)

Dr. (−)	Cr. (+)
	0
	OPENING BALANCE

Accounts Receivable (120)

Dr. (+)	Cr. (−)
0	
OPENING BALANCE	

Owner, Drawings (301)

Dr. (+)	Cr. (−)
0	
OPENING BALANCE	

Office Furniture and Equipment (159)

Dr. (+)	Cr. (−)
0	
OPENING BALANCE	

b. Complete the T-accounts based on the transactions in Practice Exercise 3.9 and add up the totals for each income and expense account; then, as a final step, total all the income and expense accounts.

T-Accounts (Income)

Fees Earned (400)

Dr. (–)	Cr. (+)

T-Accounts (Expenses)

Salaries Expense (511)

Dr. (+)	Cr. (–)

General Disbursement Expense (525)

Dr. (+)	Cr. (–)

Telephone (and Internet Service) Expense (565)

Dr. (+)	Cr. (–)

Library and Subscriptions (530)

Dr. (+)	Cr. (–)

Membership/Professional Dues (534)

Dr. (+)	Cr. (–)

Insurance/Other (528)

Dr. (+)	Cr. (–)

Equipment Lease (524)

Dr. (+)	Cr. (–)

Bank Charges (507)

Dr. (+)	Cr. (–)

Total Income and Expenses

TOTAL INCOME: $ _____   TOTAL EXPENSES: $ _____

Posting and Preparing Financial Statements

After reading this chapter, you should be able to:

- post transactions from the general journal to the general ledger
- prepare a trial balance
- prepare financial statements

In Chapter 2, we recorded the **opening balance** in a **general journal**, and in Chapter 3 we recorded transactions for the month of October in the general journal. The next step in the **accounting cycle** is to post these entries to a general ledger.

General Ledger

The **general ledger** provides a summary of the information contained in the general journal. The information from the general journal is summarized by posting or copying the information to the accounts in the general ledger. Without a summary, the firm cannot know what its bank balance is or how much money has been spent to date on any particular account. The summary is also required for preparation of financial statements.

The general ledger contains a sheet for each of the accounts listed on the company's **chart of accounts**, along with the number of the account. The example in Figure 4.1 shows the format for a simple general ledger account. The name of the account is General Bank Account; the number of the account is 100. The **post reference (PR)** is the numerical identifier for each account referenced on the chart of accounts. This makes it easy to cross-reference and identify journal entries.

The columns in the ledger sheet include a column for the year and date, an explanation, the post reference, a column for debit, a column for credit, and a column for the balance. You will notice that the column immediately before the balance is headed "Dr./Cr." This column is used to indicate whether the running balance is a debit balance or a credit balance. It does not refer to the entry made on that line. You will need to calculate the running balance after making each entry in the general ledger accounts.

A general bank account is an asset and usually has a "Dr." balance, unless the account is overdrawn (or "in the red"). If the balance in the bank is negative, you will indicate "Cr." in the column before the balance. The ledger accounts are kept by category in the same order as they appear in the chart of accounts: assets, liabilities, owner's equity, income, and expenses.

General Bank Account						Account No. 100	
Date 20**		Explanation	PR	Debit	Credit	Dr./Cr.	Balance

FIGURE 4.1   Sample general ledger account

Posting

The entries from the general journal must be copied to the individual general ledger accounts. Each debit and credit entry must be posted in the same order as it appears in the general journal. Posting is done as you transfer the debits and credits for each transaction from the general journal to the general ledger.

EXAMPLE

Justin Case, General Journal					GJ1
Date 20**		Description	PR	Debit	Credit
Oct.	1	Opening Entries			
		General Bank Account	⁶100	1,000	
		Justin Case, Capital	⁶300		1,000
		To record funds invested by owner			

FIGURE 4.2   Posting entry from the general journal

To post the general journal entry dated October 1 (Figure 4.2) to the general ledger, you would take the following steps (the numbered steps are shown in superscript in the previous and following posting entries):

STEP 1

In the general ledger, find the account called General Bank Account (Figure 4.3). Enter the amount of $1,000 in the debit column. Because the $1,000 is debited in the general journal, it must be shown as a debit in the general ledger.

STEP 2

Enter GJ1 in the post reference column of the ledger. This tells anyone looking at the books that the debit came from page 1 of the general journal.

STEP 3

Enter the transaction date in the date column of the ledger as shown in the general journal.

STEP 4

Calculate the running balance.

STEP 5

Indicate whether the balance is a debit or a credit balance in the Dr./Cr. column.

STEP 6

Put the number of the account to which the entry was posted in the post reference box of the general journal (Figure 4.2). Post referencing indicates which transactions have or have not been posted from the general journal to the general ledger, and also indicates the account to which the entry has been posted.

Repeat steps 1 to 6 to post the second line of the general journal entry (the credit side) to the Justin Case, Capital account in the general ledger (Figure 4.3).

The process provides a trail to show the ledger account to which an entry in the general journal was posted, and also shows where the number in the ledger came from. You would continue this process, entering each transaction in the correct general ledger and totalling the amounts in the general ledger to summarize the transactions.

Note that no explanation is required when completing the entry in the general ledger. This is because you have the explanation in the general journal. If you need to know what the $1,000 posted on October 1 was for, you can refer back to page 1 of the general journal, where the explanation is found. However, an explanation may be added if the bookkeeper wishes to provide extra details regarding an entry.

Once all the journal entries from pages GJ1 and GJ2 have been posted, the general journal for Justin Case's firm will appear as in Figure 4.4.

General Ledgers — Justin Case							

General Bank Account						Account No. [6]100	
Date 20**		Explanation	PR	Debit	Credit	Dr./Cr.	Balance
[3]Oct.	1		[2]GJ1	[1]1,000		[5]Dr.	[1]1,000

Justin Case, Capital						Account No. [6]300	
Date 20**		Explanation	PR	Debit	Credit	Dr./Cr.	Balance
[3]Oct.	1		[2]GJ1		[1]1,000	[5]Cr.	[1]1,000

FIGURE 4.3   Posting to the general ledgers: General Bank Account and Justin Case, Capital account

Justin Case, General Journal					GJ1
Date 20**		Description	PR	Debit	Credit
Oct.	1	Opening Entries			
		General Bank Account	100	1,000	
		Justin Case, Capital	300		1,000
		To record funds invested by owner			
	1	General Bank Account	100	4,000	
		Personal Loan	205		4,000
		To record loan from father, James Case			
	1	Computer Equipment, Hardware	155	900	
		Justin Case, Capital	300		900
		To record computer equipment invested by owner at fair market value			
	1	Office Furniture and Equipment	158	150	
		Justin Case, Capital	300		150
		To record office furniture invested by owner at fair market value			
		Totals		6,050	6,050

Justin Case, General Journal					GJ1
Date 20**		Description	PR	Debit	Credit
Oct.	5	Telephone Expense	565	300	
		General Bank Account (Cash)	100		300
		To record telephone expense for Oct.			
	5	Office Furniture and Equipment	158	2,000	
		General Bank Account (Cash)	100		500
		Credit Card Debt	210		1,500
		To record furniture purchased from IKEA			
	8	General Bank Account	100	500	
		Justin Case, Capital	300		500
		To record investment of scholarship			
	10	Office Supplies/General Expense	535	580	
		Accounts Payable/General Liabilities	200		580
		To record purchase from Legal Supplies Inc.			
	15	Office Furniture and Equipment	158	100	
		General Bank Account	100		100
		Purchased filing cabinet from Office Equipment Inc.			
	20	General Bank Account	100	3,000	
		Fees Earned	400		3,000
		To record fees billed to Sabourin and paid			
	30	Rent Expense	538	500	
		General Bank Account	100		500
		To record rent paid for one month			
		Totals		6,980	6,980

FIGURE 4.4   **All general journal entries posted for October**

After Justin Case has posted all the entries made to date on pages GJ1 and GJ2, the general ledger will have the balances shown in Figure 4.5. Note that the accounts that do not have any entries are omitted at this time. The general ledger accounts will be added as required as we complete the posting.

General Ledgers — Justin Case							

General Bank Account						**Account No. 100**	
Date 20**		Explanation	PR	Debit	Credit	Dr./Cr.	Balance
Oct.	1		GJ1	1,000		Dr.	1,000
	1		GJ1	4,000		Dr.	5,000
	5		GJ2		300	Dr.	4,700
	5		GJ2		500	Dr.	4,200
	8		GJ2	500		Dr.	4,700
	15		GJ2		100	Dr.	4,600
	20		GJ2	3,000		Dr.	7,600
	30		GJ2		500	Dr.	7,100

Computer Equipment (Hardware)						**Account No. 155**	
Date 20**		Explanation	PR	Debit	Credit	Dr./Cr.	Balance
Oct.	1		GJ1	900		Dr.	900

Office Furniture and Equipment						**Account No. 158**	
Date 20**		Explanation	PR	Debit	Credit	Dr./Cr.	Balance
Oct.	1		GJ1	150		Dr.	150
	5		GJ2	2,000		Dr.	2,150
	15		GJ2	100		Dr.	2,250

Accounts Payable/General Liabilities						**Account No. 200**	
Date 20**		Explanation	PR	Debit	Credit	Dr./Cr.	Balance
Oct.	10	Legal Supplies Inc.[1]	GJ2		580	Cr.	580

Personal Loan						**Account No. 205**	
Date 20**		Explanation	PR	Debit	Credit	Dr./Cr.	Balance
Oct.	1	James Case	GJ1		4,000	Cr.	4,000

---

1 Although an explanation is not required, it may be added if the bookkeeper wishes to provide extra details regarding an entry.

Credit Card Debt						Account No. 210	
Date 20**		Explanation	PR	Debit	Credit	Dr./Cr.	Balance
Oct.	5		GJ2		1,500	Cr.	1,500

Justin Case, Capital						Account No. 300	
Date 20**		Explanation	PR	Debit	Credit	Dr./Cr.	Balance
Oct.	1		GJ1		1,000	Cr.	1,000
	1		GJ1		900	Cr.	1,900
	1		GJ1		150	Cr.	2,050
	8		GJ2		500	Cr.	2,550

Fees Earned						Account No. 400	
Date 20**		Explanation	PR	Debit	Credit	Dr./Cr.	Balance
Oct.	20		GJ2		3,000	Cr.	3,000

Office Supplies/General Expense						Account No. 535	
Date 20**		Explanation	PR	Debit	Credit	Dr./Cr.	Balance
Oct.	10		GJ2	580		Dr.	580

Rent Expense						Account No. 538	
Date 20**		Explanation	PR	Debit	Credit	Dr./Cr.	Balance
Oct.	30		GJ2	500		Dr.	500

Telephone Expense						Account No. 565	
Date 20**		Explanation	PR	Debit	Credit	Dr./Cr.	Balance
Oct.	5		GJ2	300		Dr.	300

FIGURE 4.5   General ledger accounts after October posting completed

Preparing the Trial Balance

A **trial balance** lists all the accounts in the general ledger with the debit or credit balance shown for each account (Figure 4.6). The trial balance is not a financial report, but the information in it is used to prepare financial reports. List the accounts in the trial balance in the same order as they appear in the general ledger. The balance from each of the ledger accounts must be entered in the appropriate debit or credit column. At the end, the total is calculated for each column, and the total debits must equal the total credits. Draw a single line above the totals and a double line below the totals.

The heading of the trial balance contains three lines. The first line identifies the firm, the second line describes the statement, and the third line shows the date of the statement.

The trial balance is important because it proves that the entries were properly recorded in the general journal, that they were properly posted to the general ledger, and that the balances in the general ledger were correctly calculated.

Justin Case, Paralegal				
Trial Balance				
October 31, 20**				
#	Account		Debit	Credit
100	General Bank Account		$7,100	
155	Computer Equipment (Hardware)		900	
158	Office Furniture and Equipment		2,250	
200	Accounts Payable/General Liabilities			$580
205	Personal Loan			4,000
210	Credit Card Debt			1,500
300	Justin Case, Capital			2,550
400	Fees Earned			3,000
535	Office Supplies/General Expense		580	
538	Rent Expense		500	
565	Telephone Expense		300	
			$11,630	$11,630

FIGURE 4.6   Trial balance

If the totals in the trial balance are not equal, it is likely that one or more errors were made. These must be found before proceeding further.

Finding Errors in the Trial Balance

To find any errors, follow these steps:

1. *Wrong column:* Check to see if a debit amount was entered into the credit column in the ledger account while posting from the general journal.
2. *Wrong column:* Check to see if a credit amount was entered into the debit column in the ledger account while posting from the general journal.
3. *Calculation error:* Check the arithmetic to ensure that an error was not made in calculating one or more balances in the ledger accounts.
4. *Copying error:* Check to ensure that the amounts in the general ledger were copied correctly to the trial balance.
5. *Calculation error:* Check the calculation of the totals in the trial balance.

Some errors will not be revealed even if the debit and credit totals in the trial balance are equal:

- Amounts posted to the wrong ledger account but otherwise correctly debited or credited
- Leaving out an entire transaction when posting from the general journal to the general ledgers
- Compensating errors (an error on the debit side that offsets an error of equal value on the credit side)

Common Mistakes

Trying to find mistakes in the trial balance can be frustrating, so here are a few tricks:

1. There is probably a *mathematical error* if the difference between the total debits and credits is off by 10, 100, 1,000, and so on.
2. There is probably an *omission error* if the difference is equal to the balance in one of the general ledger accounts. The amount may accidentally have been omitted. It is also possible that the number was not posted from the general journal.
3. There is probably a *posting error* if you can divide the difference in debits and credits by two. Check to see if a debit was entered on the credit side by mistake, or vice versa, in the ledger or in the trial balance. For example, a difference of $60 divided by two is $30. This means you may have entered a $30 debit to an account instead of correctly entering the amount as a credit, or vice versa.
4. There is probably a *transposition error* if the difference is divisible by nine. A **transposition** is the accidental reversal of digits—for example, entering $91 instead of $19 or $5,520 instead of $5,250. When you subtract the numbers from each other and divide the difference by nine, you will get an even number. For example, $5,520 – $5,250 is $270. When you divide $270 by nine, you get an even $30. This result indicates a possible transposition error.
5. There is possibly a *slide error*. A **slide** is an error resulting from incorrect placement of the decimal point in writing numbers. For example, $5,250 may have been entered as $52.50.
6. There may be a *copying error*. Compare the balances in the trial balance with the ledger accounts to check for copying errors.
7. There may be a *calculation error*. Recalculate the balances in each ledger account.
8. There may be a *posting error*. Trace all postings from the journal to the ledger.

If you cannot find the error after having completed all these steps, take a break. Next time you look at the numbers, the error will probably jump out at you.

Preparing Financial Statements

The trial balance (Figure 4.7) is used to prepare **financial statements**—first the income statement, then the statement of owner's equity, and finally the balance sheet.

The financial statements will not have debit or credit columns. The left column in the income statement (Figure 4.8) and in the statement of owner's equity (Figure 4.9) is used to calculate totals, which are then placed in the column to the right. The balance sheet (Figure 4.10) is displayed with assets on the left-hand side and liabilities and owner's equity on the right-hand side. An additional column can be placed on the right-hand side to add up liabilities if necessary.

The information on the income statement is used to calculate the statement of owner's equity. Once you know the amount of the owner's equity, you are able to transfer that information to the balance sheet, so it is imperative that the statements be completed in the correct order. All the information required for each of the statements is found in the trial balance.

#	Account	Debit	Credit	
	Justin Case, Paralegal			
	Trial Balance			
	October 31, 20**			
100	General Bank Account	$7,100		
155	Computer Equipment (Hardware)	900		
158	Office Furniture and Equipment	2,250		Balance Sheet Accounts
200	Accounts Payable/General Liabilities		$580	
205	Personal Loan		4,000	
210	Credit Card Debt		1,500	
300	Justin Case, Capital		2,550	Owner's Equity Account(s)
301	Justin Case, Drawings		0	
400	Fees Earned		3,000	
535	Office Supplies/General Expense	580		Income Statement Accounts
538	Rent Expense	500		
565	Telephone Expense	300		
		$11,630	$11,630	

FIGURE 4.7 Trial balance showing balance sheet, owner's equity, and income statement accounts

Income Statement

The first statement prepared is the **income statement**, which shows the revenues and expenses for a particular **accounting period** and is sometimes called the profit and loss statement. The heading includes the name of the business, the name of the statement, and the period covered by the report.

The income statement must be prepared at the end of each fiscal year, but is usually prepared more frequently, typically each month, to inform the owner of the bottom line for the period. This information is often required by the firm's bank and investors.

The simple form of the income statement is sufficient for the purposes of a paralegal firm. It will show the revenues earned less the expenses incurred for the period to arrive at a net profit or net loss.

Justin Case, Paralegal Income Statement for the period ended October 31, 20**		
Revenue		
Fees Earned		$3,000
Expenses		
Office Supplies/General Expense	$580	
Rent Expense	500	
Telephone Expense	300	
Total Expenses		1,380
Net Income		$1,620

FIGURE 4.8   Income statement

Reporting Income and Expenses

TAX TIP

The Canada Revenue Agency (CRA) website has detailed and extensive information for businesses outlining what is to be declared as income and how expenses can be claimed. The following headings emphasize some (but not necessarily all) of the tax considerations you should be aware of as a licensee when preparing your records for tax purposes. Interpretation Bulletins published by the CRA provide detailed guidelines for interpretation of various sections of the *Income Tax Act* and should be consulted when in doubt.

Accounting for Your Earnings (Income)

Generally, business income must be reported using the accrual method of accounting. Under the accrual method, you have to report income in the fiscal period you earn it, regardless of when you receive payment. Similarly, you deduct allowable expenses in the fiscal period in which you incur them, whether or not you pay for them in that period. *Incur* usually means you either paid or will have to pay the expense.

Other Income

You must also report the total income you received from other sources, such as a recovery of an amount previously written off as a bad debt in a previous year, and interest income received for late payment of invoices.

Barter Transactions

A **barter transaction** takes place when any two persons agree to an exchange of goods or services and carry out that exchange without using money. If you are involved in a barter transaction, the goods or services you receive could be considered proceeds from a business operation. If you offer legal services to the mechanic who fixes your car, this is considered a barter transaction. You are required to include the value of the goods or services you provided in your income. Barter transactions may also have GST/HST implications.

Accounting for Your Business Expenses

A business expense is a cost you incur for the sole purpose of earning business income. You must back up business expense claims with a sales invoice, an agreement of purchase and sale, a receipt, or some other voucher that supports the expenditure. If you pay cash for any business expenses, be sure to get receipts or other vouchers. Receipts should include the vendor's name and the date as well as GST/HST information.

As a sole proprietor or partner in a partnership, when recording expenses you should enter only the business part of the expense. This means that the following are not included as part of your expenses:

- Salary or wages (including drawings) paid to self or partner(s)
- Cost of goods or services that you, your family, or your partners and their families used (including such items as food, home maintenance, or business properties)
- Interest and penalties you paid on your income tax
- Life insurance premiums
- The part of any expenses that can be attributed to non-business use of business property
- Most fines and penalties imposed after March 22, 2004, under the law of Canada or a province or a foreign country (this includes parking tickets)

Business-Use-of-Home Expenses

You can deduct expenses for the business use of a work space in your home, as long as you meet *one* of these conditions:

- It is your principal place of business OR
- You use the space only to earn your business income and you use it on a regular and ongoing basis to meet your clients or customers

You can deduct a part of your maintenance costs, such as heating, home insurance, electricity, and cleaning materials. You can also deduct a part of your property taxes, mortgage interest, and capital cost allowance. To calculate the part you can deduct, use a reasonable basis, such as the area of the work space divided by the total area of your home.

Statement of Owner's Equity

The second statement prepared is the **statement of owner's equity**. The heading includes the name of the business, the name of the statement, and the period covered by the report.

The goal of this statement is to calculate owner's equity in the firm after taking into account any profits or losses of the firm less money withdrawn by the owner. The calculation tells us how the owner's investment in the firm has been affected by the operations of the business. You can see that at the end of October, Justin Case's equity in the firm went up to $4,170 ($2,550, opening balance + $1,620, net income) because of the profit from operations during the month of October. The amount of the profit ($1,620) was added to the capital at the beginning of the period ($2,550) to calculate the balance in the capital account or owner's equity at the end of the period. If Justin had withdrawn funds from the firm, the amount withdrawn would have been deducted from the net income, resulting in a decrease in the owner's equity.

Justin Case, Paralegal Statement of Owner's Equity for the Period Ended October 31, 20**		
Justin Case, Capital, Oct. 1, 20**		$2,550
Net Income for Oct. 20**	$1,620	
Less: Withdrawals for Oct.	0	
Increase in Capital		1,620
Justin Case, Capital Oct. 31, 20**		$4,170

FIGURE 4.9   Statement of owner's equity

Balance Sheet

The third statement prepared is the balance sheet. The **balance sheet** is a snapshot of the financial position of the firm on a particular date, typically the end of the financial period being reported. The heading includes the name of the business, the name of the statement, and the date of the report.

The balance sheet provides important information about the financial position of the firm. In Figure 4.10, we can see that Justin has enough cash in the bank to meet his current liabilities. We can also see that his investment in the firm has increased since he started the business on October 1.

Justin Case, Paralegal Balance Sheet October 31, 20**			
Assets		**Liabilities**	
General Bank Account	$7,100	Accounts Payable/General Liabilities	$580
Computer Equipment (Hardware)	900	Personal Loan	4,000
Office Furniture and Equipment	2,250	Credit Card Debt	1,500
		Total Liabilities	$6,080
		Owner's Equity	
		Justin Case, Capital	4,170
Total Assets	$10,250	Total Liabilities and Owner's Equity	$10,250

FIGURE 4.10   Balance sheet

Evaluating the Financial Statements

The financial statements will help provide answers to such questions as:

- Has the firm made or lost money over the period covered by the statements?
- Are the revenues in line with the business plan for the firm or the budget that was prepared?
- Are some of the expenses out of line?
- Does the firm need to cut back, or can it expand?
- Does the firm have sufficient resources to meet its short-term liabilities?
- Does the firm have surplus cash that can be invested to produce income?
- Is the firm at risk of going bankrupt?

CHAPTER SUMMARY

The accounting cycle starts with an analysis of transactions, which are then recorded in a general journal. Once the entries have been added to the journal, they must be summarized; this is accomplished by posting the entries to general ledger accounts and calculating the balance for each general ledger account. The balances in the general ledger are then entered in a trial balance to ensure that the debits are equal to the credits. Once this is ascertained, financial statements—income statement, statement of owner's equity, and balance sheet—can be prepared.

KEY TERMS

accounting cycle, 66	financial statements, 73	post reference (PR), 66
accounting period, 74	general journal, 66	slide, 73
balance sheet, 77	general ledger, 66	statement of owner's equity, 76
barter transaction, 75	income statement, 74	transposition, 73
chart of accounts, 66	opening balance, 66	trial balance, 71

FURTHER READING

Canada Revenue Agency (CRA), "Checklist for Small Businesses," online: <http://www.cra-arc .gc.ca/tx/bsnss/sm/chcklst-eng.html>.

Canada Revenue Agency (CRA), "Reporting Business Income and Expenses" (video series), online: <http://www.cra-arc.gc.ca/vdgllry/bsnss/srs-rprtngncmxpns-eng.html?vclp=bsnss/ srs-rprtngncmxpns1-eng>. (See especially Segment 2: Record Keeping.)

Law Society of Upper Canada, *The Bookkeeping Guide for Paralegals* (Toronto: LSUC, February 2014), online: <http://www.lsuc.on.ca/uploadedFiles/PDC/Practice_Review/Paralegal%20 Bookkeeping%20Guide%20-%20February%202014.pdf>. (See especially item 7, Clients' General Ledger.)

System for Electronic Document Analysis and Retrieval (SEDAR). The official site that provides access to most public securities documents and information filed by public companies and investment funds with the 13 provincial and territorial securities regulatory authorities (Canadian Securities Administrators), online: <http://www.sedar.com/ homepage_en.htm>.

PUT IT INTO PRACTICE

Case Example: Accounting Application

1. When Ann Litigate calculates her company's trial balance, she recognizes that there was an error in the recording of a retainer received from Sam Fisher. The trial balance is understated and out by $200. How can Ann check and correct this error?

2. On April 5, a new client, Sheila McKay, advised that she would like to retain Ann to commence a small claims proceeding against her neighbour, who borrowed $10,000 but has failed to pay her back as agreed and as evidenced by a promissory note. Ann prepared the claim for Sheila, and served and filed the plaintiff's claim form at the Small Claims Court (Superior Court of Justice). On June 1, 20**, Ann invoiced Sheila for the services rendered from April 5 to May 30, 20** (invoice #101) as well as for the related disbursements. The total fee charged was equal to $1,500; the total disbursements (paid by and reimbursable to Ann) were equal to $200, which included the filing fee, the process server costs, and miscellaneous photocopy/printing costs. Harmonized sales tax (HST; 13 percent) is chargeable on both fees and disbursements. Calculate the total amount of the invoice that would be sent to the client including fees, disbursements, and HST.

REVIEW QUESTIONS

Short Answer

Give a full answer for each question:

1. Identify three kinds of financial statements that are used in financial reporting.

2. What does it mean to "post" to the general ledger?

3. When receiving a payment in cash, does this increase or decrease the general bank account? How do you record an increase in this account? How do you record a decrease?

4. How do you characterize or recognize a payment to the owner of the law firm (e.g., Justin Case) for his services?

5. What is meant by the opening balance on the ledger? What is meant by the closing balance on the ledger?

6. What information gets recorded on the trial balance?

7. How do you find and correct errors on the trial balance?

8. What information gets recorded on the income statement?

9. What information gets recorded on the statement of owner's equity?

10. What information gets recorded on the balance sheet?

11. What is a financial statement, and how do you prepare one?

12. Review, analyze, and discuss one of Air Canada's completed financial statements. To find a statement, go to <http://sedar.com/DisplayProfile.do?lang=EN&issuerType=03&issuerNo=00001324>. Choose "View" to display the company's public records, and then select the most recent audited financial statement from the list (e.g., February 11, 2015).

PRACTICE EXERCISES

Worksheets containing the forms you need to complete the practice exercises are provided separately in the working papers for this chapter.

Practice Exercise 4.1

Using the worksheets provided:

a. Prepare general journal entries for the following transactions for June Lang that occurred during September 20**.

b. Post your entries to the general ledgers.

The accounts for June Lang's firm are the following:

100	General Bank Account	200	Accounts Payable/General Liabilities
120	Accounts Receivable	300	June Lang, Capital
130	Office Supplies	350	June Lang, Drawings
140	Motor Vehicle	400	Fees Earned
158	Office Furniture and Equipment	538	Rent Expense

Transactions:

Sep.	3	June Lang invested $20,000 cash and office equipment worth $2,000 in her business
	6	Purchased a motor vehicle on account for $15,000. She paid $1,000 by cheque and the balance on credit
	13	Bought office supplies for $1,000
	15	Withdrew $500 from the business for personal use
	20	Invoiced Fred Popper $2,000 for services rendered. Account remains outstanding
	30	Paid rent expense to Minto Developments, $650

Worksheets:

PRACTICE
EXCEL

June Lang, General Journal					GJ4
Date 20**		Description	PR	Debit	Credit

General Ledgers — June Lang

General Bank Account — Account No. 100

Date 20**		Explanation	PR	Debit	Credit	Dr./Cr.	Balance

Accounts Receivable — Account No. 120

Date 20**		Explanation	PR	Debit	Credit	Dr./Cr.	Balance

Office Supplies — Account No. 130

Date 20**		Explanation	PR	Debit	Credit	Dr./Cr.	Balance

Motor Vehicle — Account No. 140

Date 20**		Explanation	PR	Debit	Credit	Dr./Cr.	Balance

Office Furniture and Equipment — Account No. 158

Date 20**		Explanation	PR	Debit	Credit	Dr./Cr.	Balance

PRACTICE

EXCEL

Accounts Payable/General Liabilities						Account No. 200	
Date 20**	Explanation	PR	Debit	Credit	Dr./Cr.	Balance	

June Lang, Capital						Account No. 300	
Date 20**	Explanation	PR	Debit	Credit	Dr./Cr.	Balance	

June Lang, Drawings						Account No. 350	
Date 20**	Explanation	PR	Debit	Credit	Dr./Cr.	Balance	

Fees Earned						Account No. 400	
Date 20**	Explanation	PR	Debit	Credit	Dr./Cr.	Balance	

Rent Expense						Account No. 538	
Date 20**	Explanation	PR	Debit	Credit	Dr./Cr.	Balance	

Practice Exercise 4.2

Using the worksheets provided, post the general journal entries for the following transactions for Frank Piper that occurred during June 20** to the general ledgers.

The partial ledger of Frank Piper uses the following accounts:

100	General Bank Account (Cash)	200	Accounts Payable/General Liabilities
158	Office Furniture and Equipment	300	Frank Piper, Capital

Frank Piper, Paralegal General Journal					GJ5
Date 20**		Description	PR	Debit	Credit
		Opening Entries			
June	1	General Bank Account (Cash)		10,000	
		Frank Piper, Capital			10,000
		To record funds invested by owner			
	1	Office Furniture and Equipment		1,000	
		Accounts Payable/General Liabilities			1,000
		Purchased photocopier from Sharp			

PRACTICE
EXCEL

General Ledgers — Frank Piper

General Bank Account (Cash) — Account No. 100

Date 20**		Explanation	PR	Debit	Credit	Dr./Cr.	Balance

Office Furniture and Equipment — Account No. 158

Date 20**		Explanation	PR	Debit	Credit	Dr./Cr.	Balance

Accounts Payable/General Liabilities — Account No. 200

Date 20**		Explanation	PR	Debit	Credit	Dr./Cr.	Balance

Frank Piper, Capital — Account No. 300

Date 20**		Explanation	PR	Debit	Credit	Dr./Cr.	Balance

Practice Exercise 4.3

a. i. Calculate the running balance for the following general ledger account. Indicate whether the balance column has a debit or credit balance.

   ii. Was the account overdrawn at any point?

   iii. What does the post reference refer to?

General Bank Account							Account No. 100	
Date 20**		Explanation	PR	Debit	Credit	Dr./Cr.	Balance	
Oct.	1		GJ1	1,000				
	1		GJ1	700				
	5		GJ2		2,000			
	5		GJ2	100				
	6		GJ2	400				
	8		GJ2		100			

PRACTICE

EXCEL

b. Calculate the running balance for the following general ledger account. Indicate whether the balance column has a debit or credit balance.

Rent Expense							Account No. 538
Date 20**		Explanation	PR	Debit	Credit	Dr./Cr.	Balance
Oct.	1		GJ2	1,000			
Nov.	1		GJ2	1,000			
	5		GJ2		30		
Dec.	1		GJ2	900			

c. Calculate the running balance for the following general ledger account. Indicate whether the balance column has a debit or credit balance.

Accounts Payable/General Liabilities							Account No. 200
Date 20**		Explanation	PR	Debit	Credit	Dr./Cr.	Balance
Oct.	1		GJ2		5,000		
Nov.	1		GJ2	300			
	5		GJ2		200		
Dec.	1		GJ2	1,000			
	15		GJ2	800			

Practice Exercise 4.4

Comprehensive Problem

The following are transactions for Ann Litigate Paralegal Services that occurred in the month of May:

#	Date 20**	Transaction	Amount
1	May 1	Ann received a cheque from her client, Alan Smith, for legal services provided in a criminal law matter	4,000
2	May 1	Ann took a draw against the firm's equity for her personal use	1,500
3	May 1	Ann paid one month's office rent	1,200
4	May 5	Ann paid for filing fees to the Landlord and Tenant Board on behalf of her client, Ellen Page, with her business credit card	145
5	May 10	Ann paid her telephone and Internet bill	120
6	May 11	Ann purchased accounting software to help manage her bookkeeping	600
7	May 15	Ann paid salary to her assistant	1,000
8	May 15	Ann paid interest expense on her bank line of credit account	90
9	May 18	Ann paid for office supplies on account to replenish her office supplies	250
10	May 25	Ann purchased new office furniture (filing cabinet)	600
11	May 30	Ann paid bank fees and charges for the month of May	30
12	May 30	Ann paid her credit card bill	100
13	May 30	Ann paid for one month of dues to the Law Society	267

Using the chart of accounts found on the inside front cover of this textbook and the worksheets provided:

- a. Prepare general journal entries for the transactions.
- b. Post (transfer) the general journal entries to the general ledger accounts.
- c. Prepare a trial balance.
- d. Prepare the income statement.
- e. Prepare the statement of owner's equity.
- f. Prepare the balance sheet.

The following balances have already been recorded for you in the general ledger for the end of April as the opening balance on May 1:

	Ann Litigate, Paralegal Trial Balance April 30, 20**		
#	Account	Debit	Credit
100	General Bank Account	$3,000	
120	Accounts Receivable	635	
130	Office Supplies	800	
158	Office Furniture and Equipment	5,000	
160	Intangible Assets (Computer Software)	1,865	
200	Accounts Payable/General Liabilities		$800
210	Credit Card Debt		1,500
250	Bank Line of Credit		5,000
300	Ann Litigate, Capital		5,500
350	Ann Litigate, Drawings	1,500	
		$12,800	$12,800

Worksheet a:

Ann Litigate, General Journal					GJ4
Date 20**		Description	PR	Debit	Credit

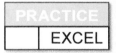

PRACTICE

EXCEL

Worksheet b:

PRACTICE

EXCEL

General Ledgers — Ann Litigate

General Bank Account — Account No. 100

Date 20**		Explanation	PR	Debit	Credit	Dr./Cr.	Balance
May	1	Opening balance	✓	3,000		Dr.	3,000

Accounts Receivable — Account No. 120

Date 20**		Explanation	PR	Debit	Credit	Dr./Cr.	Balance
May	1	Opening balance	✓	635		Dr.	635

Office Supplies — Account No. 130

Date 20**		Explanation	PR	Debit	Credit	Dr./Cr.	Balance
May	1	Opening balance	✓	800		Dr.	800

Office Furniture and Equipment — Account No. 158

Date 20**		Explanation	PR	Debit	Credit	Dr./Cr.	Balance
May	1	Opening balance	✓	5,000		Dr.	5,000

Intangible Assets (Computer Software) — Account No. 160

Date 20**		Explanation	PR	Debit	Credit	Dr./Cr.	Balance
May	1	Opening balance	✓	1,865		Dr.	1,865

Accounts Payable/General Liabilities — Account No. 200

Date 20**		Explanation	PR	Debit	Credit	Dr./Cr.	Balance
May	1	Opening balance	✓		800	Cr.	800

Credit Card Debt — Account No. 210

Date 20**		Explanation	PR	Debit	Credit	Dr./Cr.	Balance
May	1	Opening balance	✓		1,500	Cr.	1,500

Bank Line of Credit — Account No. 250

Date 20**		Explanation	PR	Debit	Credit	Dr./Cr.	Balance
May	1	Opening balance	✓		5,000	Cr.	5,000

Ann Litigate, Capital — Account No. 300

Date 20**		Explanation	PR	Debit	Credit	Dr./Cr.	Balance
May	1	Opening balance	✓		5,500	Cr.	5,500

Ann Litigate, Drawings — Account No. 350

Date 20**		Explanation	PR	Debit	Credit	Dr./Cr.	Balance
May	1	Opening balance	GJ4	1,500		Dr.	1,500

Fees Earned — Account No. 400

Date 20**		Explanation	PR	Debit	Credit	Dr./Cr.	Balance
May	1		GJ4		4,000	Cr.	4,000

Bank Charges and Credit Card Expense — Account No. 507

Date 20**		Explanation	PR	Debit	Credit	Dr./Cr.	Balance
May	25		GJ4	30		Dr.	30

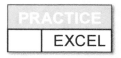
PRACTICE

EXCEL

Salaries Expense						Account No. 511	
Date 20**		Explanation	PR	Debit	Credit	Dr./Cr.	Balance
May	15		GJ4	1,000		Dr.	1,000

General Disbursement Expense						Account No. 525	
Date 20**		Explanation	PR	Debit	Credit	Dr./Cr.	Balance
May	5		GJ4	145		Dr.	145

Interest Expense						Account No. 529	
Date 20**		Explanation	PR	Debit	Credit	Dr./Cr.	Balance
May	15		GJ4	90		Dr.	90

Membership/Professional Dues						Account No. 534	
Date 20**		Explanation	PR	Debit	Credit	Dr./Cr.	Balance
May	30		GJ4	267		Dr.	267

Rent Expense						Account No. 538	
Date 20**		Explanation	PR	Debit	Credit	Dr./Cr.	Balance
May	1		GJ4	1,200		Dr.	1,200

Telephone Expense						Account No. 565	
Date 20**		Explanation	PR	Debit	Credit	Dr./Cr.	Balance
May	10		GJ4	120		Dr.	120

Worksheet c:

#	Account	Debit	Credit
	Ann Litigate, Paralegal **Trial Balance** **May 31, 20****		
	Total		

Worksheet d:

Ann Litigate, Paralegal **Income Statement** **for the period ended May 30, 20****		
Revenue		
Expenses		
Net Profit		

Worksheet e:

Ann Litigate, Paralegal Statement of Owner's Equity for the period ended May 30, 20**		

Worksheet f:

Ann Litigate, Paralegal Balance Sheet May 30, 20**			
Assets		Liabilities	
		Owner's Equity	
Total Assets		Total Liabilities and Owner's Equity	

APPENDIX 4.1

Formats for Financial Statements

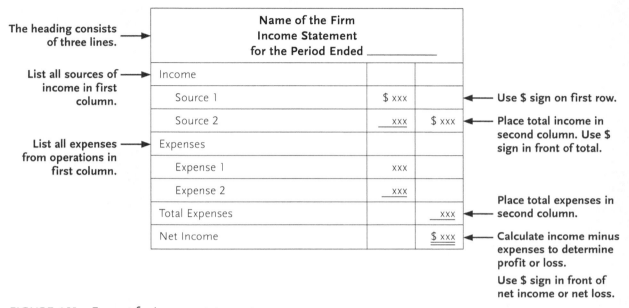

FIGURE 4.11   Format for income statement

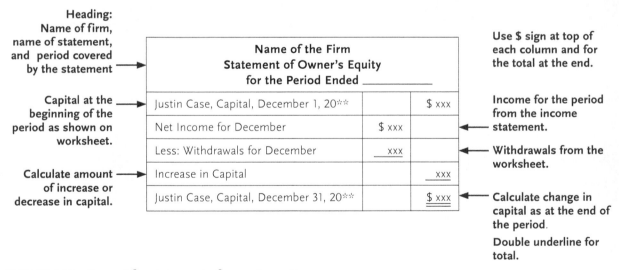

FIGURE 4.12   Format for statement of owner's equity

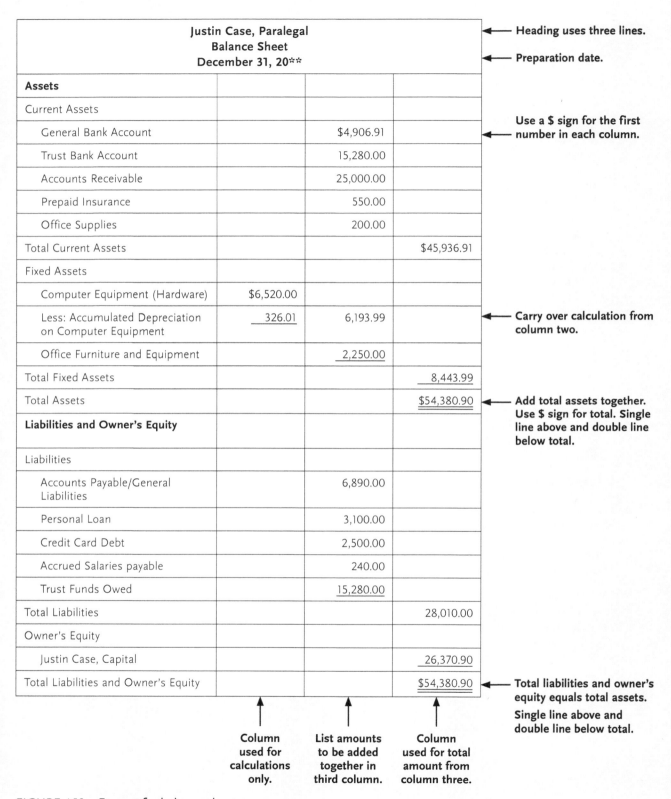

Justin Case, Paralegal Balance Sheet December 31, 20**				Heading uses three lines.
				Preparation date.
Assets				
Current Assets				
General Bank Account		$4,906.91		Use a $ sign for the first number in each column.
Trust Bank Account		15,280.00		
Accounts Receivable		25,000.00		
Prepaid Insurance		550.00		
Office Supplies		200.00		
Total Current Assets			$45,936.91	
Fixed Assets				
Computer Equipment (Hardware)	$6,520.00			
Less: Accumulated Depreciation on Computer Equipment	326.01	6,193.99		Carry over calculation from column two.
Office Furniture and Equipment		2,250.00		
Total Fixed Assets			8,443.99	
Total Assets			$54,380.90	Add total assets together. Use $ sign for total. Single line above and double line below total.
Liabilities and Owner's Equity				
Liabilities				
Accounts Payable/General Liabilities		6,890.00		
Personal Loan		3,100.00		
Credit Card Debt		2,500.00		
Accrued Salaries payable		240.00		
Trust Funds Owed		15,280.00		
Total Liabilities			28,010.00	
Owner's Equity				
Justin Case, Capital			26,370.90	
Total Liabilities and Owner's Equity			$54,380.90	Total liabilities and owner's equity equals total assets. Single line above and double line below total.

Column used for calculations only.

List amounts to be added together in third column.

Column used for total amount from column three.

FIGURE 4.13   Format for balance sheet

5 Trust Accounting

LEARNING
OUTCOMES

After reading this chapter, you should be able to:

- understand the difference between general accounts and trust accounts
- be aware of the record-keeping requirements for trust accounts
- create entries in a trust bank journal
- post from the trust bank journal to the client trust ledgers
- prepare a client trust listing and compare the total with the trust bank balance
- incorporate trust information into the firm's financial statements

Keeping track of transactions affecting the **trust bank account** and maintaining all the trust records required by the Law Society of Upper Canada (LSUC) is like maintaining a parallel set of books for the firm (Figure 5.1). Recording receipts and disbursements promptly and accurately ensures that you are able to meet your client trust obligations as they arise. Your trust records should always be up to date, and you should check clients' trust ledgers periodically to look for unusual or incorrect items. For example, was an amount entered in the wrong client's account?

Required for Trust Bank Account	Required for General Bank Account
Trust bank journal or trust receipts and disbursements journal	General journal or general receipts and disbursements journal
Trust transfer journal (matter-to-matter transfers)	Fees book
	General ledger
Client's trust ledger	Client's general ledger (recommended)
Valuable property record	
Book of duplicate cash receipts	Book of duplicate cash receipts
Trust bank reconciliation with trust listing	Bank reconciliation

FIGURE 5.1   Financial records maintained: trust bank account versus general bank account

Once all the records have been completed, the information will be merged into one set of financial reports showing a balance sheet for the firm in which the information from both the general and trust accounts is consolidated.

Difference Between a General Account and a Trust Account

In Chapter 1 we discussed the **general bank account** and the mixed trust account. Trust account records are subject to much more scrutiny by the LSUC than general bank account records because these accounts hold money that belongs to clients, not to the firm. Trust records are not required if the firm does not receive any funds in trust for clients.

You will need to use trust accounting in the following situations:

- *When money is received from another party on behalf of a client.* For example, a court case may have been settled in favour of your client, and funds are paid to the firm to be held in trust until your client signs a release and it is delivered to the other party's lawyer.

- *When money is received from a client to be paid to another party.* For example, a court case may have been settled and a client, having lost, brings funds into the firm to pay the judgment to the successful party.
- *When retainers are received from clients to pay for future legal services and future disbursements.* These receipts must be held in the mixed trust account.
- *When payments are made by the firm on behalf of your client.* These can be paid out of the trust account if the client has given a monetary retainer. For example, the client may have authorized the firm to pay a fine from funds held on her behalf in trust.
- *When reimbursement for proper expenses is paid out of the firm's general bank account on behalf of a client.* For example, the firm may have paid to issue a claim but did not have funds in trust for the client. Once the client brings in funds, the amount paid out by the firm from its general bank account can be transferred from trust to the general account to pay for the disbursement(s).
- *For payment on account after a bill has been sent to the client.* Once the client has been billed, funds can be transferred from the trust account to the general bank account to pay the amount owing, but only up to the amount held in trust for that particular client.

Deposits and Withdrawals from Trust

Bylaw 9, part I, section 1(3) of the LSUC requires that cash, cheques negotiable by the licensee, cheques drawn by the licensee on the licensee's trust account, and credit card sales slips in the possession and control of the licensee are to be deposited in the trust account *no later than the following banking day.*

Trust cheques or bank drafts cannot be made payable to "cash" or "bearer," and cash should never be withdrawn from the trust account, because an audit trail is required. Deposit records kept by the firm must indicate the date on which funds are deposited, the firm's name, the bank account number, the source of each receipt, the name of the client, and the amount of the deposit (see Figure 5.2). Each deposit slip should be stamped by a bank teller. If funds are deposited using an automated teller machine, the ATM receipt needs to be attached to the corresponding deposit slip.

Cash Receipts

Bylaw 9, part III, section 4(1) contains a provision that a licensee shall not receive or accept from a person, in respect of any one client file, cash in an aggregate amount equal to or exceeding $7,500 (Canadian).

Exceptions to this requirement are found in section 6 of the bylaw and deal mostly with funds received from public bodies or financial institutions. There is an exception if cash is received from a client for the purpose of paying a fine or penalty. There is also an exception if cash is received for fees, disbursements, expenses, or bail, provided that any refund out of such receipts is also made in cash.

As a minimum additional requirement to maintaining the usual records, a book of duplicate **cash receipts** must be kept with each receipt, identifying the date on which cash is received, the person from whom cash is received, the amount of cash received, the client for whom cash is received, and any file number in respect of which cash is received (see Figure 5.3). The signatures of the licensee or the person authorized by the licensee to receive cash, and of the person from whom cash is received, are also required (bylaw 9, part V, section 19). The receipt book must be kept for a 10-year period pursuant to bylaw 9, part V, section 23(2).

CREDIT ACCOUNT OF:			BUSINESS ACCOUNT DEPOSIT SLIP	

JUSTIN CASE, PARALEGAL
IN TRUST
ACCOUNT NUMBER   232017661

BANK OF MONEY
ONTARIO, CANADA

DATE:

DAY	MONTH	YEAR
03	OCT	20**

INITIALS:

DEPOSITOR'S	TELLER'S
JC	NM

LIST OF CHEQUES:

CHEQUE IDENTIFICATION	AMOUNT
1 HOWES, CLIFF	1,000.00
2 JONES, FRANK	500.00
3	
4	
5	
6	
7	
8	
CHEQUE SUBTOTAL	1,500.00
TOTAL # OF CHEQUES	2

CASH COUNT:

	X 5	
	X 20	
JONES 2	X 20	100.00
	X 50	
	X $1 COIN	
	X $2 COIN	

COIN TOTAL	
CASH COUNT	
CASH SUBTOTAL	100.00

DEPOSIT:

CASH SUBTOTAL	100.00
CHEQUE SUBTOTAL	1,500.00
DEPOSIT TOTAL	$ 1,600.00

FIGURE 5.2   Sample trust account deposit slip

DUPLICATE CASH RECEIPT		NUMBER	1001
RECEIVED FROM	Frank Jones	DATE	03/10/20**
			dd/mm/yr
ON BEHALF OF		FILE NO.	2
AMOUNT	One hundred dollars	DOLLARS	(100.00)

Frank Jones
Signature of Payor

Justin Case
Authorized signature on behalf of firm

GST/HST REG. NO.   RT12345

FIGURE 5.3   Sample receipt

Remember that money received on behalf of a client for future services or future disbursements must be deposited into the mixed trust bank account. You are also required to track all amounts received and paid out on behalf of clients. A company's balance sheet includes two **trust control accounts**: the trust bank account (moneys received from clients) and the trust funds owed accounts (moneys owed to clients). These trust control accounts provide a total of all moneys received in trust for each client and a total of all moneys owed to each client.

The same double-entry bookkeeping system that applies to general accounting also applies to trust accounting.

Trust Bank Journal

All the transactions we recorded in previous chapters related to general journal entries. When recording amounts related to trust receipts and disbursements, it is faster and more practical to use a special **trust bank journal**, sometimes called a trust receipts and disbursements journal, in which all financial transactions related to the mixed trust bank account are entered. Keeping trust records in a separate journal helps to eliminate errors and makes it easier to reconcile bank balances at the end of each month. This chapter will teach you how to record transactions in the trust bank journal and how to post the entries to the individual **client ledgers**, also called "**client general ledgers**." You will also note that trust balances are incorporated into the financial statements for the firm using the two control accounts Trust Bank Account (#115, an asset account) and Trust Funds Owed (#215, a liabilities account). (See the chart of accounts listed on the inside front cover of this textbook.) Some firms prefer to keep two different trust journals, one for trust receipts and one for trust disbursements.

Book of Original Entry

The trust records to be kept pursuant to the LSUC's bylaw 9, part V, section 18(1) include a book of original entry identifying the following transaction details:

- Each date on which money is received in trust for a client
- The method by which money is received
- The person from whom money is received
- The amount of money received
- The purpose for which money is received
- The client for whom money is received in trust

Steps in Using the Trust Bank Journal

1. Record the trust bank journal entry (see Examples 1 and 2).
2. Post trust receipts and disbursements to each individual client trust ledger.
3. Prepare the client trust listing (total balance is transferred/posted to Trust Funds Owed).
4. Post the total trust receipts and trust disbursements to the Trust Bank Account ledger (#115) and the Trust Funds Owed ledger (#215).

Recording Debits and Credits in the Trust Bank Journal

When funds are received by the firm and deposited into the trust bank account, the entry will be recorded as a debit to the account. This is because Trust Bank Account (#115) is an asset account, and assets have a normal debit balance. A credit entry will also be made to the client's trust ledger account to show that the funds are owed to the client. At the end of each period, the total amounts in the client trust ledgers are totalled and the amount is posted to the control account Trust Funds Owed (#215) as a credit because this is a liability account. Trust funds owed to clients must be equal to the amount in the trust bank account. Funds held in the trust account are shown as an asset on the balance sheet. Trust funds owed to clients are shown in the liabilities section of the balance sheet.

The examples that follow show the steps in recording receipts and disbursements in a trust bank journal.

EXAMPLE 1

Recording a Trust Receipt

On October 2, Cliff Howes, client file no. 1, brought Justin Case a retainer in the amount of $1,000 (in the form of a money order) for a Small Claims Court action against his neighbour, dealing with a dispute over a fence.

STEP 1

Enter the date of the receipt.

STEP 2

In the Received From/Paid To column, show the amount as "Rec." and enter the name of the person from whom the funds were received.

STEP 3

Under Client/Description, indicate the client file name and the reason the funds were received.

STEP 4

In the Method of Payment column, indicate how the client paid—via a money order, cheque, credit card, or other means.

STEP 5

In the Dr. column, enter $1,000 because funds were received and had to be deposited into the trust bank account. Trust Bank Account (#115) is an asset account, so it is debited to indicate an increase in the account.

STEP 6

Post the amount of $1,000 to the client's trust ledger sheet by entering the amount in the Receipts (Cr.) column in the Cliff Howes file no. 1 ledger sheet (Figure 5.5). Show that the amount was posted by filling in the file number in the File No. column of the journal.

Justin Case, Paralegal Trust Bank Journal						TJ1
Date 20**		Received From/Paid To	File No.	Client/Description	Method of Payment	Trust Bank Account	
						Dr.	Cr.
Oct.	2	Rec. Cliff Howes	1	Cliff Howes/Retainer	Money Order	1,000	

EXAMPLE 2

Recording a Trust Disbursement

On October 3, Justin wrote a cheque on the Cliff Howes file to Deliveries Inc. to pay the amount of $20 to send a demand letter by courier to Howes' neighbour.

STEP 1

Enter the date of the cheque.

STEP 2

In the Received From/Paid To column, show the amount as "Pd." and enter the name of the company to which the funds were paid.

STEP 3

Under Client/Description, indicate the name of the client and the reason the funds were paid out.

STEP 4

In the Method of Payment column, indicate the trust cheque number used to pay the bill.

STEP 5

Leave the Dr. column blank.

STEP 6

In the Cr. column, enter the amount of $20 paid out of the trust account.

					Trust Bank Account	
Date 20**		Received From/Paid To	File No.	Client/Description	Method of Payment	Dr.	Cr.
Oct.	2	Rec. Cliff Howes	1	Cliff Howes/Retainer	Money Order	1,000	
	3	Pd. Deliveries Inc.	1	Cliff Howes/Courier	Chq. 1		20

Justin Case, Paralegal — Trust Bank Journal — TJ1

Follow the same steps as in the examples above for the transactions that took place from October 5 to the end of the period. Figure 5.4 shows the trust bank journal entries for October once the totals have been posted to the client trust ledgers. Posting from the trust bank journal is discussed in the following section.

Transactions
On October 5, Frank Jones, client file no. 2, paid Justin a retainer in the amount of $600 using his credit card and cash for defence of charges under the *Highway Traffic Act*.
On October 15, Justin received a bank draft in the amount of $2,500 from the neighbour's firm, James Settlor, in full settlement of the claim made by Cliff Howes.
On October 16, the funds received in settlement were paid to Cliff Howes.
On October 20, Justin represented Frank Jones in court and negotiated a reduced fine of $300. He paid the Minister of Finance the amount of the fine from trust funds held on behalf of the client.

Justin Case, Paralegal Trust Bank Journal						TJ1
Date 20**		Received From/Paid To	File No.	Client/Description	Method of Payment	Trust Bank Account	
						Dr.	Cr.
Oct.	2	Rec. Cliff Howes	1	Cliff Howes/Retainer	Money Order	$1,000	
	3	Pd. Deliveries Inc.	1	Cliff Howes/Courier	Chq. 1		20
	5	Rec. Frank Jones	2	Frank Jones/Retainer	Credit Card 500 Cash 100	600	
	15	Rec. James Settlor	1	Cliff Howes/Settlement	Bank Draft	2,500	
	16	Pd. Cliff Howes	1	Cliff Howes/Settlement	Chq. 2		2,500
	20	Pd. Minister of Finance	2	Jones/Payment of Fine	Chq. 3		300
	31				Totals	$4,100	$2,820
						(115/215)	(115/215)

FIGURE 5.4   Trust bank journal entries for October (after posting)

Posting from the Trust Bank Journal

Now that you have entered all the transactions for the month of October, total the columns in the trust bank journal. Post the totals from the trust bank account Dr. and Cr. columns to the general ledger for the firm (Trust Bank Account #115). Post the individual amounts to each client trust ledger sheet.

The figures in the File No. column indicate that the individual amounts were posted to each client's trust ledger sheet. This should be done on a daily basis when the entries are recorded in the journal.

The numbers at the bottom of the trust bank account Dr. and Cr. columns (115/215) in Figure 5.4 indicate that the total deposits and cheques made to the trust account were posted to the general ledger.

The client trust ledgers in Figure 5.5 show how the information was posted from the trust bank journal to the client trust ledger accounts. Note that a running total of the balance in the client's trust ledger account was calculated after each transaction. In this way, you always know how much money each client has to his or her credit in the mixed trust bank account.

Although there is only one entry for each date in the trust bank journal, Figure 5.5 shows that double entries have been made. Each amount in the trust bank journal is transferred to the individual client ledger accounts in the client trust ledger. These transactions are posted on a daily basis.

Justin Case, Paralegal
Client Trust Ledgers

Account: HOWES, Cliff re Small Claims Court				File No. 001
		Client Trust Ledger		
Date 20**	Received From/Paid To Explanation	Disbursements (Dr.)	Receipts (Cr.)	Balance in Trust
Oct. 2	Retainer		1,000	1,000
3	Deliveries Inc.	20		980
15	James Settlor, Settlement		2,500	3,480
16	Cliff Howes, Settlement Funds	2,500		980

Account: JONES, Frank re Highway Traffic Act				File No. 002
		Client Trust Ledger		
Date 20**	Received From/Paid To Explanation	Disbursements (Dr.)	Receipts (Cr.)	Balance in Trust
Oct. 5	Retainer		600	600
20	Minister of Finance, Fine	300		300

FIGURE 5.5   Client trust ledgers after posting

Some general principles about posting from the trust bank journal:

1. The individual amounts in the Dr. column of the trust bank journal are posted to the Receipts (Cr.) column in the client's trust ledger on a daily basis. Thus you have a debit entry and a credit entry, which balance your books. Each client ledger sheet is kept up to date at all times as posting is done daily and a running total is calculated. The client file number is entered in the trust bank journal to show the client trust account to which the entry was posted.

Trust Bank Account Dr. = Client Trust Ledger Sheet Cr.

2. The individual amounts in the Cr. column of the trust bank journal are posted to the Disbursements (Dr.) column in the client's trust ledger on a daily basis, and the file number is entered in the trust bank journal to show that the entry has been posted. Again you have a double entry—a credit entry reducing the balance in the bank account and a debit entry in the respective client's trust ledger sheet.

Trust Bank Account Cr. = Client Trust Ledger Sheet Dr.

3. The totals of the trust bank account debit and credit columns are posted to the trust bank account in the general ledger. This is usually done at the end of the month.
4. A list of balances owed to clients, called the client trust listing, is prepared showing the total amounts held by each client. This information is obtained from the individual client trust ledger accounts (Figures 5.5 and 5.6). This total amount is entered in the general ledger account Trust Funds Owed (#215). The balance in this account must be equal to the balance in the Trust Bank Account (#115) (Figure 5.7).

$$\text{Trust Bank Account Balance} = \text{Total of Client Trust Listing}$$
$$(\#115) \qquad\qquad (\#215)$$

Proving That Debits Equal Credits

To prove that there are no errors in the trust bank journal after posting, check to make sure that the balance in the general ledger account Trust Bank Account (#115) is the same as the total of the list of balances owed to clients prepared at the end of the period.

	Justin Case, Paralegal List of Balances Owed to Clients October 31, 20**		
File No.	Account	Balance Owed
1	HOWES, Cliff re Small Claims Court	$980
2	JONES, Frank re *Highway Traffic Act*	300
	Total Owed to Clients	$1,280

FIGURE 5.6   Client trust listing at October 31

The total amount in the client trust listing as of October 31 is $1,280, with the individual amounts shown in Figure 5.6. After posting to the general ledger, the balance in Trust Bank Account (#115) is $1,280. This serves as proof that the amounts in the client ledgers are equal to the amount in the bank.

Trust Bank Account						Account No. 115	
Date 20**		Explanation	PR	Debit	Credit	Dr./Cr.	Balance
Oct.	31	Trust Totals for October	TJ1	4,100	2,820	Dr.	1,280

Trust Funds Owed						Account No. 215	
Date 20**		Explanation	PR	Debit	Credit	Dr./Cr.	Balance
Oct.	31	Trust Funds Owed to Clients	✓	4,100	2,820	Cr.	1,280

FIGURE 5.7   General ledger, trust bank account at October 31

Possible Error

An error to watch for when comparing the client trust listing with the trust bank account balance is whether an amount was accidentally posted to the wrong client ledger. The total client trust listing and the bank balance might be equal, but the amount debited or credited to an individual client could be incorrect.

Trial Balance

A **trial balance** of the general ledger accounts after the trust posting is completed would be as shown in Figure 5.8.

#	Account	Debit	Credit
	Justin Case, Paralegal **Trial Balance** **October 31, 20****		
100	General Bank Account	$7,100	
115	Trust Bank Account	1,280	
155	Computer Equipment (Hardware)	900	
158	Office Furniture and Equipment	2,250	
200	Accounts Payable/General Liabilities		$580
205	Personal Loan		4,000
210	Credit Card Debt		1,500
215	Trust Funds Owed		1,280
300	Justin Case, Capital		2,550
400	Fees Earned		3,000
535	Office Supplies/General Expense	580	
538	Rent Expense	500	
565	Telephone Expense	300	
		$12,910	$12,910

FIGURE 5.8   Trial balance including Trust Bank Account and Trust Funds Owed

Because the only changes made were to the trust bank account and trust funds owed to clients, this will have no effect on the firm's income statement or on the statement of owner's equity for the month of October, so these statements are not reproduced here. However, the balance sheet would show the trust bank account and the trust funds owed as in Figure 5.9.

The LSUC requires licensees to maintain a record showing a comparison made monthly of the total balances held in the trust account or accounts and the total of all unexpended balances of funds held in trust for clients as they appear from the financial records. An explanation must be provided giving the reasons for any differences between the totals in the client ledger and the reconciled bank balance (bylaw 9, part V, section 18(8)). This point will be discussed in greater detail when bank reconciliations are covered in Chapter 9.

Justin Case, Paralegal Balance Sheet October 31, 20**			
Assets		**Liabilities**	
General Bank Account	$7,100	Accounts Payable/General Liabilities	$580
Trust Bank Account	1,280	Credit Card Debt	1,500
Computer Equipment (Hardware)	900	Trust Funds	1,280
Office Furniture and Equipment	2,250	Personal Loan	4,000
		Total Liabilities	$7,360
		Owner's Equity	
		J. Case, Capital	4,170
Total Assets	$11,530	**Total Liabilities and Owner's Equity**	$11,530

FIGURE 5.9   Balance sheet including trust assets and trust liabilities

Matter-to-Matter Trust Transfer Journal

Whenever trust funds are moved from one client's trust ledger account to another client's trust ledger account, the transfer must be recorded and the reason for the transfer must be explained (bylaw 9, part IV, section 9(1)(4) and part V, section 18(4)). The **special journal** used to record these transactions is called the trust transfer journal.

Sometimes a client may instruct the firm to transfer funds held in trust on his or her behalf over to another file. This situation might arise if a parent has a file with the firm and a child is charged with an offence. The parent assumes responsibility for the child's defence and instructs the paralegal to use money held in trust in the parent's account to cover the cost.

EXAMPLE 3

On November 1, Cliff Howes, client file no. 1, has $980 left in his trust account after receiving the settlement paid in his court case. Also on November 1, he instructs the firm to transfer $280 to a new file in the name of Larry Howes as a retainer to cover legal fees in defending his son's shoplifting case.

This transaction must be recorded in a matter-to-matter trust transfer journal showing that money was moved from one client to another:

Justin Case, Paralegal Trust Transfer Journal						
Date 20**		Received From/Paid To Reason for Transfer	File No.	Client	Allocated Amount	Transfer Amount
Nov.	1	Cliff Howes	1	Cliff Howes	−280	
	1	Larry Howes	3	Larry Howes	280	280
		To transfer funds to account of Larry Howes				

Clients' instructions should be obtained before transferring funds from one matter to another matter if the two matters are for the same client. If the transfer is made from one client to another client, these instructions should be obtained in writing prior to any transfer being made.

A new client ledger would have to be opened for the Larry Howes file, and the transfer would be posted in the client ledgers as follows:

Justin Case, Paralegal
Client Trust Ledgers

Account:		HOWES, Cliff re Small Claims Court			File No. 001
Date 20**		Received From/Paid To Explanation	Disbursements (Dr.)	Receipts (Cr.)	Balance in Trust
Oct.	2	Retainer		1,000	1,000
	3	Deliveries Inc.	20		980
	15	James Settlor, Settlement		2,500	3,480
	16	Cliff Howes, Settlement Funds	2,500		980
Nov.	1	Cliff Howes, Transfer to File No. 3	280		700

Account:		HOWES, Larry			File No. 003
Date 20**		Received From/Paid To Explanation	Disbursements (Dr.)	Receipts (Cr.)	Balance in Trust
Nov.	1	Transfer from Cliff Howes		280	280

Note that the total balance in the trust bank account has not been affected by this transaction, because funds were moved only between two client trust ledger accounts. No cheque needs to be written to complete this transaction; however, the transfer must be shown in the firm's records.

The client list of trust funds owed to clients will reflect this transaction at the end of November when the trust listing is prepared.

Valuable Property Record

Another trust record required by the LSUC is the **valuable property record** (bylaw 9, part V, section 18(9)). The record is used to record all property, other than money, held in trust for clients, and describes each item and identifies the date on which the licensee took possession, the person who had possession immediately before the licensee took possession, the value, the client for whom each item is held in trust, the date on which possession is given away, and the person to whom the item is given.

Valuable property can be anything of value held for clients, such as bond certificates, share certificates, jewellery, or collector's items. Anything that a paralegal could convert to cash on his or her own authority should be included. It would be wise to investigate any insurance implications before agreeing to hold valuable property for clients. And you would certainly need to have written instructions from everyone before getting involved in such a situation.

The valuable property record is not used to record any trust moneys because these must be shown in the financial accounting records. Items such as term deposits and bank accounts held at a financial institution must be reported in the financial records, not in the valuable property record. Pursuant to bylaw 9, sections 18(9) and 23, the valuable property record must be kept for ten years plus the current year.

Although holding a client's valuable property does not typically fall within a paralegal's role, the following scenario is not an impossible one.

EXAMPLE 4

On October 20, Frank Jones brought a stamp collection in to the firm for safekeeping. This collection is still held by the firm. On November 1, Larry's parents made him turn over his hockey cards to Justin Case to ensure their son helped pay for his legal fees for the shoplifting charge. The parents insisted that if Larry did not work to contribute to his legal costs, Justin Case would be authorized to sell the cards and apply the proceeds to Larry's legal fees. Justin sold the cards on December 15 because Larry did not come up with the money as required. The proceeds from the sale would be deposited in the trust bank account to the credit of Larry Howes.

Justin Case, Paralegal Valuable Property Record						
Client	Description of Property	Date Received	Received From	Value of Property	Given To	Date Given
Jones, Frank	Stamp Collection	Oct. 20, 20**	Jones, Frank	200		
Howes, Larry	Hockey Cards	Nov. 1, 20**	Howes, Larry	60	Joe's Pawn Shop	Dec. 15, 20**

Practice Audits

Section 49.2 of the *Law Society Act* authorizes spot audits of members with a view to ensuring that licencees engage in proper management practices. Audits include an assessment of financial record-keeping practices to ensure compliance with bylaw 9. The primary goal of audits is to provide on-site guidance aimed at helping the licensee correct minor deficiencies with respect to record keeping, and to address any deficiencies that could adversely affect service to clients. Where misconduct is found, reviewers are required to report that misconduct pursuant to rule 6.10(3) of the *Rules of Professional Conduct*. Failure to meet minimum standards can result in suspension of membership until the LSUC is satisfied that the licensee is meeting the minimum standards of professional competence. It is usual to receive a two-week advance notice of a spot audit. If members try to defer or cancel audit appointments, they will be required to fax a copy of the most recent trust bank reconciliation to the auditor. Failure to do so may result in an immediate unannounced visit.

Applying GST/HST to Client Accounts

Rule 8.01(2) of the Law Society of Upper Canada's *Paralegal Rules of Conduct* requires licensees to meet promptly all financial obligations incurred in the course of practice. One responsibility is to collect and remit HST to the Canada Revenue Agency (CRA). Licensees must confirm how GST/HST applies to the specific legal services and disbursements they provide. They should consult with an accounting or tax professional to discuss how to implement HST properly within their internal accounting and invoicing systems.

The CRA has published a policy to deal with GST/HST on disbursements, which would also apply to paralegals. Its GST/HST Policy Statement P-209R is found at <http://www.cra-arc.gc.ca/E/pub/gl/p-209r/README.html>. This policy expands on the obligation to pay GST/HST on disbursements paid on behalf of clients. The disbursements described in this policy statement are characterized as either "incurred as agent" or "not incurred as agent."

The phrase "incurred as agent" indicates that the disbursement described is generally incurred in a lawyer's capacity as agent for a particular client. As such, no GST/HST is exigible (able to be charged) on the subsequent reimbursement by the client. The phrase "not incurred as agent" indicates that the disbursement described is generally incurred otherwise than in a lawyer's capacity as agent for a particular client, so GST/HST is exigible on the subsequent reimbursement by the client.

For example, in the area of civil litigation practice, common disbursements considered to be incurred as agent are court fees to start a legal proceeding, motion fees, court filing fees, or notice of trial fees. Because these fees are deemed by the CRA to be incurred as agent for a particular client, GST/HST is not charged on the disbursements when the client is invoiced.

However, in civil litigation practice, payment of witness fees, fees for recording services, transcript production or special examiner fees, service of document fees, and fees paid to have an expert prepare a report in respect of a particular proceeding or to have the expert appear at trial are subject to GST/HST because they are considered "not incurred as agent."

The CRA considers disbursements not incurred as agent to include such items as payment made for telephone charges, photocopy charges, courier costs, costs for travel by the licensee, and postage. GST/HST is charged on these amounts even though GST/HST may have been charged on the original invoice to the firm.

CHAPTER SUMMARY

There are some similarities between trust accounting and general accounting: each has books of original entry and ledgers, and the double-entry bookkeeping system applies to both types of accounting. Trust accounting requires some additional records, whereas general accounting will incorporate information from the trust records into the financial statements for the firm. Most trust records must be maintained for a period of 10 years plus the current year, whereas general records are required to be maintained for the most recent 6 full years plus the current year. See Chapter 9 for more discussion of this. All bank accounts, whether trust or general, must be reconciled at the end of each month.

In keeping with the LSUC's mandate to protect the interests of the public, licensees must be vigilant in ensuring that the obligations set out by the *Law Society Act* and its bylaws and the *Rules of Professional Conduct* are followed. The Law Society regularly conducts spot audits on members, and mishandling of trust funds can result in discipline or losing one's licence. If you purchase accounting software for a firm, it is wise to ensure that the system purchased can handle trust transactions and properly record transactions in a client ledger.

KEY TERMS

cash receipts, 99
client general ledgers, 101
client ledgers, 101
general bank account, 98
special journal, 108
trial balance, 107
trust bank account, 98
trust bank journal, 101
trust bank reconciliation, 98
trust control accounts, 101
valuable property record, 109

FURTHER READING

Law Society of Upper Canada, By-Laws. "By-law 9—Financial Transactions and Records," online: <http://www.lsuc.on.ca/by-laws/>. (See also the Appendix of this textbook.)

Law Society of Upper Canada, *Paralegal Rules of Conduct* and *Paralegal Professional Conduct Guidelines*, online: <http://www.lsuc.on.ca/paralegal-conduct-rules/>.

Law Society of Upper Canada, *The Bookkeeping Guide for Paralegals* (Toronto: LSUC, February 2014), online: <http://www.lsuc.on.ca/uploadedFiles/PDC/Practice_Review/Paralegal%20 Bookkeeping%20Guide%20-%20February%202014.pdf>. (See General Receipts Journal and General Disbursements Journal.)

PUT IT INTO PRACTICE

Case Example: LSUC Rules

Ann Litigate operates a paralegal firm, operating under the name Ann Litigate Paralegal Services, and employs a part-time secretary. Ann works as a sole practitioner and deals with all professional, business, and administrative matters of the firm. For example, Ann does all the banking to ensure that she has control over her general and trust bank accounts in accordance with the rules and regulations of the Law Society of Upper Canada, and she does all the bookkeeping.

Ann is concerned about her record-keeping responsibilities because she is so busy with the day-to-day operations of the business as well as meeting deadlines and client expectations. Although Ann keeps all her source documents, she sometimes waits until the end of the month to complete the various journals and ledgers pursuant to section 18 of the LSUC's bylaw 9, and then she becomes overwhelmed. What best-practice strategies or tools can Ann use to meet all of her obligations? Discuss.

REVIEW QUESTIONS

Short Answer

Give a full answer for each question:

1. A client bill is paid in part by trust moneys held on behalf of the client and in part by cheque. How will the paralegal record this transaction?

2. If a client has two separate matters being handled by a paralegal, can that client authorize the transfer of funds from one trust account to the other? Explain. What if the transfer of funds is from a third-party trust account? Explain.

3. When would a paralegal use a book of duplicate cash receipts? For how long would this record have to be maintained?

4. How are monetary retainers recorded? Identify the appropriate journal and/or ledger.

5. How can you verify that the trial balance after the trust posting is correct?

6. Why is it important to review client ledgers from time to time?

7. Which journal is used to track payments made from the trust bank account?

8. A client entrusts to a paralegal her certificate of authenticity of a vintage coin collection that is the subject of a small claims dispute. How would the paralegal record and track this item?

PRACTICE EXERCISES

Practice Exercise 5.1

Ann Litigate had the following trust transactions in the month of June:

#	Date 20**	Transaction	Amount
1	June 1	Ann received a cheque (#91) from a new client, Jessica Palmer, as a retainer deposit in an immigration law matter.	$2,500
2	June 1	Ann wrote trust cheque #352 on the trust bank account in payment of invoice #518 previously sent to Karen Charles. Assume that on May 30, Charles had a balance of $4,500.	$4,000
3	June 8	There is an amount of $60 charged to Daniel Pitt for photocopy charges incurred in the preparation of a document brief for use at an upcoming criminal trial. Invoice #519 was sent to Daniel Pitt, and Ann wishes to recover the charges for the disbursement from trust (trust cheque #353). Assume that on May 30, Pitt had a balance of $1,000.	$60
4	June 25	Louise Forte sent cheque #47 written on her personal bank account to the firm in the amount of $3,130. Ann deposited the cheque into the trust bank account and then wrote trust cheque #354 in payment of invoice #520 for $1,130 and held the balance remaining in trust as a retainer.	$3,130

Review the sample worksheet below and then, using the worksheets provided:

    a. Prepare the appropriate trust bank journal entries to record the transactions shown above.

    b. Post the entries to the client trust ledgers.

    c. Post the totals to the appropriate general ledger accounts.

    d. Complete the client trust listing at the end of the month. Does the listing match the amount in account #215 (Trust Funds Owed)?

Sample worksheets

On June 18, Paralegal receives $1,500 as a retainer from a new client, Anthony Johnston.							
Ann Litigate, Paralegal Trust Bank Journal							TJ1
Date 20**		Received From/ Paid To	File No.	Client/Description	Method of Payment	Trust Bank Account	
						Dr.	Cr.
June	18	Rec. Anthony Johnston	01	Johnston, retainer	Cheque	1,500	
	31				Totals	1,500	0
						(115)	(115)

Sample client ledger after posting
Ann Litigate, Paralegal Client Trust Ledgers

Account: JOHNSTON, Anthony					File No. 06
			Client Trust Ledger		
Date 20**		Received From/Paid To Explanation	Disbursements (Dr.)	Receipts (Cr.)	Balance in Trust
June	18	Retainer		1,500	1,500

Worksheet a:

Ann Litigate, Paralegal Trust Bank Journal						TJ1
Date 20**		Received From/ Paid To	File No.	Client/Description	Method of Payment	Trust Bank Account	
						Dr.	Cr.
					Totals		

Worksheet b:

Ann Litigate, Paralegal Client Trust Ledgers					
Account:					File No.
				Client Trust Ledger	
Date 20**		Received From/Paid To Explanation	Disbursements (Dr.)	Receipts (Cr.)	Balance in Trust

Worksheet c:

Ann Litigate, Paralegal General Ledger Accounts							

Trust Bank Account							Account No. 115
Date 20**		Explanation	PR	Debit	Credit	Dr./Cr.	Balance
May	30	Opening balance					5,500

Trust Funds Owed							Account No. 215
Date 20**		Explanation	PR	Debit	Credit	Dr./Cr.	Balance
June	30	Total from client listing					

Worksheet d:

Ann Litigate, Paralegal List of Balances Owed to Clients June 30, 20**		
File No.	Account	Balance Owed
06	PALMER, J. re Immigration	
04	CHARLES, K.	
03	PITT, D.	
08	FORTE, L.	
	Total Owed to Clients	

6 Special Journals

After reading this chapter, you should be able to:

- use special journals
- record fees billed in the fees book/accounts receivable journal
- record receipts in the general receipts journal
- record disbursements in the general disbursements journal
- post from the special journals to the appropriate general ledger and client general ledger
- prepare a trial balance using control accounts

A general journal is too inefficient to be useful for recording all transactions in a legal practice. Using specialized journals to record certain transactions is preferable and simplifies the bookkeeping process. The **special journals** that are most useful in a small firm are

- a fees book (also called **fees journal**),
- a general receipts journal, and
- a general disbursements journal.

You need to understand how these special journals work and their relationship to the accounts in the general ledgers.

The special journals discussed in this chapter are in addition to the specialized trust bank journal (sometimes called the trust receipts and disbursements journal) discussed in Chapter 5. You will recall that the entries from the trust bank journal were posted to the client's trust ledger, and a client trust listing was prepared summarizing how much was in the trust account for each client at the end of the period. Using this specialized journal keeps the transactions related to the trust bank account separate from the general bank entries and helps to ensure that the wrong bank account is not used in recording transactions.

Special journals are set up to efficiently process transactions with a view to eliminating the need to post every single entry made in the journals. They are usually set up using technology. As you work through this chapter, you will appreciate that learning to use special journals can be a confusing and daunting task. The manual approach demonstrated in this chapter illustrates how information moves through a computerized system. Understanding the special journals produced in this chapter will help you interpret journals and reports prepared using an electronic system. If a firm records everything manually, using special journals will make the task easier.

Client Billing

An invoice must be prepared and sent to the client before payment on account can be received. The following information is required to prepare an invoice:

- The amount billed for time spent on a file
- Disbursements paid out of the firm's general bank account on behalf of the client
- Recovery of expenses incurred in the office that can be charged to the client, such as the cost of photocopies, faxes, and postage
- A client trust ledger statement showing the amounts on the file received in trust and paid out from the trust account

Billing Out Time on a File

Many firms use accounting software to track the amount of time spent on a file and bill the client at an hourly rate that will have been discussed at the time a retainer agreement was entered into. Firms may also bill out files using a flat rate if the parties have agreed on the amount that will be charged for a specific file. More information on recording and billing time is covered in Chapter 11, which deals with computerized time and money management.

Preparing Invoices

Work done on a file is recorded using time dockets. Work may be non-billable or billable. **Non-billable work** is work performed by the licensee that will not be charged to the client. This could include, for example, a free consultation. **Billable work**—work that is charged to the client—typically includes telephone calls, preparation of legal documents, legal research, and court time.

Lawyers and paralegals generally bill for all time spent on a client file, including work done by associates, law clerks, and legal assistants. Work performed by a secretary is not charged to clients because it is considered part of the overhead incurred in running an office.

A variety of docketing methods are available to track the time spent on a file. Law firms generally express billable time in six-minute (one-tenth of an hour) intervals. A minutes-to-decimal conversion chart is included in Chapter 11 to help you make this conversion.

Expense Recovery

The firm will want to account for **expense recovery**—disbursements incurred in the office that are to be charged to the client.

The Law Society of Upper Canada (LSUC) has generally taken the position that paralegals should not profit from disbursements charged to clients.[1] Legitimate expenses that can be passed on to clients include the cost of photocopies, faxes, long-distance calls, postage, and sometimes special office supplies needed for court. The amounts passed on to clients must be fair, reasonable, and disclosed to the client in a timely manner. You must discuss with the client all items that will be charged as disbursements, and the amount charged should be shown on the statement of account sent to the client.

Expenses incurred on behalf of clients, such as charges for deliveries, service of documents, and any other charges paid by the firm from the general bank account, can be recovered from the client. These expenses also need to be journalized and posted to the client's general ledger account.

Any amounts paid out of the trust account are not included on the invoice but rather are shown on the statement of trust funds sent to the client. The trust statement included with the invoice lists all amounts received from the client and deposited into the trust account, as well as amounts paid from the trust account on the client's behalf.

Clients should be billed on a regular basis to keep them informed of the cost of the legal services being provided. This practice avoids disagreements that can arise if matters are not billed promptly, because clients can be surprised by the cost of services rendered.

Figure 6.1 shows a sample invoice for Justin Case's firm.

---

1   Law Society of Upper Canada, "Practice Management Topics: Fees and Disbursements," online: <http://www.lsuc.on.ca/FeesandDisbursements/>.

Justin Case, Paralegal
135 Main Street, Yourtown, Ontario K3P 1G9

Telephone: 905-992-8555   Facsimile: 905-992-8556

File #1

November 4, 20**

Robert Simpson
10 The Driveway
Yourtown, ON
K9G 1V8

Re: *Simpson v. Sykes*

Date		Description	Hours	Amount	Work Done By
Oct.	5	Meeting with client to receive instructions	0.5	50.00	JC
	15	Legal research	1.0	100.00	JC
	30	Document preparation	1.0	100.00	JC
		Totals		250.00	
		Total HST on Fees		32.50	

Disbursements

		Paid, Quick Courier	20.00		
		HST on Disbursements	2.60	22.60	
		Total Fees and Disbursements		305.10	
		AMOUNT DUE		305.10	

This is my account.

Justin Case
Justin Case

TRUST STATEMENT			Disbursements	Receipts
Oct.	8	Received from Robert Simpson, retainer		500.00
	27	Paid, Canada Post for registered mail	12.00	
	30	Total Trust	12.00	500.00
		Trust Balance		488.00

FIGURE 6.1   Sample invoice with trust statement

Fees Book

Part V, section 18(7) of the LSUC's bylaw 9 requires licensees to maintain a **fees book**—a chronological file of copies of billings, showing all fees charged and other billings made to clients. This can be done by recording the information in the fees book or by keeping a copy of each invoice in chronological order in a billings file. Placing each invoice in a three-ringed binder with tab dividers for each month is an excellent way to keep track of invoices sent to clients.

The information in the fees book would be completed as shown in Figure 6.2 and described below.

Justin Case, Paralegal Fees Book							FB1
Date 20**	Inv. #	Client/Re	File No.	Fees Billed Cr.	Disbursements Billed Cr.	HST Billed Cr.	Total Billed AR Dr.
Nov. 1	2	Howes, Cliff re Small Claims Court	1	800.00		104.00	904.00
10	3	Jones, Frank re *Highway Traffic Act*	2	400.00		52.00	452.00
22	4	Zimmer, Ruth re Carpenter	4	250.00	20.00	35.10	305.10
		Totals		1,450.00	20.00	191.10	1,661.10
				(400)	✓	(240)	(120)

FIGURE 6.2   **Fees book for November 20** (after posting)

Date: Record the date of the invoice.

Inv. #: Identify the invoice number. Invoices are usually numbered consecutively.

Client/Re: Write the name of the client and the name of the file. Remember that some clients may have more than one file in the office, so it is important to indicate the file to which the invoice applies.

File No.: Once the amount from the Fees Billed Cr. column is posted to the general client ledger, enter the file number in the File No. column.

Fees Billed Cr.: Enter the total amount of fees for services rendered in this column. The amount billed for fees should be posted to the client's general ledger as soon as the bill is recorded.

Disbursements Billed Cr.: Enter the amount billed for disbursements out of the general bank account in this column. Note that this number is obtained from the client general ledger sheet for the particular client when the bill is prepared. You will not need to post this amount to the client general ledger because the total disbursements were posted when the entries were made in the general disbursements journal (discussed later in the chapter). Note that any amounts paid out of the trust account do not show up on the invoice. The amounts paid out of trust are shown on a trust statement, which is attached to the invoice (as in Figure 6.1).

HST Billed Cr.: The amount billed for HST on fees and disbursements as shown on the invoice to the client must be entered in this column.

Total Billed AR (accounts receivable) Dr.: Enter the total amount billed to the client in this column. Once an invoice is sent out, the total amount of the invoice is an account receivable (which is an asset on the balance sheet). The total amount billed is entered in this column and is the sum of the three previous columns: fees, disbursements, and HST.

Posting from the Fees Book

Some notes about posting from the fees book:

1. The individual amounts in the Fees Billed Cr. column are posted to each client's general ledger account on a daily basis. The amount of HST billed would also be posted daily to the individual client's general ledger account. Posting to the client ledgers every day keeps each client's balance up to date at all times.

2. The total of the Fees Billed Cr. column is posted as a credit to the Fees Earned account (#400) in the general ledger. Once the total is posted, show the account number below the total in parentheses to show that the total was posted (see Figure 6.2).

3. Disbursements billed are not posted to the client's general ledger, because the entry was posted when the disbursement was paid out of the general bank account when the expense was incurred. For example, in Figure 6.2, the amount of $20 paid by the firm on the Zimmer file was recorded in the client's general ledger at the time the payment was made on the client's behalf. This is indicated by placing a check mark below the total.

4. The total of the HST Billed Cr. column will be posted to the HST/GST Payable account (#240) as a credit. HST billed by the firm is remitted to the Canada Revenue Agency minus any HST paid for the period. Once the total is posted, show the account number below the total to show that the total was posted.

5. The total of the Total Billed AR Dr. column is posted to a control account in the general ledger called Accounts Receivable (#120). Once the total is posted, show the account number below the total to show that it was posted. (Note that the individual amounts in this column are not posted.)

Once the entries have been posted, the fees book would appear as shown in Figure 6.2.

Recording Payment of an Invoice

You will need to track invoices sent to clients and payments received for those invoices. Figure 6.3 illustrates the steps in this process:

1. An invoice is sent to the client.
2. The amount billed is entered in the fees book.
3. The client pays the bill to the firm.   *OR*   The firm writes a cheque on the trust account from funds held on behalf of the client in trust.

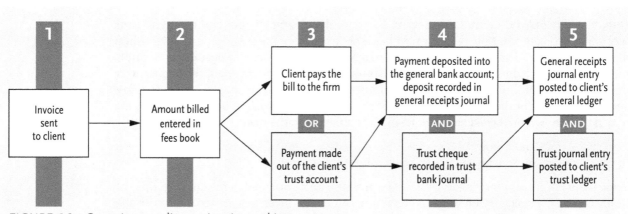

FIGURE 6.3   Steps in recording an invoice and its payment

4. Client's payment on account is deposited into the general bank account and the deposit is recorded in the general receipts journal. *AND* If payment was made out of the client's trust account, the trust cheque is recorded in the disbursement column of the trust bank journal (or in the trust disbursements journal if separate journals are kept).
5. The entry from the general receipts journal is posted to the client's general ledger account to show that payment has been received. *AND* If payment was made out of the client's trust account, the trust cheque that was entered in the trust bank journal (or trust disbursements journal) is posted to the client's trust ledger sheet.

Accounts Receivable Journal

Some firms may wish to maintain an accounts receivable journal where amounts billed to and paid by clients are tracked. Typically, accounts receivable journals will provide details of amounts billed to clients and amounts collected. They may be organized by client or by lawyer/paralegal, showing dates and amounts billed and amounts paid. The amounts receivable may be shown by amounts outstanding for more than 30 days, for 31–60 days, for 61–90 days, etc. Tracking accounts receivable in this manner helps to ensure accounts are paid in a timely fashion and that follow-up of delinquent accounts is not neglected. Most legal accounting software can automatically produce an accounts receivable journal on demand. If an accounts receivable journal is not used, a column can be added to the client general ledger to track accounts receivable and used to summarize the accounts receivable by way of a list, as shown in Figure 6.12.

Other Specialized Journals

In addition to the fees book and the accounts receivable journal, other specialized journals used for tracking transactions are the general receipts journal and the general disbursements journal. Many of the entries we made in Chapter 2 that were recorded in the general journal can be recorded in these specialized journals. In Chapter 5, we saw examples of the use of the trust bank journal, as well as the specialized trust receipts and trust disbursements journals. The trust bank is a general journal that can be used in place of the specialized trust (receipts and disbursements) journals.

The general journal, used as a book of original entry in Chapter 2, is still required for use when a particular transaction does not fit into the specialized journal and for recording adjusting and closing entries. For example, for the purposes of this course we have not created a specialized purchases journal for recording accounts payable. Accounts payable could be recorded using the general journal, or a specialized journal could be developed for the purpose of recording accounts payable.

Why Use Special Journals?
- A specialized or combination journal saves time and effort by reducing the amount of unnecessary writing.
- Special or combination journals are more efficient and capture specific information.
- Posting to ledger accounts from specialized journals is simpler and more efficient, because not every entry must be posted individually. For example, instead of posting each deposit or cheque made individually to the general bank account ledger sheet, totals are posted at the end of a period.

Recording Transactions in Specialized Journals

Figure 6.4 lists transactions made by Justin Case in November, a brief description of the journal that must be used to record the transaction, and to which ledger the transaction will be posted. The completed journals and ledgers used for posting are included at the end of the

Date 20**		Transaction	Journal Used	Post to Ledger
Nov.	1	Invoice #2 was sent to Cliff Howes re Small Claims Court for $800 plus HST of $104.	Fees book	Client's general ledger
	1	Rent was paid to Lucky Landlord in the amount of $300 plus $39 HST, general cheque #4.	General disbursements journal	General ledger
	3	A new client file was opened for *Ruth Zimmer v. Bud Carpenter* re work improperly done on her property. She is claiming damages in the amount of $24,000 for repairs that had to be made. Open a file for Ruth Zimmer (file #4). No retainer was received.	N/A. This does not require a journal entry because no financial transaction occurred	Client's general and trust ledger sheets must be opened for client in order to record future transactions
	4	Justin paid $268.75 plus $34.94 HST for a total of $303.69 to cover Law Society of Upper Canada membership dues for October, November, and December—general cheque #5.	General disbursements journal	General ledger
	5	Justin wrote a cheque to himself for $800 for personal expenses. General cheque #6.	General disbursements journal	General ledger
	6	A letter was sent to Bud Carpenter on the Zimmer file setting out the claim. The letter was sent by Quick Courier at a cost of $20 plus $2.60 for HST for a total of $22.60. The amount was paid by general cheque #7.	General disbursements journal	Client's general ledger (excluded HST amount)
	10	Fees were billed to Frank Jones re *Highway Traffic Act* for $400 plus $52 HST (invoice #3). There were no disbursements.	Fees book	Client's general ledger
	10	Partial payment on account was received from Cliff Howes for $700 (trust cheque #4).	General receipts journal	Client's general ledger
	15	Justin paid the telephone bill in the amount of $80, plus $10.40 for HST, general cheque #8, general bank account.	General disbursements journal	General ledger
	20	Justin received the amount of $300 from Frank Jones to be applied to invoice #3.	General receipts journal	Client's general ledger
	21	Justin sold the printer he had invested in the firm to Jane Crozier. He received $50 for the printer.	General journal	General ledger
	22	Justin sent an interim bill to Ruth Zimmer in the amount of $250 for fees and for disbursements of $20 plus HST of $35.10 for a total of $305.10 (invoice #4). The bill was paid immediately in cash when it was handed to Ruth.	Fees book and general receipts journal	Client's general ledger
	30	Justin received a bill from the Law Society for $1,075 plus HST of $139.75 for a total of $1,214.75. The first payment on account is not due until April 14 next year. He wishes to enter this as an account payable.	General journal, because we do not have an accounts payable journal	General ledger

FIGURE 6.4   Transactions made by Justin Case, November 20**

chapter (Figures 6.8 through 6.13). Trust transactions are not shown here because they were covered in Chapter 5.

General Receipts Journal

The **general receipts journal** is used to record money received by the firm and deposited in the general bank account. Pursuant to the LSUC bylaws, licensees are required to maintain a book of original entry showing all money received[2] by the firm and must record

- the date on which money is received,
- the method by which money is received,
- the amount of money received, and
- the person from whom money is received.

The types of entries that are entered in the general receipts journal are:

- Money received from a client for payment on account.
- Money transferred from the trust bank account to the general bank account for payment of an invoice sent to the client.
- Money transferred from the trust bank account to the general bank account to cover payment of disbursements properly made by the firm. This can be done even if the amount has not yet been billed to the client.

The headings used in a general receipts journal designed to suit the requirements of a paralegal firm are illustrated in Figure 6.5. Additional columns could be added at the discretion of the bookkeeper to capture specific information. The journal in Figure 6.5 contains the information required by the LSUC.

Justin Case, Paralegal General Receipts Journal						GRJ1
Date 20**		Name of Account	Particulars/ Method of Payment	File No.	General Bank Dr.	Accounts Receivable Cr.
Nov.	10	Howes, Cliff re Small Claims Court	Transfer from trust chq. #4, inv. #2	1	700.00	700.00
	15	Jones, Frank re *Highway Traffic Act*	Transfer from trust chq. #5, inv. #3	2	300.00	300.00
	22	Zimmer, Ruth re Carpenter	Payment on inv. #4, cash	4	305.10	305.10
	30		Totals		1,305.10	1,305.10
					(100)	(120)
			Proof		Dr.	Cr.
					1,305.10	
						1,305.10
					1,305.10	1,305.10

FIGURE 6.5   General receipts journal for November 20** (after posting)

---

2 Law Society of Upper Canada, bylaw 9, part V, s 18(5).

Date: The date column is used to record the date the transaction occurs.

Name of Account: The name of the client and the name of the matter for which payment is being made is shown in this column. Be sure to record sufficient information so you will know to which client ledger account the amount needs to be posted.

Particulars/Method of Payment: An explanation providing details regarding the transaction is placed here. These details should include the invoice number to which the payment is to be applied, if applicable. The Law Society of Upper Canada also requires that the method of payment be shown—for example, whether payment is made by cheque, cash, debit, money order, or other means. The client file number is entered in this column when posting is done to the client ledger.

General Bank Dr.: The total amount received and being deposited in the general bank account is recorded in this column.

Accounts Receivable Cr.: When payment is received from a client on an outstanding invoice, the amount paid on the account for fees and disbursements is recorded in the accounts receivable column. Entries recorded in this column should be posted immediately to the client's general ledger account so that client accounts are kept current.

All receipts deposited into the general bank account are recorded in the general receipts journal. The total of the General Bank Dr. column is posted to the general bank account as a debit at the end of the period. The individual amounts will be posted to the individual ledgers, either in the general ledger or in the client general ledger, wherever appropriate.

You may wonder what happened to debit and credit. Even though you are using special journals, the entries will be posted to two places. The sum of the General Bank Dr. column is posted as a debit to the general bank account ledger sheet in the general ledger. The individual amounts in the Accounts Receivable Cr. column are posted as a credit to the client general ledger accounts.

Each line recorded in the general receipts journal must be a balanced entry. The General Bank Dr. amount must be equal to the Accounts Receivable Cr. amount.

After all the entries for the month are recorded, the columns are totalled and the balance is proven by comparing the credit total to the debit total. Figure 6.5 shows the proof for the journal. Although bookkeepers do not usually show the proof at the bottom of the journal sheet, students are encouraged to show the proof on every journal.

Posting from the General Receipts Journal

Entries in the general receipts journal must be posted to the appropriate ledgers, where information is summarized.

1. *General Bank Dr.:* Individual amounts do not need to be posted. The total of this column is debited to the general ledger in the account called General Bank Account (#100). The advantage of using the general receipts journal is that the need to post each individual receipt to the general bank account is avoided.

2. *Accounts Receivable Cr.:* The individual amounts listed in this column must be posted as a debit to each client account affected by the transaction. The amount is entered in the Payments from Client" column in the client's general ledger. The client file number is placed in the PR column in the journal to indicate that the individual amounts were posted to each client's general ledger sheet in the client general ledgers. At the end of

the month, a list of the accounts receivable is prepared listing the amount owed by each client on that date.

The column total is credited to the Accounts Receivable account (#120) in the general ledger. It is a good practice to prepare a list of accounts receivable each period by listing the client files and the balance owed as shown in the client's general ledger at the end of the month.

General Disbursements Journal

Payments made out of the general bank account can be recorded in the **general disbursements journal**. A general disbursements journal designed to suit the requirements of a paralegal firm is illustrated in Figure 6.6. Additional columns may be added at the discretion of the bookkeeper if specific information needs to be captured.

Licensees are required to maintain a book of original entry showing all money paid out[3] by the firm and must record

- the date on which money is disbursed,
- the method by which money is disbursed, including the identifier of any document used to disburse money (such as a cheque number, debit transaction number, and so on),
- the amount of money disbursed, and
- the person to whom money is paid.

The information in the general disbursements journal would be completed as shown in Figure 6.6.

Justin Case, Paralegal General Disbursements Journal							GDJ1
Date 20**	Method/ Ref. #	Paid To/Particulars Client/RE	File No./ PR	General Ledger Acct. Dr.	Client's General Ledger Dr.	HST Paid Dr.	General Bank Acct. Cr.
Nov. 1	chq. #4	Lucky Landlord, Rent Exp.	538	300.00		39.00	339.00
4	chq. #5	LSUC re Dues Oct. – Dec.	534	268.75		34.94	303.69
5	chq. #6	J. Case, Drawings	350	800.00			800.00
6	chq. #7	Quick Courier, Zimmer re Courier Exp.	4		20.00	2.60	22.60
15	chq. #8	Unitel re Telephone Exp.	565	80.00		10.40	90.40
30		Totals		1,448.75	20.00	86.94	1,555.69
						(240)	(100)
		Proof		Dr.	Cr.		
				1,448.75	1,555.69		
				20.00			
				86.94			
				1,555.69	1,555.69		

FIGURE 6.6   General disbursements journal for November 20** (after posting)

---

3 Law Society of Upper Canada, bylaw 9, part V, s 18(6).

Date: The date column is used to record the date the transaction occurs.

Method/Ref. #: Indicate how the payment was made by showing the cheque number, the debit reference, or other relevant information.

Paid To/Particulars: Record the name of the payee (person or company paid) and what the payment was for (e.g., telephone expense, salaries, filing court documents). If you are recording a disbursement made on behalf of a client, record the name of the payee, the file name, and the reason the funds were paid (e.g., Quick Courier, Zimmer, re Courier Exp.). You may use more than one line to make the entry.

General Ledger Acct. Dr.: Record the amount to be debited to the general ledger account for the expense incurred. For example, in Figure 6.6, $90.40 was paid to Unitel for telephone expense (phone $80 plus $10.40 HST), so $80 was recorded in this column. This amount should be posted to the general ledger account called Telephone Expense (#565). You will put the $10.40 amount paid for HST in the HST Paid Dr. column in the general ledger.

Client's General Ledger Dr.: When the firm pays expenses on behalf of a client from the general bank account, the amount paid will be entered in this column and it will be posted to the client's general ledger sheet. The amount paid out for the client's file will be charged to the client at the time of billing.

HST Paid Dr.: The amount of HST paid on the transaction should be entered in this column. Once the firm starts to remit HST, the amount collected and the amounts paid out will be deducted from one another and any payment owing will have to be remitted to the Canada Revenue Agency. HST will be dealt with more thoroughly in Chapter 8.

General Bank Acct. Cr.: Enter the total amount of the cheque written in this column.

Posting from the General Disbursements Journal

Entries in the general disbursements journal must be posted to the appropriate ledgers, where information is summarized.

1. *General Ledger Acct. Dr.:* The amounts in this column must be posted to the individual accounts affected. The number in the preceding PR column indicates the account to which the entry was posted.
2. *Client's General Ledger Dr.:* This amount paid out on behalf of a client is recorded in the client's general ledger account. The number in the PR column corresponds to the client file number in the client's general ledger.
3. *HST Paid Dr.:* The total amount is posted to the HST/GST Payable account (this is a liability account (#240), but note that the entry is a debit, which means it is a decrease in the liability for HST). The HST/GST Payable account number (240) is entered at the bottom of the column to show that the amount was posted.
4. *General Bank Acct. Cr.:* The total for this column is posted to the general bank account in the general ledger and the General Bank Account number (100) is entered at the bottom of the column to show that the amount was posted.

General Journal Entries

When a particular transaction does not fit into one of the special journals used by the firm, the entry can be made using the general journal. Each line is then posted to the appropriate ledger account. Figure 6.8 at the end of this chapter shows examples of such general journal entries.

Posting from Special Journals

We saw in Chapter 2 how a general journal is used to record transactions for a business and how the transactions are then posted to the general ledger. There are several different types of ledgers that you will encounter when working in a legal practice.

- *General ledger:* This ledger records receipts and disbursements for the firm that are used for the purposes of preparing the financial statements—the income statement, statement of owner's equity, and balance sheet. The general ledger will have a ledger sheet for each of the accounts listed in the chart of accounts. The entries made in the general journal are posted to the general ledger.
- *Client's general ledger:* This ledger contains a separate sheet for each client file. All the payments received from a client for payment on invoices, payments made from the firm's general bank account on behalf of a client, and expense recovery items, such as charges for photocopies and faxes charged to a client, are recorded in the client's general ledger. A running total of the balance is calculated.
- *Client's trust ledger:* This ledger contains a separate sheet for each client file. All the receipts and payments from the trust bank account related to a client file will have to be posted to the client's trust ledger. It is important to keep a running total of the balance in the client's trust ledger account so that the balance held for each client is always up to date. The entries made in the trust bank journal are posted to the individual client trust ledger sheet for each client. The total receipts and payments from the trust bank journal are posted to the account in the general ledger. Because the trust bank journal and trust ledgers were covered in Chapter 5, we have not included them again in this chapter.
- *Combined client's general and trust ledger:* It is sometimes convenient to combine the client's general ledger sheets and the client's trust ledger sheets for each file on one page. In that way, you need look at only one ledger sheet to view the status of a client's account. The information you will find in a ledger that combines both the client general ledger and client trust ledger transactions will include the following items:

  - All transactions that were posted from the trust bank journal showing all receipts and payments made in trust on behalf of a client
  - All transactions that were posted from the general journal to the client ledger accounts for individual clients
  - All invoices recorded in the fees book that have been billed to the client
  - All payments received from a client and the balance owing on account, if any

Analysis of Each Transaction in November

Figure 6.7 shows an analysis of all the transactions referred to above. The completed journal and ledgers are shown at the end of this chapter (Figures 6.8 through 6.13).

Nov. 1—Invoice #2 was sent to Cliff Howes re Small Claims Court for $800 plus HST of $104.		
1.	Which journal is to be used?	• The amount of fees charged on an invoice must be recorded in the fees book in the column Fees Billed Cr.
2.	How will this entry be posted?	• The amounts $800 and $104 are entered in the client's general ledger for Cliff Howes under the appropriate columns for fees and HST.
Nov. 1—Rent was paid to Lucky Landlord in the amount of $300 plus $39 HST, general cheque #4.		
3.	Which journal is to be used?	• This is a disbursement out of the general bank account, so the total amount of the entry must be placed in the general disbursements journal under the General Bank Acct. Cr. column. • Record the amount for rent ($300) in the General Ledger Acct. Dr. column. • Record the amount of HST in the HST Paid Dr. column.
4.	How will this entry be posted?	• Post the amount of $300 for rent expense to the general ledger account. • Do not post the individual amounts for the other two columns because the totals will be posted at the end of the month.
Nov. 3—A new client file was opened for *Ruth Zimmer v. Bud Carpenter* re work improperly done on her property. She is claiming damages in the amount of $24,000 for repairs that had to be made. Open a file for Ruth Zimmer (file #4). No retainer was received.		
5.	Which journal is to be used?	• N/A. Opening of a file does not require a journal entry.
6.	How will this entry be posted?	• You will need to open a client ledger sheet for Zimmer in the client's general and trust ledgers for the purpose of making entries in the future.
Nov. 4—Justin Case paid $268.75 plus $34.94 HST for a total of $303.69 to cover LSUC membership dues for October, November, and December—general cheque #5.		
7.	Which journal is to be used?	• This is a payment out of the general bank account, so record the transaction in the general disbursements journal: – General Ledger Acct. Dr. column: $268.75 – HST Paid column: $34.94 – General Bank Acct. Cr. column: $303.69
8.	How will this entry be posted?	• Post the expense of $268.75 for Law Society membership dues to the general ledger account called Membership/Professional Dues.
Nov. 5—Justin wrote a cheque to himself for $800 for personal expenses. General cheque #6.		
9.	Which journal is to be used?	• This is a payment out of the general bank account, so record the transaction in the general disbursements journal: – General Ledger Acct. Dr. column: $800 – General Bank Acct. Cr. column: $800
10.	How will this entry be posted?	• Post the withdrawal of $800 to the general ledger account called Justin Case, Drawings.

Nov. 6—A letter was sent to Bud Carpenter on the Zimmer file setting out the claim. The letter was sent by Quick Courier at a cost of $20 plus $2.60 for HST for a total of $22.60. The amount was paid by general cheque #7.

11.	Which journal is to be used?	• This is a disbursement out of the general bank account, so the total amount of the entry should be placed in the general disbursements journal under the General Bank Acct. Cr. column. • Also enter the amount of $20 in the Client's General Ledger Dr. column of the general disbursements journal.
12.	How will this entry be posted?	• Post the amount from the Client's General Ledger Dr. column to the ledger sheet for Zimmer. Do not post the amount of $2.60 for HST because this will be included in the total posted to the general ledger at the end of the month.

Nov. 10—Fees were billed to Frank Jones re *Highway Traffic Act* for $400 plus HST of $52 (invoice #3).

13.	Which journal is to be used?	• The $400 amount of fees charged is to be recorded in the fees book in the column Fees Billed Cr.
14.	How will this entry be posted?	• The amount of $400 is posted to the client's general ledger for Frank Jones under the column Fees. HST will be posted at the end of the month to the general ledger account.

Nov. 10—Partial payment on account was received by transferring funds from the trust account for Cliff Howes. There was $700 in the Cliff Howes trust account, so Justin wrote cheque #4 from trust for $700, then deposited the cheque in his general bank account. Record the receipt of payment in this transaction. (Trust entries not included here.)

15.	Which journal is to be used?	• The deposit of $700 in the firm's general bank account is recorded in the general receipts journal in the General Bank Dr. column and also in the Accounts Receivable Cr. column.
16.	How will the entry be posted?	• The amount received from the client will be posted to the client's general ledger to show that the client paid $700 on account.

Nov. 15—Justin paid the telephone bill in the amount of $80, plus $10.40 for HST, general cheque #8, general bank account.

17.	Which journal is to be used?	• Record the amount of $90.40 for telephone expense to the general disbursements journal in the column General Bank Acct. Cr. • Enter the amount of $80 in the General Ledger Acct. Dr. column and the $10.40 in the HST Paid Dr. column.
18.	How will this entry be posted?	• Post the amount of $80 to the general ledger on the sheet for telephone expense.

Nov. 20—Justin transferred the amount of $300 held in trust for Frank Jones by writing cheque #5 on the trust account. He then deposited the cheque in the general bank account and applied payment to invoice #3. Record receipt of the payment of $300 in the general bank account.

19.	Which journal is to be used?	• The deposit of $300 in the firm's general bank account is recorded in the general receipts journal in the General Bank Dr. column and also in the Accounts Receivable Cr. column.
20.	How will this entry be posted?	• The amount received from the client will be posted to the client's general ledger to show that the client paid $300 on account.

Nov. 21—Justin sold the printer he had invested in the firm to Jane Crozier. He received $50 for the printer.

21.	Which journal is to be used?	• Record the receipt from the sale of the printer as a debit in the general journal. • Record the decrease in the asset computer equipment on the next line in the general journal.
22.	How will this entry be posted?	• Post the entries to the general ledger as a debit to the General Bank Account and as a credit to the Computer Equipment account.

Nov. 22—Justin presented an interim bill to Ruth Zimmer in the amount of $250 for fees and for disbursements of $20 plus HST of $35.10 for a total of $305.10 (invoice #4). Ruth Zimmer immediately paid the bill in cash when the bill was presented to her.

23.	Which journal is to be used?	• Record the fees billed in the fees book under the Fees Billed Cr. column. • Record the $20 billed under the Disbursements Billed column and the HST under the HST Billed column. • Show the total amount of the bill ($305.10) in the Total Billed AR Dr. column.
24.	How will this entry be posted?	• Post the amount billed ($250) to the client's general ledger for Ruth Zimmer and post the HST of $35.10. You do not need to post the amount of $20 because it was already entered on November 6.
25.	Which journal is to be used?	• You have received payment in cash from Ruth Zimmer. Record the amount received in the general receipts journal under the General Bank Dr. column and also under the Accounts Receivable Cr. column.
26.	How will this entry be posted?	• Post the amount of $305.10 received to the client's general ledger for Zimmer to show that she has paid the fee.

Nov. 30—Justin received a bill from the Law Society of Upper Canada for $1,075 plus HST of $139.75 for a total of $1,214.75. The first payment on account is not due until April 14 next year.

27.	Which journal is to be used?	• This entry should be made using the general journal. It is a compound entry. • Record the LSUC dues of $1,075 as an expense (debit) on the first line: Membership/Professional Dues. • Record the HST of $139.75 as a debit on the second line, and record the account payable of $1,214.75 as a credit on the third line. Enter the explanation on the fourth line.
28.	How will the entry be posted?	• Post each entry to the accounts in the general ledger.

FIGURE 6.7   Analysis of all transactions for Justin Case, November 20**

Completed Journal and Ledgers to November 30

Justin Case, Paralegal General Journal					GJ3
Date 20**		Description	PR	Debit	Credit
Nov.	21	General Bank Account	100	50.00	
		Computer Equipment	155		50.00
		To record funds received on sale of printer			
	30	Membership/Professional Dues	534	1,075.00	
		HST/GST Payable	240	139.75	
		Accounts Payable	200		1,214.75
		To record professional dues payable			
		Totals		1,264.75	1,264.75

FIGURE 6.8   Justin Case, general journal entries for November 20**

Justin Case, Paralegal
General Ledgers

General Bank Account — Account No. 100

Date 20**		Explanation	PR	Debit	Credit	Dr./Cr.	Balance
Oct.	1		GJ1	1,000.00		Dr.	1,000.00
	1		GJ1	4,000.00		Dr.	5,000.00
	5		GJ2		300.00	Dr.	4,700.00
	5		GJ2		2,000.00	Dr.	2,700.00
	6		GJ2	500.00		Dr.	3,200.00
	15		GJ2		100.00	Dr.	3,100.00
	20		GJ2	3,000.00		Dr.	6,100.00
	30		GJ2		500.00	Dr.	5,600.00
Nov.	21	Sale of Printer to Crozier	GJ3	50.00		Dr.	5,650.00
	30	Totals from General Receipts Journal	GRJ1	1,305.10		Dr.	6,955.10
	30	Totals from General Disb. Journal	GDJ1		1,555.69	Dr.	5,399.41

Trust Bank Account — Account No. 115

Date 20**		Explanation	PR	Debit	Credit	Dr./Cr.	Balance
Oct.	30	Trust Totals for October	TJ1	4,100.00	2,820.00	Dr.	1,280.00
Nov.	30	Trust Totals for November	TJ2		1,000.00	Dr.	280.00

Accounts Receivable — Account No. 120

Date 20**		Explanation	PR	Debit	Credit	Dr./Cr.	Balance
Nov.	30	Total A/R—November	FB1	1,661.10		Dr.	1,661.10
Nov.	30	Totals for November	GRJ1		1,305.10	Dr.	356.00

Computer Equipment (Hardware) — Account No. 155

Date 20**		Explanation	PR	Debit	Credit	Dr./Cr.	Balance
Oct.	1		GJ1	900.00		Dr.	900.00
Nov.	21	Sale of Printer to Crozier	GJ3		50.00	Dr.	850.00

Office Furniture and Equipment — Account No. 158

Date 20**		Explanation	PR	Debit	Credit	Dr./Cr.	Balance
Oct.	1		GJ1	150.00		Dr.	150.00
	5		GJ2	2,000.00		Dr.	2,150.00
	15		GJ2	100.00		Dr.	2,250.00

Accounts Payable/General Liabilities — Account No. 200

Date 20**		Explanation	PR	Debit	Credit	Dr./Cr.	Balance
Oct.	10	Legal Supplies Inc.	GJ2		580.00	Cr.	580.00
Nov.	30	Law Society Dues	GJ3		1,214.75	Cr.	1,794.75

Personal Loan — Account No. 205

Date 20**		Explanation	PR	Debit	Credit	Dr./Cr.	Balance
Oct.	1	J. Case	GJ1		4,000.00	Cr.	4,000.00

Trust Funds Owed — Account No. 215

Date 20**		Explanation	PR	Debit	Credit	Dr./Cr.	Balance
Oct.	31	Trust Funds Owed to Clients	TJ1	4,100.00	2,820.00	Cr.	1,280.00
Nov.	30	Trust Funds Owed November 30	TJ2		1,000.00	Cr.	280.00

HST/GST Payable — Account No. 240

Date 20**		Explanation	PR	Debit	Credit	Dr./Cr.	Balance
Nov.	31	Total Billed to Clients	FB1		191.10	Cr.	191.10
Nov.	30	Total Disbursed for November	GDJ1	86.94		Cr.	104.16
	30	HST on Professional Dues	GJ3	139.75		Dr.	35.59

Justin Case, Capital — Account No. 300

Date 20**		Explanation	PR	Debit	Credit	Dr./Cr.	Balance
Oct.	1		GJ1		1,000.00	Cr.	1,000.00
	1		GJ1		900.00	Cr.	1,900.00
	1		GJ1		150.00	Cr.	2,050.00
	5		GJ2		500.00	Cr.	2,550.00

Justin Case, Drawings						Account No. 350	
Date 20**		Explanation	PR	Debit	Credit	Dr./Cr.	Balance
Nov.	5	Withdrawal of funds for personal expenses	GDJ1	800.00		Dr.	800.00

Fees Earned						Account No. 400	
Date 20**		Explanation	PR	Debit	Credit	Dr./Cr.	Balance
Oct.	20		GJ2		3,000.00	Cr.	3,000.00
Nov.	30	Total Fees Billed—November	FB1		1,450.00	Cr.	4,450.00

Membership/Professional Dues						Account No. 534	
Date 20**		Explanation	PR	Debit	Credit	Dr./Cr.	Balance
Nov.	4	Law Society Dues	GDJ1	268.75		Dr.	268.75
	30	Law Society Dues—next year	GJ3	1,075.00		Dr.	1,343.75

Office Supplies/General Expense						Account No. 535	
Date 20**		Explanation	PR	Debit	Credit	Dr./Cr.	Balance
Oct.	10		GJ2	580.00		Dr.	580.00

Rent Expense						Account No. 538	
Date 20**		Explanation	PR	Debit	Credit	Dr./Cr.	Balance
Oct.	30		GJ2	500.00		Dr.	500.00
Nov.	1		GDJ1	300.00		Dr.	800.00

Telephone Expense						Account No. 565	
Date 20**		Explanation	PR	Debit	Credit	Dr./Cr.	Balance
Oct.	5		GJ2	300.00		Dr.	300.00
Nov.	15	Unitel	GDJ1	80.00		Dr.	380.00

FIGURE 6.9   Justin Case, general ledgers as of November 20**

<table>
<tr><td colspan="11" align="center">Justin Case, Paralegal
Client General Ledger and Client Trust Ledger</td></tr>
</table>

		Client General Ledger					Client Trust Ledger			File No. 001

Account: HOWES, Cliff   re Small Claims Court — File No. 001

Date 20**		Received From/Paid To Explanation	Disburse-ments Expenses Paid	HST	Fees	Payments from Client	Balance Owed	Disburse-ments (Dr.)	Receipts (Cr.)	Balance in Trust
Oct.	1	Retainer							1,000.00	1,000.00
	3	Deliveries Inc.						20.00		980.00
	15	James Settlor, Settlement							2,500.00	3,480.00
	15	Cliff Howes, Settlement Funds						2,500.00		980.00
	30	Cliff Howes, Transfer to File No. 3						280.00		700.00
Nov.	1	Invoice #2		104.00	800.00		904.00			
	10	Justin Case, on Account						700.00		0.00
	10	Transfer from Trust				700.00	204.00			

Account: JONES, Frank   re *Highway Traffic Act* — File No. 002

Date 20**		Received From/Paid To Explanation	Disburse-ments Expenses Paid	HST	Fees	Payments from Client	Balance Owed	Disburse-ments (Dr.)	Receipts (Cr.)	Balance in Trust
Nov.	1	Retainer							600.00	600.00
	8	Minister of Finance, Fine						300.00		300.00
	10	Fees Billed, invoice #3		52.00	400.00		452.00			
	15	Justin Case, on Account							300.00	0.00
	20	Justin Case, Payment on invoice #3				300.00	152.00			

Account: HOWES, Larry   re Shoplifting — File No. 003

Date 20**		Received From/Paid To Explanation	Disburse-ments Expenses Paid	HST	Fees	Payments from Client	Balance Owed	Disburse-ments (Dr.)	Receipts (Cr.)	Balance in Trust
Oct.	30	Transfer from Cliff Howes, File No. 1							280.00	280.00

Account: ZIMMER, Ruth re *Ruth Zimmer v. Bud Carpenter*						File No. 004			
		Client General Ledger					**Client Trust Ledger**		
Date 20**	Received From/Paid To Explanation	Disburse-ments Expenses Paid	HST	Fees	Payments from Client	Balance Owed	Disburse-ments (Dr.)	Receipts (Cr.)	Balance in Trust
Nov. 6	Quick Courier	20.00				20.00			
22	Fees Billed, invoice #4		35.10	250.00		305.10			
22	Zimmer, on Account				305.10	0.00			

FIGURE 6.10   Justin Case, client general ledger and client trust ledger for October and November 20**

	Justin Case, Paralegal Trial Balance November 30, 20**		
#	Account	Debit	Credit
100	General Bank Account	$5,399.41	
115	Trust Bank Account	280.00	
120	Accounts Receivable	356.00	
155	Computer Equipment (Hardware)	850.00	
158	Office Furniture and Equipment	2,250.00	
200	Accounts Payable		$1,794.75
205	Personal Loan		4,000.00
215	Trust Funds Owed		280.00
240	HST/GST Payable	35.59	
300	Justin Case, Capital		2,550.00
350	Justin Case, Drawings	800.00	
400	Fees Earned		4,450.00
534	Membership/Professional Dues	1,343.75	
535	Office Supplies/General Expense	580.00	
538	Rent Expense	800.00	
565	Telephone Expense	380.00	
		$13,074.75	$13,074.75

FIGURE 6.11   Justin Case, trial balance, November 30, 20**

	Justin Case, Paralegal List of Accounts Receivable November 30, 20**	
File No.	Name of Client/RE	Balance Owed
1	HOWES, Cliff re Small Claims Court	$204.00
2	JONES, Frank re *Highway Traffic Act*	152.00
	Total Owed by Clients	$356.00

FIGURE 6.12   Justin Case, list of accounts receivable

	Justin Case, Paralegal List of Balances Owed to Clients November 30, 20**	
File No.	Account	Balance Owed
1	HOWES, Cliff re Small Claims Court	$0.00
2	JONES, Frank re *Highway Traffic Act*	0.00
3	HOWES, Larry re Shoplifting	280.00
	Total Owed to Clients	$280.00

FIGURE 6.13   Justin Case, client trust listing at November 30, 20**

Supporting Documents

The Canada Revenue Agency (CRA) requires that you keep organized accounting and financial documents that summarize the information from your supporting documents. Examples of such documents include ledgers, journals, and financial statements, statements of accounts, income tax returns, and GST/HST tax credit returns.

Documents you must keep that support transactions identified in your records include invoices for fees, purchase receipts, vouchers, contracts (such as a lease), bank deposit slips, cancelled cheques, credit card receipts, logbooks, emails, and correspondence supporting transactions.

These records can be kept in English or French.

CHAPTER SUMMARY

Learning how to use special journals can seem complicated, but ultimately they simplify your record-keeping. Special journals do this by grouping certain transactions in one column so that you do not need to post as many entries. This saves time and avoids errors. Keeping the client general ledger and the client trust ledger on the same page will help you to see the flow of transactions between the two ledgers.

Technology is a useful tool for using special journals because the software usually records and posts the information automatically to the correct place. The manual approach used in this chapter helps you to understand how the information flows through a computerized system. If you do not understand how the information is processed manually, you will have difficulty understanding the information created by a computerized system. Further, some paralegals may not be able to afford specialized computer bookkeeping software when they start out—so it is good to know how books must be set up and maintained.

KEY TERMS

billable work, 121
expense recovery, 121
fees book, 123
fees journal, 120
general disbursements journal, 129
general receipts journal, 127
non-billable work, 121
special journals, 120

FURTHER READING

Canvas Network, Intro to Accounting, "Study: Subsidiary Ledgers and Special Journals," online: <https://learn.canvas.net/courses/37/pages/study-subsidiary-ledgers-and-special-journals>. For additional information, select "Special Journals and Subsidiary Ledgers" under Additional Resources to link to a video on an external site.

Lawyers' Professional Indemnity Company, *Managing the Finances of Your Practice*, online: <http://www.practicepro.ca/practice/pdf/Managing_Finances_booklet.pdf>. See sections related to established practices (fee agreements, docketing, billing).

LexisNexis Canada, PCLaw billing and accounting software FAQ, online: <http://law.lexisnexis.com/literature/back_office_faqs.pdf>. See sections related to billing, client disbursements, and time entries.

PUT IT INTO PRACTICE

Case Example: Special Journals

Ann Litigate has prepared the following invoices dated May 30, 20**:

Client Matter #21-xx:	$1,250.00 (Total Fees, Disbursements, and HST)
Fees Billed:	$1,000.00
Disbursement Recoverable:	$120.00, Court Filing Fees (no HST)
HST Billed:	$130.00

Client Matter #08-xx:	$583.20 (Total Fees, Disbursements, and HST)
Fees Billed:	$500.00
Disbursement Recoverable:	$16.10, Courier Fees (Speedy Courier)
HST Billed:	$67.10

Client Matter #11-xx:	$1,672.40 (Total Fees, Disbursements, and HST)
Fees Billed:	$1,440.00
Disbursement Recoverable:	$40.00, Travel Expense (Mileage)
HST Billed:	$192.40

Client Matter #29-xx:	$864.45 (Total Fees, Disbursements, and HST)
Fees Billed:	$750.00
Disbursement Recoverable:	$15.00, Photocopy Charges (Kwick Print)
HST Billed:	$99.45

Answer the following questions and list the steps that Ann will need to take for these transactions. Identify the appropriate special journals and ledgers.

1. How can Ann keep track of the balance owing by her clients once the invoices are issued?
2. When Ann receives payment on an invoice, how can she keep track of the payments made by her clients?
3. Suppose Ann paid $100 in disbursements or expenses on behalf of her client and wishes to recover the cost from the client.
   a. What entries should Ann make when the expense is incurred?
   b. What entries should Ann make when the expenses paid by Ann are not yet paid by the client?
   c. What entries should Ann make when the client subsequently pays the expense?

REVIEW QUESTIONS

True or False

_____ 1. A fees book includes only information about legal fees charged to clients.

_____ 2. An accounts receivable journal is an example of a special journal.

_____ 3. The general disbursements journal is used only for disbursements made on behalf of clients, which are recoverable by the paralegal.

_____ 4. If a credit is given to a client (as a result of overpayment or as a result of holding unused trust funds), the transaction should be recorded on both the appropriate client trust ledger and the general ledger.

_____ 5. Every receipt shown on the general receipts journal will have a corresponding entry on the general disbursements journal for the same accounting period.

_____ 6. An invoice should be created each and every time disbursements are billed to a client.

_____ 7. Entries from a special journal do not need to be posted to the general ledger.

_____ 8. The Accounts Receivable account found on the general ledger can be further subdivided by clients.

_____ 9. The general journal replaces the need for special journals.

_____ 10. The "control account" and the "trial balance" are accounting terms that can be used interchangeably.

Short Answer

1. Which of the following entries would be recorded in the general receipts journal?

   a. The firm was paid $300 on account by a client.

   b. The firm received a credit of $50 from the landlord for rent.

   c. The firm paid photocopies expense to be recovered from a client.

   d. The firm wrote a cheque to itself from the trust account to pay for an invoice sent to the client.

   e. The firm paid money out of trust to cover filing fees of $150 paid the previous week from the firm's general bank account and deposited the amount in its general bank account.

2. What is the purpose of the general disbursements journal?

3. What is the benefit of maintaining a fees book?

4. Which columns in the fees book are posted as a total, and to which account are they posted?

5. Which individual items in the fees book get posted to the client's general ledger?

PRACTICE EXERCISES

Practice Exercise 6.1

Prepare the appropriate special journals and client general ledgers based on the following transactions for Ann Litigate in the operation of her paralegal practice:

1. July 1: Paid rent expense (invoice #1001 payable to Magnum Office Managers), $1,200, general chq. #217, A. Litigate

2. July 7: Paid courier invoice account (invoice #A0-111 payable to Fast Courier), $120 plus HST for a total of $135.60 ($60 plus HST of $7.80 recoverable from client, L. Forte), chq. #218, A. Litigate

3. July 9: Billed L. Forte for legal services (invoice #400), $500 disbursement plus $67.80 HST for a total of $641.61

4. July 9: Paid court filing fees, $240 ($120 recoverable from client L. Bailey; $120 recoverable from R. Smythe) (no HST payable on court fees), chq. #219, A. Litigate

5. July 15: Billed L. Bailey for legal services (invoice #401), $1,000 disbursement plus $120 HST (billed on fees only) for a total of $1,250

6. July 15: Paid professional liability insurance (payable to ABC Insurance), $167, chq. #220, A. Litigate

7. July 23: Received payment for invoice #400 (L. Forte), $641.61 ($500 disbursement plus $67.80 HST)

8. July 30: Paid salary to assistant, $2,000, general chq. #221

9. July 30: Received payment for invoice #401 (L. Bailey), $1,000 disbursement plus $120 HST for a total of $1,250

10. July 31: Capital investment (from Ann to the firm), $2,500, chq. #24, A. Litigate (personal account)

11. July 31: Billed client (R. Smythe) on invoice #402, $120 (no HST payable) for a total of $120

a. Prepare the entries for the above transactions by completing the appropriate journals: fees book, general journal, general receipts journal, general disbursements journal. Post the individual entries that need to be posted to the client ledgers and the general ledgers.

b. Post the totals for the journals that need to be posted to the appropriate general ledger accounts.

c. Prepare the trial balance.

> **HINT**
>
> Also prepare a list of the total accounts receivable owed to Ann for the month.

Date 20**		Description	PR	Debit	Credit

Ann Litigate, Paralegal
General Journal — GJ3

PRACTICE

EXCEL

Ann Litigate, Paralegal
Fees Book — FB1

Date 20**	Inv. #	Client/Re	Ref.	Fees Billed	Disbursements Billed	HST Billed Cr.	Total Billed AR Dr.

Ann Litigate, Paralegal
General Receipts Journal — GRJ1

Date 20**		Name of Account	Particulars/ Method of Payment	PR	General Bank Dr.	Accounts Receivable Cr.

Ann Litigate, Paralegal General Disbursements Journal							GDJ1
Date 20**	Method/ Ref. #	Paid To/Particulars Client/RE	PR /File	General Ledger Acct. Dr.	Client's General Ledger Dr.	HST Paid Dr.	General Bank Account Cr.

Ann Litigate, Paralegal
Client General Ledgers and Client Trust Ledger

Account: FORTE, L. | **File No. 04**

| | | Client General Ledger | | | | | Client Trust Ledger | | |
Date 20**	Received From/ Paid To Explanation	Disburse- ments Expenses Paid	HST	Fees	Payments from Client	Balance Owed	Disburse- ments (Dr.)	Receipts (Cr.)	Balance in Trust

Account: BAILEY, L. | **File No. 05**

| | | Client General Ledger | | | | | Client Trust Ledger | | |
Date 20**	Received From/ Paid To Explanation	Disburse- ments Expenses Paid	HST	Fees	Payments from Client	Balance Owed	Disburse- ments (Dr.)	Receipts (Cr.)	Balance in Trust

Account: SMYTHE, R. | **File No. 06**

| | | Client General Ledger | | | | | Client Trust Ledger | | |
Date 20**	Received From/ Paid To Explanation	Disburse- ments Expenses Paid	HST	Fees	Payments from Client	Balance Owed	Disburse- ments (Dr.)	Receipts (Cr.)	Balance in Trust

Ann Litigate, Paralegal
General Ledgers as of July 31

General Bank Account   **Account No. 100**

Date 20**		Explanation	PR	Debit	Credit	Dr./Cr.	Balance

Accounts Receivable   **Account No. 120**

Date 20**		Explanation	PR	Debit	Credit	Dr./Cr.	Balance

Office Furniture and Equipment   **Account No. 158**

Date 20**		Explanation	PR	Debit	Credit	Dr./Cr.	Balance

Accounts Payable/General Liabilities   **Account No. 200**

Date 20**		Explanation	PR	Debit	Credit	Dr./Cr.	Balance

HST Payable   **Account No. 240**

Date 20**		Explanation	PR	Debit	Credit	Dr./Cr.	Balance

Ann Litigate, Capital   **Account No. 300**

Date 20**		Explanation	PR	Debit	Credit	Dr./Cr.	Balance

Ann Litigate, Drawings						Account No. 350	
Date 20**	Explanation	PR	Debit	Credit	Dr./Cr.	Balance	

Fees Earned						Account No. 400	
Date 20**	Explanation	PR	Debit	Credit	Dr./Cr.	Balance	

Salaries Expense						Account No. 511	
Date 20**	Explanation	PR	Debit	Credit	Dr./Cr.	Balance	

Insurance—Professional Liability						Account No. 527	
Date 20**	Explanation	PR	Debit	Credit	Dr./Cr.	Balance	

Office Supplies/General Expense						Account No. 535	
Date 20**	Explanation	PR	Debit	Credit	Dr./Cr.	Balance	

Rent Expense						Account No. 538	
Date 20**	Explanation	PR	Debit	Credit	Dr./Cr.	Balance	

Delivery Expense						Account No. 550	
Date 20**	Explanation	PR	Debit	Credit	Dr./Cr.	Balance	

PRACTICE

EXCEL

	Ann Litigate, Paralegal Trial Balance November 30, 20**		
#	Account	Debit	Credit

Practice Exercise 6.2

Complete the invoices provided based on the following time docket entries prepared by Ann Litigate.

HINT

To calculate billable time, divide X minutes billed by 60 (minutes) and round up to the nearest 0.10.

Time Docket Entries
A. Johnston—Matter No. 01 (Small Claims Matter—*Johnston v. Delaney*)

Date 20**	Description	Start Time	End Time	Total Time
June 18	Initial consultation with client to discuss options for small claim matter	10:30 a.m.	11:00 a.m.	0.50 hours (30 min/60 min)
June 20	Conduct research on issues related to trespass	3:00 p.m.	4:15 p.m.	1.30 hours (75 min/60 min)
June 22	Prepare initial draft of statement of claim and email to client for review	11:20 a.m.	12:50 p.m.	1.50 hours (90 min/60 min)
June 28	Follow-up meeting with client to discuss draft statement of claim for the purpose of finalizing same statement of claim based on client comments	10:00 a.m.	10:45 a.m.	0.80 hours (45 min/60 min)

Time Docket Entries
J. Palmer—Matter No. 06 (Provincial Offences Matter)

Date 20**	Description	Start Time	End Time	Total Time
May 15	Phone call and initial consultation with J. Palmer	1:55 p.m.	2:15 p.m.	0.40 hours (20 min/60 min)
May 20	Meeting with client to discuss upcoming court date	5:30 p.m.	6:00 p.m.	0.50 hours (30 min/60 min)
June 5	Review disclosure and conduct research (section 130, *Highway Traffic Act*) in preparation for upcoming court date	10:15 a.m.	11:00 a.m.	0.80 hours (45 min/60 min)
June 12	Attend at Provincial Offences Court and negotiate a settlement with the Crown	9:00 a.m.	10:15 a.m.	1.30 hours (75 min/60 min)

Invoice for A. Johnston

Ann Litigate Paralegal Services   Invoice #1015
11 Any Street, Ottawa, Ontario K1A 0B0

June 30, 20**

Mr. Anthony Johnston
123 Avenue Road
Ottawa, Ontario K1A 0C0

FOR SERVICES RENDERED RE SMALL CLAIMS MATTER:

Date	Hours Billed	Description	Billable Rate (/h)	Amount Billed
		FEES:	**Subtotal**	
			HST (13%)	

DISBURSEMENTS

	Quantity	Description	Unit Price	Amount
	45 pages	Photocopies	0.25/page	
	15 pages	Fax transmissions	1.00/page	
		DISBURSEMENTS:	**Subtotal**	
			HST (13%)	

TOTAL (FEES, DISBURSEMENTS, AND HST)

	Total	
	Total Balance Owing	

Invoice for J. Palmer

Ann Litigate Paralegal Services   Invoice #1016
11 Any Street, Ottawa, Ontario K1A 0B0

June 30, 20**

Ms. Janet Palmer
567 Jane Street
Ottawa, Ontario K1A 0C1

FOR SERVICES RENDERED RE HIGHWAY TRAFFIC ACT MATTER:

Date	Hours Billed	Description	Billable Rate (/h)	Amount Billed
		FEES:	Subtotal	
		DISCOUNT, FLAT RATE SERVICE ($450.00):	Subtotal	
			HST (13%)	

DISBURSEMENTS

Quantity	Description	Unit Price	Amount
25 pages	Photocopies	0.25/page	
35 km	Travel to/from Provincial Offences Court	0.40/km	
	DISBURSEMENTS:	Subtotal	
		HST (13%)	

TOTAL (FEES, DISBURSEMENTS, AND HST)

	Total	
	Total Balance Owing	

7 Adjusting Accounts for Financial Statements

After reading this chapter, you should be able to:

- record the trial balance in a worksheet
- prepare adjusting entries at the end of a period
- prepare an adjusted trial balance
- complete the income statement and balance sheet portions of a worksheet

Once the trial balance is prepared, the next step in the accounting cycle is to prepare a worksheet on which required adjustments are made before financial statements can be prepared. In this chapter you will learn how to prepare a **worksheet**, adjusting entries, and an **adjusted trial balance**. You will also use this information to complete the financial statements portion of the worksheet.

Figure 7.1 highlights these next steps in the accounting cycle.

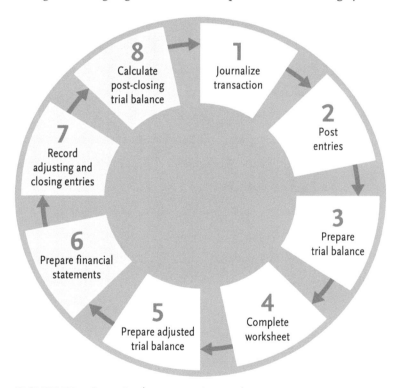

FIGURE 7.1 Steps in the accounting cycle

Adjusting Entries

At the end of the fiscal year, the firm is required to prepare an accurate and detailed statement of its revenues and expenses for income tax purposes. This is called an income statement and is used to calculate the profit (or loss) for the year. If the firm is a sole proprietorship, the business owner will have to include the amount of the profit on his or her personal income tax return. A worksheet enables the accountant to organize and check data, and make any necessary adjustments, before financial statements are prepared.

Before preparing his personal income tax return, Justin Case will want to ensure his records have been maintained in accordance with Canadian generally accepted accounting principles (GAAP). In particular, he will want to make certain that the **matching principle** has been respected, that is, that expenses incurred during the current accounting period are related to or have contributed toward the revenue that was generated during the same period. This principle is fundamental to the **accrual basis of accounting**.

Justin does not want to pay more income tax than he has to, so the statements will be reviewed and the entries adjusted with a view to ensuring that the numbers are accurate and that all expenses and deductions he is entitled to claim have been recorded. The reverse is also true: when reporting income for tax purposes, Justin must not understate his profit as a result of income or expenses not being recorded in the correct period.

The adjustment process will include the following steps:

- Completing an accurate **office supplies inventory** and writing off supplies used as an expense
- Calculating capital cost allowance or depreciation on Justin's assets and recording the amount of depreciation as an expense
- Reviewing his accounts receivable to determine whether there are any bad debts to be written off
- Reviewing the accuracy of his liabilities and making any necessary corrections
- Ensuring there are no revenues and expenses that are to be carried over to the next operating year
- Preparing an adjusted trial balance

Preparing a Worksheet

The worksheet consolidates all adjustments to a firm's revenues and expenses. If the worksheet is prepared by hand, it can be completed in pencil because it is not a permanent record. Once the worksheet has been completed, the adjusting entries will be entered in the books of the firm using the general journal, and these entries will be posted to each of the ledger accounts affected.

The worksheet enables the bookkeeper to make sure that the books are balanced at each stage up to completion of the financial statements before starting the accounting cycle over again for the next period. A worksheet includes the following six column headings, as shown in Figure 7.2:

Account Titles		Trial Balance		Adjustments			Adjusted Trial Balance		Income Statement		Balance Sheet	
		Dr.	Cr.		Dr.		Cr.	Dr.	Cr.	Dr.	Cr.	Dr.	Cr.

FIGURE 7.2   Typical worksheet headings

1. *Account Titles:* The account numbers and names in the far left column of the worksheet are taken from the general ledger. The account number is not a requirement, but can be included if the bookkeeper finds it helpful. For the purposes of this chapter, account numbers are included.

2. *Trial Balance:* This section contains a list of all the accounts in the same order as they are found in the general ledger. Accounts with a zero balance are not listed. Additional account titles from the ledger will be added as they are needed once we start making adjustments.

3. *Adjustments:* Each amount in the trial balance must be reviewed by the business owner, bookkeeper, or accountant to determine whether any adjustments are required. An adjusting entry can be recorded at the end of each accounting period, for example, each month. Some business owners may be satisfied with doing adjusting entries annually at the end of the fiscal year. Others may want to do them more often. Once the adjustments have been made, the debit and credit columns must be totalled to ensure that the debits are equal to the credits. The entries in the Adjustments column are assigned a letter for reference purposes, giving the corresponding debit and credit entries for a particular adjustment the same letter. This is helpful in tracking the entries that were made if you are looking for errors.

4. *Adjusted Trial Balance:* After the adjusting entries are recorded in the worksheet, the balance in each account is recalculated to arrive at the new balance for each account, and the amount is placed in the Adjusted Trial Balance column. Amounts from the trial balance that have not been adjusted are simply carried over to the Adjusted Trial Balance column. If there was an adjustment made to an account, a calculation of the new balance must be done. Debits are added to debits, credits are added to credits, and debits and credits are subtracted from one another. Once the horizontal calculations have been completed, the debit and credit column totals of the Adjusted Trial Balance column must be equal.

5. *Income Statement:* Extend the amounts for the income and expense accounts from the Adjusted Trial Balance column to the Income Statement column of the worksheet. These are the accounts with the numbers 400 to 599. Be careful to enter the amounts in the correct column for debit and credit. Revenue will normally be in the credit column, whereas expenses will normally be in the debit column. The difference between the income (credit) column and the expense (debit) column is the profit or loss for the period.

6. *Balance Sheet:* Extend the amounts of assets, liabilities, and owner's equity from the Adjusted Trial Balance column to the Balance Sheet column. The asset accounts are the accounts starting with the numbers 100 to 199, the liabilities are the accounts starting with the numbers 200 to 299, and the owner's equity accounts start with the numbers 300 to 399. Total the debit and credit columns once the entries have been copied from the Adjusted Trial Balance column. These totals will not be equal. The amount calculated as profit or loss from the income statement will be used to balance the debit and credit columns in the Balance Sheet column in the bottom portion of the worksheet.

Types of Adjusting Entries

The common types of adjustments include:

- Prepaid expenses
- Amortization or depreciation
- Work in progress (WIP)
- Accrued expenses
- **Accrued revenues**

Prepaid Expenses

Prepaid expenses are sometimes referred to as unexpired expenses. They represent items that have been paid for in advance. As the asset is used the cost becomes an expense, and the amount used must be shifted from the balance in the asset account to the expense section of the ledger. Common examples of prepaid expenses are prepaid insurance, office supplies and other assets, and prepaid rent.

Amortization or Depreciation

Amortization or **depreciation** refers to the amount of wear and tear of an asset for which a reduction is made over time in the valuation of that asset. The diminished value will be shown on the firm's balance sheet. The amount claimed for depreciation is an expense. Assets such as computers and office furniture have a certain life and are expected to be used by the firm for more than one accounting period. They cannot totally be written off as expenses in the year they are purchased. The cost of the item will be written off as an expense over the estimated useful life of the asset. For income tax purposes, the amount expensed is called **capital cost allowance (CCA)**. When amortization expense is recorded it is considered an operating expense, even though no cash is actually spent. (The cash was spent when the asset was acquired.)

There are some terms with which you need to be familiar when discussing depreciation:

- **Historical cost** refers to the original price paid for an item.
- **Class** refers to assets included in a particular account. For example, the account for office furniture will include desks, chairs, waiting room furniture, and so on.
- **Accumulated depreciation** refers to the total amount that has been written off as an expense against a particular asset over time.
- **Book value** is the historical cost of the asset minus the accumulated depreciation. The number will decrease from period to period if no new assets have been added to the class.
- **Residual value** refers to the estimated value of the asset at the end of its useful life.
- **Contra-asset account** is an account in the chart of accounts that is linked to an asset account, such as Office Furniture and Equipment, and has a normal credit balance on the asset side of the balance sheet. In the case of accumulated depreciation, this contra-asset account records the depreciation of an asset. This account totals the amount of depreciation taken from time to time and is used to reduce the value of the asset on the balance sheet.

Depreciation will affect both the balance sheet and the income statement. The value of the asset on the balance sheet is being reduced by the amount of amortization taken. The expenses of the firm on the income statement are increased by the depreciation expense taken, resulting in lower income for the firm.

EXAMPLE 1

Depreciation

Suppose Justin Case purchased a photocopier costing $10,000 and took $79.17 depreciation in the month of December. The asset account would appear as follows on the balance sheet:

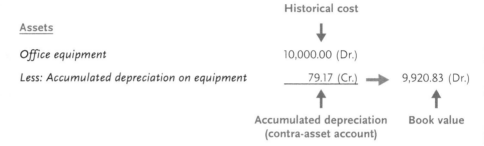

FIGURE 7.3   Depreciation of an asset

The amount of $79.17 will be posted as a debit to depreciation expense to balance the entry. The value of the office equipment account shows the original cost of the photocopier. However, the accumulated depreciation for the period is linked to the office equipment account and the depreciation is subtracted (or credited) against the value. Once it is credited, the amount $9,920.83 represents the book value of the asset. You know how much was originally paid for the photocopier because the historical cost does not change on the balance sheet. Amortization will increase from period to period, reducing the book value of the asset as time goes by.

Calculating Amortization

To depreciate an asset, you have to calculate how much of its cost is used up each period. The Canada Revenue Agency (CRA) has specific rules that tell businesses in Canada how they can depreciate their assets for tax purposes. It is not necessary to use this calculation for financial reports because the value allowed by the CRA may be different from what the business owner feels is the useful life of an asset.

For the purposes of this textbook, we will discuss two methods of calculating amortization on assets, but we will use the straight-line amortization method for doing adjusting entries.

Straight-Line Amortization Method

The **straight-line amortization method** depreciates the value of an asset over its useful life after deducting its residual value, which refers to the estimated value of the asset at the end of its useful life. The amount of depreciation remains constant for each period.

The following formula is used to calculate the rate of amortization using the straight-line method:

$$\text{Depreciation} = \frac{\text{Cost of Equipment} - \text{Residual Value}}{\text{Estimated Useful Life}}$$

EXAMPLE 2

Suppose Justin purchased a photocopier that cost $10,000 and it was expected to last 10 years, at which time he expected the residual value would be $500. The calculation of depreciation would be as follows:

$$\frac{\$10,000 - \$500}{10 \text{ years}} = \frac{\$9,500}{10 \text{ years}} = \$950 \text{ per year or } \$79.17 \text{ per month } (\$950/12)$$

The photocopier is depreciating at a constant rate of $950 per year or $79.17 per month ($950/12 months). Using the straight-line method for calculating depreciation on Justin's photocopier, the book value at the end of four years would be $6,200:

Office Equipment	Life	Historical Cost	Residual Value	Year	Depreciation 9,500/10 yrs.	Accumulated Depreciation	Book Value
Photocopier	10	10,000	500	1	950	950	9,050
		10,000	500	2	950	1,900	8,100
		10,000	500	3	950	2,850	7,150
		10,000	· 500	4	950	3,800	6,200

FIGURE 7.4   Calculation of depreciation using the straight-line method

Declining Balance Amortization Method

The Canada Revenue Agency requires a business to calculate capital cost allowance using the declining balance method.[1] This means you claim CCA on the capital cost (original cost) of the property minus the CCA you claimed in previous years, if any. The remaining balance—the **undepreciated capital cost (UCC)**—declines over the years as you claim CCA.

The CCA that a business can claim depends on the type of property being depreciated and the date it was acquired. Classes of assets are set out by the CRA and assigned a specific rate of depreciation. For example, class 1 includes most buildings acquired after 1987 (unless they specifically belong in another class), and they can be depreciated at a rate of 4 percent. Furniture and appliances are categorized as class 8 and can be depreciated at a rate of 20 percent. If you claim CCA, and you later dispose of the property, you may have to add an amount to your income as a recapture of CCA. Alternatively, you may be able to deduct an additional amount from your income as a terminal loss. You are not required to claim the maximum amount of CCA in any given year. You can claim any amount you like, from zero to the maximum allowed for the year.

---

1   Canada Revenue Agency, "Claiming Capital Cost Allowance (CCA)," online: <http://www.cra-arc.gc.ca/tx/bsnss/tpcs/slprtnr/rprtng/cptl/menu-eng.html>.

EXAMPLE 3

Using the declining balance method for calculating depreciation on Justin's photocopier, the calculation would be:

Item	Class	%	Year	Cost	Capital Cost Allowance (CCA)	Undepreciated Capital Cost (UCC)
Photocopier	8	20%	1	10,000	1,000*	9,000
UCC × 20%			2		1,800	7,200
UCC × 20%			3		1,440	5,760
UCC × 20%			4		1,152	4,608
Total CCA					5,392	

FIGURE 7.5   CCA calculation using the declining balance method

* In the year you acquire property, you can usually claim CCA on only half of your net additions to a class, so the amount is calculated on $5,000 instead of $10,000. In this instance, only half of the CCA of $2,000 is allowed in the first year. If the business has operated for less than one year, the amount should be prorated. If Justin claimed CCA in his first year of business and he acquired the photocopier on December 1, he could claim $1,000/365 × 31 days or $84.93 as capital cost allowance.

Work in Progress

Work in progress (WIP) refers to services that have not been completed or that have been performed in part but are still in progress and, therefore, not yet included as earned income or revenue. As mentioned in Chapter 2, paralegals do not have the opportunity to exclude the value of work in progress from their income as is allowed for lawyers and accountants. An adjustment might be required to include as revenue the value of work in progress that has not yet been billed in income for the period. Usually, invoices are recorded when they are sent out and are shown as income. However, work in progress is recorded only when the invoice is sent. The **revenue recognition principle** of GAAP and the CRA rules governing paralegals require paralegals to include the value of work done on a file that has not yet been billed as revenue for the period. The balance sheet would also show the value of this work as an account receivable.

Accrued Expenses

Accrued expenses refer to costs incurred in a period that are both unpaid and unrecorded. For example, a business could have **accrued interest expense** owing on an unpaid account. Salaries often must be adjusted because the employee may be owed a certain number of days' pay at the end of the period, but payday is in the next period. Accrued vacation pay is a debt owing to the employee for which an adjustment may be required.

Accrued Revenues

Accrued revenues refer to income that has been earned but has not yet been recorded. For example, **accrued interest revenue** on an investment may have accumulated over the period, but may not have been received and not have been recorded in the records of the business. If Justin Case had a guaranteed investment certificate of $10,000 invested at the rate of 2 percent per annum, the daily interest accruing on the investment would be $10,000 × 2 percent per annum/365 days, or 55 cents a day. If he held the investment for 90 days, the adjustment would be $49.50.

Value of Work in Progress

One of the adjustments you will be required to calculate for income tax purposes is the value of WIP if it has not already been included. The income statement you prepare for the purposes of filing an income tax return must include all fees you receive for goods or services you provide, whether you receive or will receive money. As a professional, your income generally includes the value of your work in progress. Your professional fees for the current year are the total of

- all amounts you received during the year for professional services, whether you provided the services before or during the current year or after your current year-end; plus
- all amounts receivable at the end of the current year for professional services you provided during the current year; and
- the value of your WIP at the end of your current year for which you have not received any amount during the year; minus
- all amounts receivable at the end of your previous year-end; and
- the value of your WIP that was included.

TAX TIP

Preparing Adjusting Entries

Justin Case selected December 31 as his fiscal year-end. Once the accounting entries were completed, he prepared the trial balance as of December 31, and the balances were entered in the Trial Balance column of the completed worksheet in Figure 7.9 at the end of the chapter.

Adjusting Entries for Year-End

Upon reviewing the trial balance for his books at the end of December (Figure 7.6), Justin realizes that some transactions need to be adjusted before the financial statements for the year can be finalized. Each type of **adjusting entry** is demonstrated using the accounts described below.

Remember that even when doing adjusting entries, you must have a debit and a credit entry for the books to remain balanced. Each adjustment is identified with a letter of the alphabet (a, b, c, d, e, and so on) to track the corresponding debit and credit. Once you complete an adjustment, you must total the columns across the page to calculate the new balance in each account. This calculated amount is placed in the Adjusted Trial Balance column, as shown in Figure 7.7.

		Trial Balance	
	Justin Case, Paralegal **Worksheet** **for the Month Ended December 31, 20****		
	Account Titles	*Dr.*	*Cr.*
100	General Bank Account	$4,906.91	
115	Trust Bank Account	15,280.00	
120	Accounts Receivable	25,000.00	
125	Prepaid Insurance	600.00	
130	Office Supplies	630.00	
155	Computer Equipment (Hardware)	6,520.00	
158	Office Furniture and Equipment	2,250.00	
200	Accounts Payable/General Liabilities		$6,890.00
205	Personal Loan		3,000.00
210	Credit Card Debt		2,500.00
215	Trust Funds Owed		15,280.00
300	Justin Case, Capital		2,550.00
350	Justin Case, Drawings	1,800.00	
400	Fees Earned		31,580.00
511	Salaries Expense	960.00	
533	Meals and Entertainment Expense	350.00	
534	Membership/Professional Dues	1,343.75	
535	Office Supplies/General Expense	580.00	
538	Rent Expense	1,100.00	
565	Telephone Expense	479.34	
	Total	$61,800.00	$61,800.00

FIGURE 7.6   Trial balance at December 31

Adjustment a: Prepaid Expenses

Justin has prepaid insurance of $600 on the trial balance. The insurance premiums cover one year; the policy starts on December 1 of this year and expires on November 30 next year. He must allocate the cost of the insurance over a 12-month period and cannot take the whole expense this year. This insurance covers liability for fire and theft on his premises.

The adjustment is calculated as follows:

$$\$600 \text{ per } 12 \text{ months} = \$50 \text{ per month}$$

Justin must expense $50 for the month of December and leave the rest of the insurance premium in the prepaid insurance account. The adjusting entry required is a credit of $50 to the prepaid insurance account and a debit to the insurance expense account for $50.

The steps followed to enter this adjustment in the worksheet are as follows (and are shown in Figure 7.7):

1. Enter $50 in the credit column of prepaid insurance and place the letter (a) next to the entry.
2. The account named Insurance Expense (#527) is not listed in the trial balance. You must add the name at the end of the list in the Account Titles column.
3. Enter the expense of $50 as a debit in the Adjustments column. Place the letter (a) next to the entry in the space provided.
4. Calculate the new account balance, taking the adjustments into consideration. The adjusted balance for prepaid insurance is $600 − $50, or $550. The insurance expense account has a new balance of $50. Calculate the new balances and place them in the Adjusted Trial Balance column in the correct column for debit or credit.

Adjustment b: Office Supplies

Justin did an inventory of the supplies he has on hand in his supply cupboard. The amount remaining on December 31 is worth $200. His trial balance shows a value of $630 in the office supplies account.

Calculation of the adjustment:

Inventory shown in trial balance	$630
Less: Amount left in stock	$200
Amount used over the period	$430

The goal of this adjustment is to show the correct value of what is left as an asset, which is $200, and to record the amount of $430 that was used as an expense.

Justin must record the amount of $430 as an expense, and he has to credit the asset account Office Supplies (#130) to reduce the amount of the asset.

The adjusting entry required is as follows:

535	Office Supplies/General Expense	Dr.	$430
130	Office Supplies	Cr.	$430

The steps followed to enter this adjustment in the worksheet are as follows, and are shown in the completed worksheet in Figure 7.9 at the end of the chapter:

1. Enter $430 in the credit column of the asset account Office Supplies (#130) and place the letter (b) next to the entry.
2. The account Office Supplies/General Expense (#535) is listed in the Account Titles column, so it does not have to be added for this entry. Enter the expense of $430 as a debit in the Adjustments column. Place the letter (b) next to the entry in the space provided.
3. Calculate the new account balances after making the adjustments. The adjusted balance for Office Supplies (#130) is $630 less the credit of $430, or $200. The adjusted balance for Office Supplies/General Expense (#535) is $580 plus $430, or $1,010.

	Account Titles	Trial Balance		Adjustments		Adjusted Trial Balance		Calculating the Balances in the Adjusted Trial Balance
		Dr.	Cr.	Dr.	Cr.	Dr.	Cr.	
100	General Bank Account	4,906.91				4,906.91		When there is no adjustment, simply place the trial balance amount in the Adjusted Trial Balance column, respecting Dr. and Cr.
125	Prepaid Insurance	600.00		a	50.00	550.00		Place the letter identifying the transaction in the column provided. Each transaction will have the same letter in two locations, one for the debit (see account 527 below) and one for the credit. Calculate the new balance: $600 Dr. – $50 Cr. = $550. Place the difference of $550 in the debit column because the balance is a debit.
200	Accounts Payable		6,890.00	d			6,890.00	If the trial balance has a credit balance, and there are no adjustments, enter the amount in the credit column of the Adjusted Trial Balance column.
205	Personal Loan		3,000.00 +	+	100.00	=	3,100.00	If the trial balance has a credit balance and the adjustment is a credit, add the two credits together to obtain the new balance.
511	Salaries Expense	960.00 +		e 240.00	=	1,200.00		Add both debits together to get the new amount for salaries expense and place the total in the debit column of the Adjusted Trial Balance column.
	Total	61,800.00	61,800.00		Leave this space blank			Totals for the trial balance must be equal.
527	Insurance Expense			a 50.00		50.00		For the new accounts added at the end of the trial balance, the balance will be the amount entered in the Adjustments column. Place the amount in the Adjustment Trial Balance column, respecting Dr. and Cr. This is the entry that corresponds to entry "a" above.
	Totals			1,146.01	1,146.01	62,466.01	62,466.01	Total Dr. and Cr. for adjusting entries must be equal. Total Dr. and Cr. for the adjusted trial balance must be equal.

FIGURE 7.7   Extending balances to the adjusted trial balance

Adjustment c: Depreciation

The account for Computer Equipment (Hardware) (#155) has a value of $6,520 in the trial balance. Justin believes the assets have a useful life of about five years and that there will be no residual value for this equipment.

Calculation of depreciation using the straight-line method:

$$\frac{\text{Cost of Equipment} - \text{Residual Value}}{\text{Estimated Useful Life}} = \frac{\$6,520 - 0}{5} = \$1,304/12 \text{ months} = \$108.67$$

The annual depreciation of the equipment is $1,304. Suppose Justin has had the equipment in his business for only three months and wishes to take three months' worth of depreciation. He would multiply the monthly amount, or $108.67, by three months, for total depreciation of $326.01.

The adjusting entry required is as follows:

522	Depreciation Expense		Dr.	$326.01
156	Depreciation—Computer Equipment		Cr.	$326.01

The steps followed to enter this adjustment in the worksheet are as follows and are shown in Figure 7.9:

1. The account Depreciation Expense (#522) is not listed in the Account Titles column, so you need to add the name below the last entry in the Account Titles column.
2. Enter the amount of depreciation expense ($326.01) as a debit in the Adjustments column. Place the letter (c) next to the entry.
3. The contra-asset account Depreciation—Computer Equipment (#156) is not listed in the Account Titles column, so it also must be added. Add this below the account Depreciation Expense (#522). Enter $326.01 as a credit in the Adjustments column and place the letter (c) next to the entry.
4. Calculate the new account balances after making the adjustments. The adjusted balance for Depreciation—Computer Equipment (#156) is $326.01, and for Depreciation Expense (#522) is $326.01.
5. Note that the account Computer Equipment (Hardware) (#155) has not been changed. The value of this account has remained at $6,520, its historical value.

Adjustment d: Personal Loan

Justin paid $1,000 to his father on the loan he accepted, but $100 of that was interest. His records show that he owes his father $3,000, but in fact he owes his father $3,100 because the $100 for interest did not reduce the principal amount owing. Justin should have recorded the payment as a debit to Interest Expense (#529) of $100 and $900 to the Personal Loan liability account (#205). Because Justin's books show the amount of the loan outstanding at $3,000, he must correct this entry. He can do this using the following adjusting entry:

529	Interest Expense	Dr.	$100
205	Personal Loan	Cr.	$100

The steps required to enter this adjustment in the worksheet are as follows and are shown in Figure 7.9:

1. The account Interest Expense (#529) is not listed in the Account Titles column, so you have to add the name below the last entry in the column.
2. Enter the amount of interest expense of $100 as a debit in the Adjustments column. Place the letter (d) next to the entry.
3. The personal loan secured by Justin was recorded in the account Personal Loan (#205) in the liabilities section of the balance sheet. This account is listed on the trial balance, so the amount of $100 can be entered as a credit in the Adjustments column. Place the letter (d) next to the entry.
4. Calculate the new account balances after making the adjustments. The adjusted balance for Personal Loan (#205) is $3,100, and Interest Expense (#529) has a debit balance of $100. These amounts are shown in the Adjusted Trial Balance column.

Adjustment e: Accrued Salaries Expense

Justin has an employee who works five days a week, from Monday to Friday, and receives $80 a day or $400 a week. She gets paid every two weeks on Friday. She was paid on the 12th and 26th of December and will receive her next paycheque on the next payday, which is January 9, next year. However, at the end of the fiscal period, December 31, the employee is owed three days' pay for December 29, 30, and 31. This payment will be made on January 9. An adjusting entry is therefore required to reflect the **accrued salaries expense** payable for three days at the rate of $80 a day for a total of $240. This can be done using the following adjusting entry:

| 511 | Salaries Expense | Dr. | $240 |
| 220 | Accrued Salaries Payable | Cr. | $240 |

The steps required to enter this adjustment in the worksheet are as follows and are shown in Figure 7.9:

1. The account Salaries Expense (#511) is already listed in the Account Titles column. Debit the Adjustments column $240 to show the expense for salaries, and place the letter (e) in the box next to the entry.
2. Accrued Salaries Payable (#220) is not listed in the Account Titles column and must be added at the end.
3. Enter the amount of accrued salaries payable of $240 as a credit in the Adjustments column. Place the letter (e) in the box next to the entry.
4. Calculate the new account balances after making the adjustments. The adjusted balance for Salaries Expense (#511) will be $1,200, and Accrued Salaries Payable (#220) will have a credit balance of $240. These amounts are shown in the Adjusted Trial Balance column.

Checking the Adjusting Entries

To ensure that no mistakes were made in entering the adjusting entries, total the debit and credit columns of the Adjustments column in the worksheet (see Figure 7.9). The total debits must equal the total credits. If the totals are not equal, you should stop and look for errors using the same strategies for finding errors that were explained in Chapter 4. Do not proceed until these columns are balanced.

Adjusted Trial Balance Column

All account balances from the trial balance must be extended to the Adjusted Trial Balance column (see Figure 7.9). If you did not already calculate the balances across the accounts as you prepared the adjustments, you may do so at this point. Many people prefer to wait until all the adjustments are completed before calculating the adjusted trial balance. Remember to add debits together and to add credits together. Take the difference when calculating debits plus or minus credits and make sure you enter the result in the correct column. Keep in mind what the normal balance is supposed to be for each category of account (see Chapter 3):

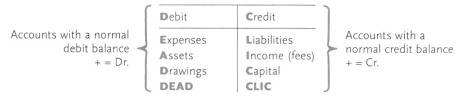

If the balance is not the normal balance associated with that category of account, ask yourself: "why not?"

Looking for Errors

Consider the following possible causes of errors:

- Calculation error: Two debits were not added together, and instead were subtracted from one another or vice versa.
- Calculation error: You did not subtract debits and credits.
- Entry in wrong column: The entry was put in the debit column instead of the credit column or vice versa.
- You did not carry over the balances from the trial balances for the accounts that had no adjustment.

Once the debit and credit columns in the adjusted trial balance are equal, you are ready to move on to preparation of the financial statements.

Income Statement and Balance Sheet Columns

The totals from the adjusted trial balance should be carried over to the Income Statement column or the Balance Sheet column, depending on the category of account. Figure 7.8 shows the balances once they have been extended. Copy the amounts one by one from the adjusted trial balance over to the correct statement. Remember that the accounts numbered 100 to 399 belong in the Balance Sheet column and should be extended to the respective debit or credit columns. The accounts numbered 400 to 599 belong in the Income Statement column, so these amounts should be extended to the respective debit or credit columns.

Take care not to include the asset accounts listed at the bottom of the worksheet in the wrong category or statement. Pay particular attention to the contra-asset account for accumulated depreciation and the salaries payable account. These are credit balances that belong on the balance sheet.

Completing the Worksheet

Total the debit and credit columns of the Income Statement and Balance Sheet columns of the worksheet. Your next task is to balance the Income Statement and Balance Sheet columns.

Calculating Net Profit or Loss

Figure 7.8 shows the following steps (in superscript) in calculating the net profit or net loss:

	Income Statement		Balance Sheet	
	Dr.	Cr.	Dr.	Cr.
	Totals	Totals	Totals	Totals
Totals	[1]5,959.10	[1]31,580.00	[5]56,506.91	[5]30,886.01
[4]Net Profit	[2]25,620.90	_____	_____	[6]25,620.90
	[3]31,580.00	[3]31,580.00	[7]56,506.91	[7]56,506.91 [8]

Justin Case, Paralegal
Worksheet
for the Month Ended December 31, 20**

FIGURE 7.8 Completing the bottom portion of the worksheet

1. Total the Dr. and Cr. columns in the income statement section. They will not be equal.
2. Subtract the total credits and debits. If your credits on the income statement are higher than the debits, you have a net profit, but if the debits are higher than the credits, you have a net loss. Enter this figure in the space below whichever column has the smaller total.
3. Add the numbers at the bottom of the columns. The total debits should now equal the total credits at the bottom of the Income Statement column.
4. Write "Net Profit" or "Net Loss" in the Account Titles column.

Completing the Balance Sheet Portion of the Worksheet

5. Total the Dr. and Cr. columns in the balance sheet portion of the worksheet. They will not be equal.
6. Place the amount of the net profit or loss from step 2 in the space below whichever column has the smaller total.
7. Add the balance sheet debit and credit columns on the last line of the worksheet. The debit and credit columns must be equal.
8. Rule the columns by placing a single line above and a double line below the totals.

A completed worksheet with all the adjustments and balances extended is shown in Figure 7.9.

Once you have calculated the net profit or loss and used the result to balance the columns under the balance sheet heading, you have the information you need to prepare financial statements for the firm.

Justin Case, Paralegal
Worksheet
for the Month Ended December 31, 20**

	Account Titles	Trial Balance Dr.	Trial Balance Cr.	Adjustments Dr.	Adjustments Cr.	Adjusted Trial Balance Dr.	Adjusted Trial Balance Cr.	Income Statement Dr.	Income Statement Cr.	Balance Sheet Dr.	Balance Sheet Cr.
100	General Bank Account	4,906.91				4,906.91				4,906.91	
115	Trust Bank Account	15,280.00				15,280.00				15,280.00	
120	Accounts Receivable	25,000.00				25,000.00				25,000.00	
125	Prepaid Insurance	600.00			a 50.00	550.00				550.00	
130	Office Supplies	630.00			b 430.00	200.00				200.00	
155	Computer Equipment (Hardware)	6,520.00				6,520.00				6,520.00	
158	Office Furniture and Equipment	2,250.00				2,250.00				2,250.00	
200	Accounts Payable/ General Liabilities		6,890.00				6,890.00				6,890.00
205	Personal Loan		3,000.00		d 100.00		3,100.00				3,100.00
210	Credit Card Debt		2,500.00				2,500.00				2,500.00
215	Trust Funds Owed		15,280.00				15,280.00				15,280.00
300	Justin Case, Capital		2,550.00				2,550.00				2,550.00
350	Justin Case, Drawings	1,800.00				1,800.00				1,800.00	
400	Fees Earned		31,580.00				31,580.00		31,580.00		
511	Salaries Expense	960.00		e 240.00		1,200.00		1,200.00			

	Account Titles	Trial Balance Dr.	Trial Balance Cr.	Adjustments Dr.		Adjustments Cr.	Adjusted Trial Balance Dr.	Adjusted Trial Balance Cr.	Income Statement Dr.	Income Statement Cr.	Balance Sheet Dr.	Balance Sheet Cr.
533	Meals and Entertainment Expense	350.00					350.00		350.00			
534	Membership/Professional Dues	1,343.75					1,343.75		1,343.75			
535	Office Supplies/General Expense	580.00		430.00	b		1,010.00		1,010.00			
538	Rent Expense	1,100.00					1,100.00		1,100.00			
565	Telephone Expense	479.34					479.34		479.34			
	Total	61,800.00	61,800.00									
527	Insurance Expense			50.00	a		50.00		50.00			
522	Depreciation Expense			326.01	c		326.01		326.01			
156	Depreciation—Computer Equipment				c	326.01		326.01				326.01
529	Interest Expense			100.00	d		100.00		100.00			
220	Accrued Salaries Payable				e	240.00		240.00				240.00
	Totals			1,146.01		1,146.01	62,466.01	62,466.01	5,959.10	31,580.00	56,506.91	30,886.01
	Net Profit								25,620.90			25,620.90
	Totals								31,580.00	31,580.00	56,506.91	56,506.91

FIGURE 7.9 Completed worksheet

CHAPTER SUMMARY

The accrual basis of accounting requires that financial statements reflect revenues when earned and expenses when incurred so that they are reported in the correct accounting period. The adjustment process enables the record-keeper to adjust account balances to ensure that what is reported in the financial statements accurately reflects the financial position of the firm. A paralegal wishing to know how his or her business is doing will want to prepare an income statement fairly frequently. This practice tells the owner whether the company is making or losing money. The balance in the bank account is not always an indication of how your business is doing. The bank balance may show income from various sources, such as an investment by the owner, a transfer from the line of credit, or revenue earned.

Remember that a paralegal working as a sole proprietor does not receive a salary. Money is taken out of the firm by way of drawings. The income statement and balance sheet will tell the owner whether or not there is a profit from which a draw can be taken. Recording amortization on assets and preparing the common adjustments help to ensure that the financial records of the firm accurately reflect its financial position.

KEY TERMS

accrual basis of accounting, 157
accrued interest expense, 162
accrued interest revenue, 163
accrued revenues, 158
accrued salaries expense, 168
accumulated depreciation, 159
adjusted trial balance, 156
adjusting entry, 163

amortization, 159
book value, 159
capital cost allowance (CCA), 159
class, 159
contra-asset account, 159
depreciation, 159
historical cost, 159
matching principle, 157

office supplies inventory, 157
prepaid expenses, 159
residual value, 159
revenue recognition principle, 162
straight-line amortization method, 160
undepreciated capital cost (UCC), 161
work in progress (WIP), 162
worksheet, 156

FURTHER READING

Canada Revenue Agency, "Accounting Methods," online: <http://www.cra-arc.gc.ca/tx/bsnss/tpcs/slprtnr/ccntng-eng.html>.

Canada Revenue Agency, "Claiming Capital Cost Allowance (CCA)," online: <http://www.cra-arc.gc.ca/tx/bsnss/tpcs/slprtnr/rprtng/cptl/menu-eng.html>.

Canada Revenue Agency, Guide T4002(E), "Business and Professional Income," online: <http://www.cra-arc.gc.ca/E/pub/tg/t4002/t4002-14e.pdf>.

Canada Revenue Agency, "Information for Canadian Small Businesses," RC4070, online: <http://www.cra-arc.gc.ca/E/pub/tg/rc4070/rc4070-14e.pdf>. See especially Chapter Six: Income Tax.

Canada Revenue Agency, "Small Businesses and Self-Employed," online: <http://www.cra-arc.gc.ca/selfemployed>. Topics of interest: capital cost allowance, WIP, accruals.

Michael Cooke, "2014-0531461E5 E—Paralegals and Work in Progress Election," 28 May 2014, online: <http://taxinterpretations.com/?p=27323>.

PUT IT INTO PRACTICE

Case Example: Financial Statements

Ann Litigate has scheduled a meeting with her small-business bank manager to discuss getting an additional line of credit. However, the bank manager has concerns about Ann's current debt ratio because this would be an additional credit facility. She has asked Ann to provide her with an interim financial statement. Ann does not understand why the bank manager needs this information because the bank produces statements for her general bank account and trust account each month. She thought that these bank statements, together with last year's tax return and financial statement, would be sufficient. Also, Ann does not know what information to provide to her accountant to prepare the interim financial statement, because she tends to contact the accountant only at the end of the year when she does her tax reporting.

1. Why would the bank manager need to see an interim, year-to-date financial statement as part of the bank approval process?
2. What are some of the things that Ann will need to discuss with her accountant? Which items on the balance sheet or income statement will likely require an adjustment? (Hint: Assess the before-adjustment and after-adjustment journal entries that may be required for such items on the balance sheet or income statement.)
3. What records will Ann need to review and update so that the accountant is in a good position to prepare the financial statement?

REVIEW QUESTIONS

True or False

_____ 1. The worksheet is an example of a financial statement.

_____ 2. A contra-asset account reduces the value of an asset.

_____ 3. An accrual is an adjustment that recognizes when cash is received or used to make a payment.

_____ 4. Each entry on the adjusted trial balance represents an account that has been adjusted.

_____ 5. The debit (Dr.) and credit (Cr.) entries in the Balance Sheet portion of the worksheet are equal.

_____ 6. Book value means the same thing as fair market value.

_____ 7. Prepaid expense is an asset account reflected on the balance sheet.

_____ 8. Paralegals can elect to exclude WIP in reporting income at the end of the financial year.

_____ 9. Capital cost allowance is a tax reporting term used in the calculation of depreciating assets.

_____ 10. Accumulated depreciation has a normal credit balance (Cr.).

Short Answer

1. When Ann Litigate purchased $1,000 worth of stationery and supplies for the office, she recorded the purchases in the asset account Office Supplies (#130). At the end of the year, she calculated the value of her office supply stock as $350.

   a. What must Ann do to correctly reflect the accrued assets and expenses over the course of the past three months?

   b. Calculate the value of the office supplies used during the period.

   c. Which accounts need to be adjusted to record the office supplies used?

   d. If Ann does not make the necessary adjustment to her books, which account will be overstated and which will be understated?

   e. How would failure to make the adjustment affect

   i. the income statement?

   ii. the balance sheet?

2. What is the relationship between the adjusted trial balance and the income statement, balance sheet, and statement of owner's equity?

PRACTICE EXERCISES

Practice Exercise 7.1

Complete the following table by calculating depreciation using the straight-line method for five years.

Calculation of depreciation using the straight-line method							
Office Equipment	Life	Historical Cost	Residual Value	Year	Depreciation 3,500/10 yrs.	Accumulated Depreciation	Book Value
Computers	10	4,000	500	1	350	350	3,650
				2	350	700	3,300
				3			
				4			
				5			

Practice Exercise 7.2

Complete the following table by calculating amortization using the declining balance method.

Calculation of amortization using the declining balance method						
Item	Class	%	Year	Cost	CCA	UCC
Computer	10	30%	1	5,000.00	750.00*	4,250.00
UCC x 30%			2		1,275.00	2,975.00
			3			
			4			
			5			
Total CCA						

* Note: Only half of depreciation allowed was taken in year 1.

Practice Exercise 7.3

Using the worksheet provided, prepare the adjusting entries for Ann Litigate's financial records, which her accountant will use in preparing her year-end financial statements.

a. Dec. 31: Payment on account received (invoice #xx501, M. Arbor), $1,000.

b. Dec. 31: Prepaid professional insurance used up, $2,500 (one-year policy, from February of this year until February of next year, valued at $3,000).

c. Dec. 31: Rent expense recognized (Magnum Office Managers), $1,200.

d. Dec. 31: Office supplies used up, $200.

e. Dec. 31: Depreciation of computer equipment, $1,360/year based on the declining balance amortization calculation. Assume that Ann purchased the computer equipment for $6,800 in the previous year and that the annual depreciation being claimed is 20 percent.

PRACTICE
EXCEL

	Ann Litigate, Paralegal Worksheet for the Month Ended December 31, 20**							
	Account Titles	Trial Balance		Adjustments		Adjusted Trial Balance		
		Dr.	Cr.	Dr.	Cr.	Dr.	Cr.	
100	General Bank Account	15,360						
115	Trust Bank Account	18,500						
120	Accounts Receivable	3,500						
125	Prepaid Insurance	3,000						
128	Prepaid Expense (Rent)	1,200						
130	Office Supplies	800						
155	Computer Equipment (Hardware)	6,800						
156	Depreciation—Computer Equipment							
200	Accounts Payable/General Liabilities		6,500					
210	Credit Card Debt		4,500					
215	Trust Funds Owed		18,500					
300	A. Litigate, Capital		12,500					
350	A. Litigate, Drawings	2,000						
400	Fees Earned		10,550					
511	Salaries Expense	1,000						
522	Depreciation Expense							
527	Insurance—Professional Liability							
534	Membership/Professional Dues	230						
535	Office Supplies/General Expense							
538	Rent Expense							
565	Telephone Expense	160						
	Totals	52,550	52,550					

Practice Exercise 7.4

Prepare the income statement and balance sheet portion of the worksheet from the adjusted trial balance for Ann Litigate's firm.

	Account Titles	Adjusted Trial Balance		Income Statement		Balance Sheet	
		Dr.	Cr.	Dr.	Cr.	Dr.	Cr.
100	General Bank Account	16,360					
115	Trust Bank Account	18,500					
120	Accounts Receivable	2,500					
125	Prepaid Insurance	500					
128	Prepaid Expense (Rent)	0					
130	Office Supplies	600					
155	Computer Equipment (Hardware)	6,800					
156	Depreciation—Computer Equipment		1,360				
200	Accounts Payable/General Liabilities		6,500				
210	Credit Card Debt		4,500				
215	Trust Funds Owed		18,500				
300	A. Litigate, Capital		12,500				
310	A. Litigate, Withdrawals	2,000					
400	Fees Earned		10,550				
511	Salaries Expense	1,000					
522	Depreciation Expense	1,360					
527	Insurance—Professional Liability	2,500					
534	Membership/Professional Dues	230					
535	Office Supplies/General Expense	200					
538	Rent Expense	1,200					
565	Telephone Expense	160					
	Totals	53,910	53,910				
	Net Profit						

The table title (above the worksheet):

Ann Litigate, Paralegal
Worksheet
for the Month Ended December 31, 20**

Practice Exercise 7.5

Prepare the following adjusting entries for Peter Bitter's Legal Services firm and complete all columns of the worksheet.

a. An adjustment for office supplies is required. The ending inventory as of December 31 is $300. Expense the office supplies used up over the period.

b. The landlord required prepayment of rent when Peter's firm moved into the premises. The amount of $1,200 has now been used up and needs to be written off as an expense.

c. At year-end, the firm owes three days' salary to the assistant at the rate of $90 per day.

d. The firm is taking $300 depreciation on office furniture and equipment.

Peter Bitter's Legal Services
Worksheet
for the Month Ended December 31, 20**

	Account Titles	Trial Balance		Adjustments		Adjusted Trial Balance		Income Statement		Balance Sheet	
		Dr.	Cr.	Dr.	Cr.	Dr.	Cr.	Dr.	Cr.	Dr.	Cr.
100	General Bank Account	5,230									
115	Trust Bank Account	3,200									
120	Accounts Receivable	3,500									
128	Prepaid Expense (Rent)	3,000									
130	Office Supplies	1,200									
158	Office Furniture and Equipment	22,000									
159	Dep. Office Furniture and Equipment		600								
200	Accounts Payable/General Liabilities		6,500								
215	Trust Funds Owed		3,200								
220	Accrued Salaries Payable										
300	Peter Bitters, Capital		13,170								
350	Peter Bitters, Drawings	6,000									
400	Fees Earned		29,000								
511	Salaries Expense	4,000									
522	Depreciation Expense	250									
527	Insurance—Professional Liability	450									
534	Membership/Professional Dues	230									
535	Office Supplies/General Expense	250									
538	Rent Expense	3,000									
565	Telephone Expense	160									
	Totals	52,470	52,470								
	Net Profit										

8

Final Steps in the Accounting Cycle

After reading this chapter, you should be able to:

- prepare and interpret financial statements
- journalize and post adjusting entries to the general ledger
- journalize and post closing entries
- prepare a post-closing trial balance

Once the worksheet is completed, you have the information needed to prepare **financial statements** for the period. In our case, we will prepare the statements as of the end of the year for Justin Case. The financial statements must be prepared in the following order:

1. Income statement
2. Statement of owner's equity
3. Balance sheet

Figure 8.1 highlights these final steps in the accounting cycle.

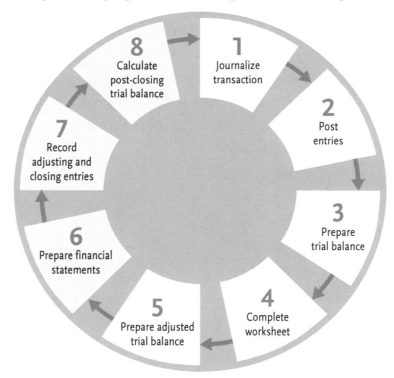

FIGURE 8.1   Steps in the accounting cycle

The worksheet prepared in Chapter 7 will be used for preparation of the **income statement**, the **statement of owner's equity**, and the **balance sheet**. You will also need the worksheet to record the adjusting entries in the general journal in order to make them part of the firm's permanent record.

Preparing the Income Statement

Income statements show the income earned less expenses incurred over a period of time to determine whether the firm has made a profit or a loss. If the firm's total income is higher than the total expenses, the firm has a profit. If the firm's expenses are higher than total income, the firm has suffered a loss. The profit or loss for the period affects the owner's capital account because losses are deducted from the capital account and profits are added to the capital account. The amount of profit or loss calculated on the income statement is needed in order to prepare the statement of owner's equity.

Steps in Preparing the Income Statement

The information you need to prepare the income statement is found on the worksheet for the end of the period.

When preparing the income statement, keep the following points in mind:

1. The heading section has three lines: the name of the firm, the name of the statement, and the period covered by the statement.
2. Although the form used has two columns for calculations, they are not debit and credit columns. The inside column is used to list numbers and for subtotalling, and the outside column is used for the totals.
3. The amounts you need are found on the worksheet in the Income Statement column.
4. The statement has four main parts:
   a. *Heading:* Place the name of the firm, the name of the statement, and the period covered by the statement in the heading. Income statements report on the income earned over a period of time, whether a month, a quarter, or a year. The heading should have a statement saying "for the Period Ended _____ ."
   b. *Income:* List each source of income below the heading "Income" (or "Revenue") in the body of the statement. If there is only one source of income, place the amount in the outside column. If there is more than one source of income, list the source account name, indented under the heading "Income." Then place the amounts in the inside column. Draw a line under the last number entered, and place the total income in the outside column.
   c. *Expenses:* List each expense account that has a balance and enter the amount in the inside column. Place a line under the last number and enter the total in the outside column on the "Total Expenses" line at the end of the list.
   d. *Net income or net loss:* Take the difference between the total income and the total expenses to calculate the net income or net loss. The net income or net loss should be the same as the amount that was calculated on the worksheet. Negative values are recorded in parentheses to indicate net loss.

Figure 8.2 illustrates these points.

The information contained in the income statement is not only useful to the owner of the firm, but will also be of interest to the firm's banker if there is an outstanding line of credit and, of course, to the Canada Revenue Agency for income tax purposes. In a sole proprietorship, the net income shown on the income statement represents the taxable income of the owner. Remember that drawings (withdrawals) are what the owner took out of the business for personal use. Income tax will be payable on the net income for the firm if it is a sole proprietorship.

Justin Case, Paralegal Income Statement for the Period Ended December 31, 20**		
Income		
Fees Earned		$31,580.00
Expenses		
Meals and Entertainment Expense	$350.00	
Membership/Professional Dues	1,343.75	
Office Supplies/General Expense	1,010.00	
Rent Expense	1,100.00	
Salaries Expense	1,200.00	
Telephone Expense	479.34	
Insurance Expense—Professional Liability	50.00	
Depreciation Expense	326.01	
Interest Expense	100.00	
Total Expenses		5,959.10
Net Income		$25,620.90

FIGURE 8.2   Income statement

Interpreting Information from the Income Statement

The income statement will help to provide answers to the following questions.

With regard to income:

1. Is the income earned during the period covered by the statement reasonable considering the amount of time and effort spent?
2. Should a review of billing practices be done to see if work completed is being billed effectively?
3. Does the owner need to work harder to increase the amount of income being earned?
4. Is the income earned during the period enough to cover the expenses incurred over the same period? If not, what needs to be done to improve the situation?

With regard to expenses:

1. Review each of the expenses listed to determine whether the amount being spent on each account is reasonable.
2. Can the firm afford to increase salaries expense? Would bringing in extra help assist in increasing revenues?
3. Does the firm need to cut back to reduce expenses (especially if expenses are higher than income)? If so, where can the firm cut back?

Preparing the Statement of Owner's Equity

The second statement that must be prepared is the statement of owner's equity. This statement will calculate the owner's equity in the firm, taking into account any additional investment made by the owner over the period and the net income or net loss for the period. Withdrawals also serve to reduce the owner's equity in the firm. The amount calculated for owner's equity at the end of the period will be carried over to the balance sheet.

The statement of owner's equity shows how the net income or net loss affects owner's equity. Remember the expanded accounting equation (see also Figure 2.3 in Chapter 2):

$$\text{Assets} = \text{Liabilities} + \text{Capital} - \text{Withdrawals} + (\text{Income} - \text{Expenses})$$

The statement of owner's equity calculates the increase or decrease in the owner's equity in the firm over the period covered by the statement. This number obtained for owner's equity can then be inserted when completing the balance sheet.

The steps for preparing the statement of owner's equity are as follows:

1. The heading section has three lines: the name of the firm, the name of the statement, and the period covered by the statement.
2. The form used for preparing the statement of owner's equity also uses columns for calculations. The columns do not designate debit and credit entries.
3. The amounts are taken from the worksheet in both the Income Statement and the Balance Sheet columns.
4. You must first enter the owner's capital at the beginning of the period as shown on the Balance Sheet column in the worksheet. Place this amount in the outside column.
5. The net income was calculated using the income statement. The next line is the net income or net loss for the period. Take the amount shown on the income statement you just prepared and place that amount in the inside column.
6. On the next line, you need to show any withdrawals that were made by the owner during the period. This amount needs to be deducted from the net income. If there was a net loss, the net loss and the amount of withdrawals will be added together.
7. On the next line, indicate whether there was an increase or a decrease in the capital account.
   a. In the case of a net profit: calculate net income less withdrawals. If the figure is positive, there has been an increase in the capital account. If the figure is negative, there has been a decrease in capital.
   b. In the case of a net loss: total the net loss and the withdrawals taken during the period. The total is the decrease in capital that occurred over the period.
   c. Enter the amount of the increase or decrease in capital and extend the calculation to the outside column.
8. Total the outside column to arrive at the capital at the end of the period. In the case of a decrease in capital, subtract the decrease from the first line (owner's capital at the beginning of the period). In the case of an increase in capital, add the increase to the first line (owner's capital at the beginning of the period). This total amount will be used in completing the owner's equity portion of the balance sheet.

Figure 8.3 illustrates these points.

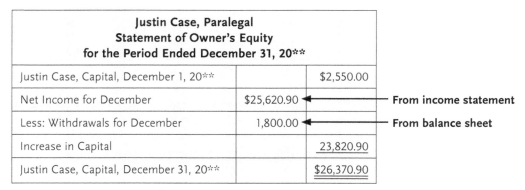

Justin Case, Paralegal Statement of Owner's Equity for the Period Ended December 31, 20**		
Justin Case, Capital, December 1, 20**		$2,550.00
Net Income for December	$25,620.90	
Less: Withdrawals for December	1,800.00	
Increase in Capital		23,820.90
Justin Case, Capital, December 31, 20**		$26,370.90

FIGURE 8.3   Statement of owner's equity

Interpreting Information on the Statement of Owner's Equity

The statement of owner's equity at the end of a period helps to provide answers to the following questions:

1. Has the owner's investment in the firm increased or decreased? In other words, is the investment in the firm worth more or less than at the beginning of the period?
2. How much could the owner justify asking for the firm if he or she decided to sell it?
3. How much should the owner ask a partner to invest in the firm if the owner wanted to take one on? If a partner were to receive a 50 percent interest in the firm, it would be wise to ask that he or she invest 50 percent of the amount of capital at the end of the period.

Preparing the Balance Sheet

Now that you have calculated the owner's equity at the end of the period, you are able to complete the balance sheet. This form can be laid out in different ways. The balance sheet is often laid out with the assets on one side and the liabilities and owner's equity on the other in the shape of a T-account (see, for example, Figure 2.2 in Chapter 2).

Accounting software tends to lay out the balance sheet by placing the assets at the top of the page and the liabilities and owner's equity below. This is the format we will use for the purposes of this chapter. When the balance sheet is laid out this way, the three last columns are usually used for calculations, two for calculating subtotals and the last one for calculating the final numbers, as shown in Figure 8.4.

Follow these steps to prepare the balance sheet:

1. The amounts you will enter on the balance sheet are found in the Balance Sheet column of the worksheet and on the statement of owner's equity.
2. The heading for the balance sheet should show the name of the firm, the name of the financial statement, and the date. A balance sheet gives a snapshot of the firm at a particular date, so the date at the top does not refer to a period as in the income statement and statement of owner's equity. Rather, it shows the date for which the statement is being prepared.
3. Place the title "Assets" above the first column. Place the title "Current Assets" below near the margin, and place the value of each asset in the third column. Total the value of the current assets, and enter the total current assets in the outside column.

4. Note that the first number in the column has a dollar sign, and then the grand totals. Follow this convention.
5. Place the title "Fixed Assets" below and list the value of the assets in the third column, except for any assets that have been depreciated. You will need to place their value in the second column so that you can show the historical cost and the accumulated depreciation, and then place the resulting value in the third column (see Figure 8.4).

Justin Case, Paralegal Balance Sheet December 31, 20**			
Assets			
Current Assets			
General Bank Account		$4,906.91	
Trust Bank Account		15,280.00	
Accounts Receivable		25,000.00	
Prepaid Insurance		550.00	
Office Supplies		200.00	
Total Current Assets			$45,936.91
Fixed Assets			
Computer Equipment (Hardware)	$6,520.00		
Less: Accumulated Depreciation on Computer Equipment	326.01	6,193.99	
Office Furniture and Equipment		2,250.00	
Total Fixed Assets			8,443.99
Total Assets			$54,380.90
Liabilities and Owner's Equity			
Liabilities			
Accounts Payable/General Liabilities		6,890.00	
Personal Loan		3,100.00	
Credit Card Debt		2,500.00	
Accrued Salaries Payable		240.00	
Trust Funds Owed		15,280.00	
Total Liabilities			28,010.00
Owner's Equity			
Justin Case, Capital			26,370.90 ← From Statement of Owner's Equity
Total Liabilities and Owner's Equity			$54,380.90

FIGURE 8.4   Balance sheet

6. Once you have completed the calculations, the totals are carried over to the last column and totalled.

7. Place the total value of assets in the outside column. Place a dollar sign in front of the number and a double underline under the total.

8. Complete the liabilities section by listing the liabilities as shown on the worksheet. They should be totalled and the sum placed in the outside column.

9. Enter the amount of the capital that was calculated on the statement of owner's equity in the owner's equity section.

10. Add the total liabilities and owner's equity together. This number should be equal to the total assets shown above.

11. You have now completed the balance sheet. Place a double underline under the total for liabilities and owner's equity.

Interpreting Information from the Balance Sheet

The balance sheet will help to provide answers to the following questions:

1. Does the firm have sufficient resources to meet its liabilities?

2. Does the firm need to seek additional investment to meet its expenses or to expand?

3. How old are the outstanding accounts receivable? Should steps be taken to have accounts paid more quickly so that they do not become bad debts? In that regard, does the firm need to consider increasing the amounts charged for retainers from clients so that accounts are paid in a timely manner?

4. Does the firm have excess cash that should be invested in short-term or long-term investment vehicles to gain interest income?

5. Are the debts excessive in relation to the owner's investment? If so, is the firm at risk of going bankrupt?

Once you have completed the financial statements, you are ready to close the books for the year. You will need to record the adjusting entries that were entered in the worksheet and also prepare the year-end **closing entries**.

Recording the Year-End Adjustments

The year-end adjustments that were made on the worksheet must be recorded in the permanent records of the firm. You will make these entries using the general journal (see Figure 8.5).

Follow these steps to record adjusting entries:

1. Enter the title "Adjusting Entries" on the first line.

2. Copy the entry for each adjustment from the worksheet to the general journal, listing the debit entry first and the credit entry on the second line.

3. An explanation is not required because you have placed the title "Adjusting Entries" at the top of the column. Skip one line and enter the next adjusting entry.

4. Record the entries in the Adjustments column of the worksheet (a to e in our case) by repeating steps 2 and 3 for each entry until they have all been recorded.

5. Total the debits and credits in the general journal. The totals should be the same as the totals in the Adjustments column of the worksheet.

6. Once you have entered all the adjusting entries in the general journal, post each entry to the respective account in the general ledger, indicating that the entry is an adjusting entry in the description. Remember to complete the PR numbers in the general journal and in the reference in the general ledger account as you post each entry.

Justin Case, Paralegal General Journal					GJ4
Date 20**		Description	PR	Debit	Credit
		Adjusting Entries			
Dec.	31	Insurance—Professional Liability	527	50.00	
		Prepaid Insurance	125		50.00
	31	Office Supplies/General Expense	535	430.00	
		Office Supplies	130		430.00
	31	Depreciation Expense	522	326.01	
		Depreciation—Computer Equipment	156		326.01
	31	Interest Expense	529	100.00	
		Personal Loan	205		100.00
	31	Salaries Expense	511	240.00	
		Accrued Salaries Payable	220		240.00
		Totals		1,146.01	1,146.01

FIGURE 8.5   Adjusting entries

Preparing Closing Entries

Before starting to record transactions for the new year, the books for the previous fiscal period must be closed. **Balance sheet accounts** are referred to as **permanent accounts** because their balances carry over from one fiscal period to the next. If you think about it, the balance in the bank on December 31 will carry over to the next year—it does not disappear just because your fiscal year-end has arrived. This is true of all the assets. The same goes for any liabilities outstanding—they unfortunately do not disappear just because the end of the year has come. However, income, expense, and withdrawal accounts need to be zeroed out because you need to start fresh each year. It is for that reason that these three categories of account are referred to as **temporary accounts**.

Closing entries are used to set the temporary account balances to zero at the end of the fiscal year. Closing entries:

- Allow you to accumulate new data for the income, expense, and withdrawal accounts starting with the first day of the new fiscal year.
- Enable you to update the capital account going forward by transferring the net income or net loss to a permanent account (called income summary or retained earnings).

As illustrated in the journal entries shown below, there are four steps in the process for preparing closing entries:

1. Clear the balance in the income accounts and transfer the balance to the income summary.
   - Debit income accounts/credit income summary.
2. Clear the balance in the individual expense accounts and transfer the total to the income summary.
   - Debit income summary/credit expense accounts.
3. Clear the balance in the income summary (net income) account and transfer the balance to the capital account.
   - Debit income summary/credit capital (if net income).
4. Clear the balance in the drawings account and transfer the balance to the capital account.
   - Debit capital/credit drawings.

Step 1: Closing the Income (Revenue) Accounts

Use the information shown on the income statement to close accounts.

Close all accounts with a credit balance by debiting each **income account** with a credit balance to get a zero balance. For example, in the Justin Case income statement (Figure 8.2), the Fees Earned account has a credit balance of $31,580. Debit the Fees Earned account by that amount. To have a balanced entry, credit the **income summary account**.

General Journal					GJ5
Date 20**		Description	PR	Debit	Credit
		Closing Entries			
Dec.	31	Fees Earned	400	31,580	
		Income Summary	355		31,580
		To close income accounts			

FIGURE 8.6   General journal closing entries—income accounts

Step 2: Closing the Expense Accounts

Close all the accounts on the income statement with a debit balance (**expense accounts**) by crediting each account. This will bring each account down to zero. Debit the income summary account. Remember that in the general journal, debits are entered on the first line and credits below so the first line of your closing entry will be income summary, followed by a list of each expense account that is being closed. Each entry must be posted to the general ledger. Once you have completed posting, all the expense accounts should have a zero balance.

General Journal				GJ5
Date 20**	Description	PR	Debit	Credit
Dec. 31	Income Summary	355	5,959.10	
	Depreciation Expense	522		326.01
	Insurance—Professional Liability	527		50.00
	Interest Expense	529		100.00
	Meals and Entertainment Expense	533		350.00
	Membership/Professional Dues	534		1,343.75
	Office Supplies/General Expense	535		1,010.00
	Rent Expense	538		1,100.00
	Salaries Expense	511		1,200.00
	Telephone Expense	565		479.34
	To close expense accounts			

FIGURE 8.7   General journal closing entries—expense accounts

Step 3: Closing the Income Summary Account

Once the closing entries for the income and expense accounts have been posted, the general ledger shows a credit balance in the income summary account. After posting, the balance in this account is equal to the net income (or net loss) of the firm. Figure 8.8 shows the income summary account after the closing entries for the income and expense accounts have been posted.

Income Summary					Account No. 355	
Date 20**	Explanation	PR	Debit	Credit	Dr./Cr.	Balance
Dec. 31	To close income accounts	GJ5		31,580.00		
31	To close expense accounts	GJ5	5,959.10		Cr.	25,620.90

FIGURE 8.8   Income summary account in general ledger

In order to clear the net income amount from the income summary account, you must create a closing entry by debiting the income summary account and crediting the capital account.

The general journal closing entry made to close the income summary account is as shown in Figure 8.9.

General Journal				GJ5
Date 20**	Description	PR	Debit	Credit
Dec. 31	Income Summary	355	25,620.90	
	Justin Case, Capital	300		25,620.90
	To close income summary account			

FIGURE 8.9   Closing entries—income summary

Step 4: Closing the Drawings Account

Clear the balance in the drawings account and transfer the balance to the capital account. The owner of a sole proprietorship takes withdrawals for personal use over the course of the year, and this account needs to be cleared. As was seen on the statement of owner's equity, withdrawals decrease the owner's equity in the firm. For this reason, the amount taken by way of withdrawals will be transferred to the capital account and used to decrease the owner's equity in the firm. This account is cleared at the end of the fiscal year. Drawings taken in the subsequent year will start from zero and be accumulated over the next year.

The closing entry required to close the drawings account is as shown in Figure 8.10.

General Journal					GJ5
Date 20**		Description	PR	Debit	Credit
Dec.	31	Justin Case, Capital	300	1,800.00	
		Justin Case, Drawings	350		1,800.00
		To close drawings into capital			

FIGURE 8.10   General journal closing entries—drawings

Once the closing entries are posted, the general ledger capital and drawings accounts will appear as in Figure 8.11.

Justin Case, Capital							Account No. 300
Date 20**		Explanation	PR	Debit	Credit	Dr./Cr.	Balance
Dec.	1	Balance Forward	✓		2,550.00	Cr.	2,550.00
	31	Closing Entry—Income Summary			25,620.90	Cr.	28,170.90
	31	Closing Entry—Drawings		1,800.00		Cr.	26,370.90

Justin Case, Drawings							Account No. 350
Date 20**		Explanation	PR	Debit	Credit	Dr./Cr.	Balance
Dec.	1	Balance Forward	✓	1,800.00		Dr.	1,800.00
	31	Closing Entry	GJ5		1,800.00		0.00

Justin Case, Income Summary							Account No. 355
Date 20**		Explanation	PR	Debit	Credit	Dr./Cr.	Balance
Dec.	31	Closing Entry—Income Account	GJ5		31,580.00	Cr.	31,580.00
	31	Closing Entry—Expense Accounts	GJ5	5,959.10		Cr.	25,620.90
	31	Closing Entry—Net Income transfer to Capital	GJ5	25,620.90			0.00

FIGURE 8.11   General ledger capital, drawings, and income summary accounts after posting

Preparing the Post-Closing Trial Balance

Once all the adjusting entries and closing entries have been recorded and posted, a **post-closing trial balance** must be prepared. All temporary accounts will have been closed, and the only balances remaining in the general ledger should be in the permanent accounts. Prepare a list of all the general ledger accounts with a balance. They have been placed in numerical order in the post-closing trial balance shown in Figure 8.12.

	Justin Case, Paralegal Post-Closing Trial Balance December 31, 20**		
		Dr.	*Cr.*
100	General Bank Account	$4,906.91	
115	Trust Bank Account	15,280.00	
120	Accounts Receivable	25,000.00	
125	Prepaid Insurance	550.00	
130	Office Supplies	200.00	
155	Computer Equipment (Hardware)	6,520.00	
156	Depreciation—Computer Equipment		$326.01
158	Office Furniture and Equipment	2,250.00	
200	Accounts Payable/General Liabilities		6,890.00
205	Personal Loan		3,100.00
210	Credit Card Debt		2,500.00
215	Trust Funds Owed		15,280.00
220	Accrued Salaries Payable		240.00
300	Justin Case, Capital		26,370.90
	Totals	$54,706.91	$54,706.91

FIGURE 8.12   **Post-closing trial balance**

General Ledger Accounts at the End of the Fiscal Year

Figure 8.13, below, shows Justin's general ledger accounts at the end of December once the year-end was completed. Note that only those accounts from December 1 (where a balance forward was recorded) to the end of December are included here. The asset, liability, and capital accounts show a balance, but the drawings, income, and expense accounts are at zero, ready to start the new fiscal year.

Justin Case, Paralegal
General Ledgers

General Bank Account — Account No. 100

Date 20**		Explanation	PR	Debit	Credit	Dr./Cr.	Balance
Dec.	1	Balance Forward	✓	4,906.91		Dr.	4,906.91

Trust Bank Account — Account No. 115

Date 20**		Explanation	PR	Debit	Credit	Dr./Cr.	Balance
Dec.	1	Balance Forward	✓	15,280.00		Dr.	15,280.00

Accounts Receivable — Account No. 120

Date 20**		Explanation	PR	Debit	Credit	Dr./Cr.	Balance
Dec.	1	Balance Forward	✓	25,000.00		Dr.	25,000.00

Prepaid Insurance — Account No. 125

Date 20**		Explanation	PR	Debit	Credit	Dr./Cr.	Balance
Dec.	1	Prepaid Insurance	✓	600.00		Dr.	600.00
Dec.	31	Adjusting Entry	GJ4		50.00	Dr.	550.00

Office Supplies — Account No. 130

Date 20**		Explanation	PR	Debit	Credit	Dr./Cr.	Balance
Dec.	1	Balance Forward	✓	630.00		Dr.	630.00
	31	Adjusting Entry	GJ4		430.00	Dr.	200.00

Computer Equipment (Hardware) — Account No. 155

Date 20**		Explanation	PR	Debit	Credit	Dr./Cr.	Balance
Dec.	1	Balance Forward	✓	6,520.00		Dr.	6,520.00

Depreciation—Computer Equipment — Account No. 156

Date 20**		Explanation	PR	Debit	Credit	Dr./Cr.	Balance
Dec.	1	Adjusting Entry	GJ4		326.01	Cr.	326.01

Office Furniture and Equipment						Account No. 158
Date 20**		Explanation	PR	Debit	Credit	Dr./Cr.	Balance
Dec.	1	Balance Forward	✓	2,250.00		Dr.	2,250.00

Accounts Payable/General Liabilities						Account No. 200
Date 20**		Explanation	PR	Debit	Credit	Dr./Cr.	Balance
Dec.	1	Balance Forward	✓		6,890.00	Cr.	6,890.00

Personal Loan						Account No. 205
Date 20**		Explanation	PR	Debit	Credit	Dr./Cr.	Balance
Dec.	1	Balance Forward	✓		3,000.00	Cr.	3,000.00
	31	Adjusting Entry	GJ4		100.00	Cr.	3,100.00

Credit Card Debt						Account No. 210
Date 20**		Explanation	PR	Debit	Credit	Dr./Cr.	Balance
Dec.	1	Balance Forward	✓		2,500.00	Cr.	2,500.00

Trust Funds Owed						Account No. 215
Date 20**		Explanation	PR	Debit	Credit	Dr./Cr.	Balance
Dec.	1	Balance Forward	✓		15,280.00	Cr.	15,280.00

Accrued Salaries Payable						Account No. 220
Date 20**		Explanation	PR	Debit	Credit	Dr./Cr.	Balance
Dec.	31	Adjusting Entry	GJ4		240.00	Cr.	240.00

Justin Case, Capital						Account No. 300
Date 20**		Explanation	PR	Debit	Credit	Dr./Cr.	Balance
Dec.	1	Balance Forward	✓		2,550.00	Cr.	2,550.00
	31	Closing Entry—Income Summary	GJ5		25,620.90	Cr.	28,170.90
	31	Closing Entry—Drawings	GJ5	1,800.00		Cr.	26,370.90

Justin Case, Drawings						Account No. 350	
Date 20**		Explanation	PR	Debit	Credit	Dr./Cr.	Balance
Dec.	1	Balance Forward	✓	1,800.00		Dr.	1,800.00
	31	Closing Entry	GJ5		1,800.00		0.00

Income Summary						Account No. 355	
Date 20**		Explanation	PR	Debit	Credit	Dr./Cr.	Balance
Dec.	31	To close income accounts	GJ5		31,580.00	Cr.	31,580.00
	31	To close expense accounts	GJ5	5,959.10		Cr.	25,620.90
	31	To transfer balance to Capital	GJ5	25,620.90			0.00

Fees Earned						Account No. 400	
Date 20**		Explanation	PR	Debit	Credit	Dr./Cr.	Balance
Dec.	1	Balance Forward	✓		31,580.00	Cr.	31,580.00
	31	Closing Entry	GJ5	31,580.00			0.00

Salaries Expense						Account No. 511	
Date 20**		Explanation	PR	Debit	Credit	Dr./Cr.	Balance
Dec.	1	Balance Forward	✓	960.00		Dr.	960.00
	31	Adjusting Entry	GJ4	240.00		Dr.	1,200.00
	31	Closing Entry	GJ5		1,200.00		0.00

Depreciation Expense						Account No. 522	
Date 20**		Explanation	PR	Debit	Credit	Dr./Cr.	Balance
Dec.	31	Adjustment—Computer Equipment	GJ4	326.01		Dr.	326.01
	31	Closing Entry	GJ5		326.01		0.00

Insurance—Professional Liability						Account No. 527	
Date 20**		Explanation	PR	Debit	Credit	Dr./Cr.	Balance
Dec.	31	Adjusting Entry	GJ4	50.00		Dr.	50.00
	31	Closing Entry	GJ5		50.00		0.00

Interest Expense							Account No. 529
Date 20**		Explanation	PR	Debit	Credit	Dr./Cr.	Balance
Dec.	31	Adjusting Entry	GJ4	100.00		Dr.	100.00
	31	Closing Entry	GJ5		100.00		0.00

Meals and Entertainment Expense							Account No. 533
Date 20**		Explanation	PR	Debit	Credit	Dr./Cr.	Balance
Dec.	1	Balance Forward	✓	350.00		Dr.	350.00
	31	Closing Entry	GJ5		350.00		0.00

Membership/Professional Dues							Account No. 534
Date 20**		Explanation	PR	Debit	Credit	Dr./Cr.	Balance
Dec.	1	Balance Forward	✓	1,343.75		Dr.	1,343.75
	31	Closing Entry	GJ5		1,343.75		0.00

Office Supplies/General Expense							Account No. 535
Date 20**		Explanation	PR	Debit	Credit	Dr./Cr.	Balance
Dec.	1	Balance Forward	✓	580.00		Dr.	580.00
	31	Adjusting Entry	GJ4	430.00		Dr.	1,010.00
	31	Closing Entry	GJ5		1,010.00		0.00

Rent Expense							Account No. 538
Date 20**		Explanation	PR	Debit	Credit	Dr./Cr.	Balance
Dec.	1	Balance Forward	✓	1,100.00		Dr.	1,100.00
	31	Closing Entry	GJ5		1,100.00		0.00

Telephone Expense							Account No. 565
Date 20**		Explanation	PR	Debit	Credit	Dr./Cr.	Balance
Dec.	1	Balance Forward	✓	479.34		Dr.	479.34
	31	Closing Entry	GJ5		479.34		0.00

FIGURE 8.13   General ledgers after closing

Legal Requirements for Keeping Records

All records, such as paper documents as well as those stored in an electronic medium (such as on computer disk), must be kept in Canada or made available in Canada at the request of the Canada Revenue Agency (CRA). The records must be in English or French.

A business is required to keep orderly records of all income received. All receipts, invoices, vouchers, and cancelled cheques indicating outlays of money must also be kept. Such outlays include

- salaries and wages,
- operating expenses such as rent, advertising, and capital expenditures, and
- miscellaneous items such as charitable donations.

Records must be permanent and contain a systematic account of income, deductions, credits, and other information needed to file income tax and GST/HST returns. Incomplete records that use approximations instead of exact amounts are not acceptable. The records must

- allow you to determine how much tax you owe, or the tax, duties, or other amounts to be collected, withheld, or deducted, or any refund or rebate you may claim; and
- be supported by vouchers or other necessary source documents. If you do not keep your receipts or other vouchers to support your expenses or claims, and there is no other evidence available, the CRA will probably reduce the expenses or claims you have made.

The Six-Year Requirement

If tax returns are filed on time, records must be retained (other than certain documents for which there are special rules) for six years from the end of the last tax year to which they relate. You must keep every record necessary for dealing with an objection or appeal until it is resolved and the time for filing any further appeal has expired, or until the six-year period has expired, whichever is later.

CHAPTER SUMMARY

In this chapter you have completed the accounting cycle up to preparation of the post-closing trial balance. The post-closing trial balance serves as a check to ensure that the ledger accounts are in balance. All the temporary accounts have been cleared, and you are ready to begin the accounting cycle over again for the next fiscal period. The post-closing trial balance contains the balances for opening the books for the new fiscal year.

The financial statements were prepared for the end of the year. They can be prepared more frequently if you need to see how the business is doing or for submitting to a lender who requires the information.

KEY TERMS

balance sheet, 182
balance sheet accounts, 189
closing entries, 188
expense accounts, 190
financial statements, 182
income account, 190

income statement, 182
income summary account, 190
permanent accounts, 189
post-closing trial balance, 193
statement of owner's equity, 182
temporary accounts, 189

FURTHER READING

Canada Revenue Agency, *Business and Professional Income 2014*, online: <http://www.cra-arc.gc.ca/E/pub/tg/t4002/t4002-e.html>. Financial reporting for sole proprietors.

Canada Revenue Agency, "General Index of Financial Information (GIFI)," online: <http://www.cra-arc.gc.ca/tx/bsnss/tpcs/crprtns/rtrn/wht/gifi-ogrf/menu-eng.html>. Corporate financial statements.

L Kenway, "Accounting and Bookkeeping Checklists," *Bookkeeping-Essentials.com*, online: <http://www.bookkeeping-essentials.com/bookkeeping-checklist.html>. Select the "Year End Accountant Checklist" link.

L Kenway, "Learn How to Read Your Internal Financial Reports," *Bookkeeping-Essentials.com*, online: <http://www.bookkeeping-essentials.com/accounting-training.html>. Select the "Balance sheet" and "Income statement" links.

MaRS Discovery District, online: <http://www.marsdd.com/collections/accounting/financial-statements>. See the following topics:

- "Reading a Financial Statement: The Balance Sheet (Assets, Liabilities and Equity)." <http://www.marsdd.com/mars-library/reading-financial-statement-balance-sheet-assets-liabilities-equity>.
- "Reading a Financial Statement: The Income Statement." <http://www.marsdd.com/mars-library/reading-financial-statement-income-statement>.
- "Accounting Mechanics: An Example of Financial Statements." <http://www.marsdd.com/mars-library/financial-statement-example>.

PUT IT INTO PRACTICE

Case Example: Year-End Financial Statements

Ann Litigate had a meeting with her accountant, who advised her that there were some discrepancies in the information Ann provided. Consequently, the year-end financial statement will have to be adjusted and revised.

1. What steps can Ann take to ensure that the accountant has all the relevant information and that such information is accurate? Discuss.
2. What are some common issues with financial statement preparation that Ann can avoid next time? Discuss.

REVIEW QUESTIONS

True or False

_____ 1. The income statement calculation will determine the taxable income for a business owner.

_____ 2. At closing, all temporary and permanent account balances are brought to zero.

_____ 3. The post-closing trial balance includes only the permanent accounts: assets, liabilities, and equity.

_____ 4. To close the revenue accounts, you debit the revenue accounts.

_____ 5. The income summary is a permanent account that is transferred to the opening balance in the next fiscal period.

_____ 6. To close the expense account, you debit the expense account.

_____ 7. To close the income summary account, you transfer the ending balance to the capital account.

_____ 8. The ending balances on the general ledger and the post-closing trial balance become the opening balances in the new fiscal period.

_____ 9. At the close of the fiscal year, the general ledger accounts must be updated to reflect all adjustments.

_____ 10. The post-closing trial balance serves as a check to ensure that the ledger accounts are in balance.

Short Answer

1. What information does the statement of owner's equity report? Why is this important?

2. What happens to the drawings account at the end of the accounting cycle?

3. What information does the general ledger report at the end of the accounting cycle?

4. What are the four steps involved in closing the accounts at the end of the accounting cycle?

5. Name two categories of accounts that are "permanent accounts."

6. Name three categories of accounts that are "temporary accounts."

PRACTICE EXERCISES

Practice Exercise 8.1

a. Using the balances obtained in Practice Exercise 7.4, prepare the financial statements for the period ended December 31, 20**.

PRACTICE

EXCEL

Ann Litigate, Paralegal Income Statement for the Period Ended December 31, 20**		
Income		
Fees Earned		
Expenses		
Salaries Expense		
Depreciation Expense		
Insurance—Professional Liability		
Membership/Professional Dues		
Office Supplies/General Expense		
Rent Expense		
Telephone Expense		
Total Expenses		
Net Income		

Ann Litigate, Paralegal Statement of Owner's Equity for the Period Ended December 31, 20**		
Ann Litigate, Capital, December 1, 20**		
Net Income for December		
Less: Withdrawals for December		
Increase in Capital		
Ann Litigate, Capital, December 31, 20**		

Ann Litigate, Paralegal Balance Sheet December 31, 20**			
Assets			
Current Assets			
General Bank Account			
Trust Bank Account			
Accounts Receivable			
Prepaid Insurance			
Office Supplies			
Total Current Assets			
Fixed Assets			
Computer Equipment (Hardware)			
Less: Accumulated Depreciation on Computer Equipment			
Total Fixed Assets			
Total Assets			
Liabilities and Owner's Equity			
Liabilities			
Accounts Payable/General Liabilities			
Credit Card Debt			
Trust Funds Owed			
Total Liabilities			
Owner's Equity			
Ann Litigate, Capital			
Total Liabilities and Owner's Equity			

b. Record the adjusting entries in Ann's general journal, then post the amounts to the individual general ledger accounts.

PRACTICE

EXCEL

Date 20**		Description	PR	Debit	Credit
		Ann Litigate, Paralegal **General Journal**			GJ8
		Adjusting Entries			
Dec.	31				

c. In the same general journal, once the adjusting entries have been posted, prepare the closing entries and post them to the general ledger. Use the same general journal and general ledgers you used for part (b).

| Ann Litigate, Paralegal |
| General Ledgers |

General Bank Account — Account No. 100

Date 20**		Explanation	PR	Debit	Credit	Dr./Cr.	Balance
Dec.	31	Opening balance December 1	✓			Dr.	15,360

Trust Bank Account — Account No. 115

Date 20**		Explanation	PR	Debit	Credit	Dr./Cr.	Balance
Dec.	31	Opening balance December 1	✓			Dr.	18,500

Accounts Receivable — Account No. 120

Date 20**		Explanation	PR	Debit	Credit	Dr./Cr.	Balance
Dec.	31	Opening balance December 1	✓			Dr.	3,500

Prepaid Insurance — Account No. 125

Date 20**		Explanation	PR	Debit	Credit	Dr./Cr.	Balance
Dec.	31	Opening balance December 1	✓			Dr.	3,000

Prepaid Expense — Account No. 128

Date 20**		Explanation	PR	Debit	Credit	Dr./Cr.	Balance
Dec.	31	Opening balance December 1 (rent)	✓			Dr.	1,200

Office Supplies — Account No. 130

Date 20**		Explanation	PR	Debit	Credit	Dr./Cr.	Balance
Dec.	31	Opening balance December 1	✓			Dr.	800

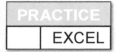

| | | Computer Equipment (Hardware) | | | | | Account No. 155 |
Date 20**		Explanation	PR	Debit	Credit	Dr./Cr.	Balance
Dec.	31	Opening balance December 1	✓			Dr.	6,800

| | | Depreciation—Computer Equipment | | | | | Account No. 156 |
Date 20**		Explanation	PR	Debit	Credit	Dr./Cr.	Balance
Dec.	31	Opening balance December 1	✓				0

| | | Accounts Payable/General Liabilities | | | | | Account No. 200 |
Date 20**		Explanation	PR	Debit	Credit	Dr./Cr.	Balance
Dec.	31	Opening balance December 1	✓			Cr.	6,500

| | | Credit Card Debt | | | | | Account No. 210 |
Date 20**		Explanation	PR	Debit	Credit	Dr./Cr.	Balance
Dec.	31	Opening balance December 1	✓			Cr.	4,500

| | | Trust Funds Owed | | | | | Account No. 215 |
Date 20**		Explanation	PR	Debit	Credit	Dr./Cr.	Balance
Dec.	31	Opening balance December 1	✓			Cr.	18,500

| | | Ann Litigate, Capital | | | | | Account No. 300 |
Date 20**		Explanation	PR	Debit	Credit	Dr./Cr.	Balance
Dec.	31	Opening balance December 1	✓			Cr.	12,500

Ann Litigate, Drawings Account No. 350

Date 20**		Explanation	PR	Debit	Credit	Dr./Cr.	Balance
Dec.	31	Opening balance December 1	✓			Dr.	2,000

Income Summary Account No. 355

Date 20**		Explanation	PR	Debit	Credit	Dr./Cr.	Balance

Fees Earned Account No. 400

Date 20**		Explanation	PR	Debit	Credit	Dr./Cr.	Balance
Dec.	31	Opening balance December 1				Cr.	10,550

Salaries Expense Account No. 511

Date 20**		Explanation	PR	Debit	Credit	Dr./Cr.	Balance
Dec.	31	Opening balance December 1	✓			Dr.	1,000

Depreciation Expense Account No. 522

Date 20**		Explanation	PR	Debit	Credit	Dr./Cr.	Balance
Dec.	31	Opening balance December 1	✓				0

Insurance—Professional Liability Account No. 527

Date 20**		Explanation	PR	Debit	Credit	Dr./Cr.	Balance
Dec.	31	Opening balance December 1	✓				0

PRACTICE

EXCEL

Membership/Professional Dues							Account No. 534	
Date 20**		Explanation	PR	Debit	Credit	Dr./Cr.	Balance	
Dec.	31	Opening balance December 1	✓			Dr.	230	

Office Supplies/General Expense							Account No. 535	
Date 20**		Explanation	PR	Debit	Credit	Dr./Cr.	Balance	
Dec.	31	Opening balance December 1	✓				0	

Rent Expense							Account No. 538	
Date 20**		Explanation	PR	Debit	Credit	Dr./Cr.	Balance	
Dec.	31	Opening balance December 1	✓				0	

Telephone Expense							Account No. 565	
Date 20**		Explanation	PR	Debit	Credit	Dr./Cr.	Balance	
Dec.	31	Opening balance December 1	✓			Dr.	160	

d. Using the general journal and general ledgers from parts (b) and (c), close the income summary and drawings accounts to the Ann Litigate, Capital account. Then prepare the post-closing trial balance.

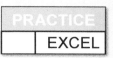

	Ann Litigate, Paralegal Post-Closing Trial Balance December 31, 20**		
	Account Titles	Dr.	Cr.
100	General Bank Account		
115	Trust Bank Account		
120	Accounts Receivable		
125	Prepaid Insurance		
128	Prepaid Expense (Rent)		
130	Office Supplies		
155	Computer Equipment (Hardware)		
156	Depreciation—Computer Equipment		
200	Accounts Payable/General Liabilities		
210	Credit Card Debt		
215	Trust Funds Owed		
300	Ann Litigate, Capital		
	Totals		

Practice Exercise 8.2

a. Using the worksheets provided, prepare the financial statements for ABC Legal Services based on the adjusted trial balance shown below. Assume that the adjustments have been entered in the journal (GJ2) and have been entered and posted to the account ledgers.

ABC Legal Services Adjusted Trial Balance December 31, 20**		
Account Titles	Dr.	Cr.
General Bank Account	$15,000	
Trust Bank Account	35,000	
Accounts Receivable	20,250	
Prepaid Insurance	700	
Prepaid Expense (Rent)	700	
Office Supplies	150	
Computer Equipment (Hardware)	4,750	
Depreciation—Computer Equipment		$950
Accounts Payable/General Liabilities		2,025
Personal Loan		6,000
Credit Card Debt		4,500
Trust Funds Owed		35,000
ABC, Capital		17,165
ABC, Drawings	5,000	
Fees Earned		23,000
Expense Recovery		750
Salaries Expense	1,700	
Depreciation Expense	950	
Insurance—Professional Liability	2,500	
Membership/Professional Dues	200	
Office Supplies/General Expense	500	
Rent Expense	1,800	
Telephone Expense	190	
Total	$89,390	$89,390

ABC Legal Services Income Statement for the Period Ended December 31, 20**		
Income		
Fees Earned		
Expense Recovery		
Total Income		
Expenses		
Salaries Expense		
Depreciation Expense		
Insurance—Professional Liability		
Membership/Professional Dues		
Office Supplies/General Expense		
Rent Expense		
Telephone Expense		
Total Expenses		
Net Income		

ABC Legal Services Statement of Owner's Equity for the Period Ended December 31, 20**		
ABC, Capital, December 31, 20**		
Net Income for December		
Less: Withdrawals for December		
Increase in Capital		
ABC Legal Services, Capital, December 31, 20**		

ABC Legal Services Balance Sheet December 31, 20**			
Assets			
Current Assets			
General Bank Account			
Trust Bank Account			
Accounts Receivable			
Prepaid Insurance			
Prepaid Expense (Rent)			
Office Supplies			
Total Current Assets			
Fixed Assets			
Computer Equipment (Hardware)			
Less: Accumulated Depreciation on Computer Equipment			
Total Fixed Assets			
Total Assets			
Liabilities and Owner's Equity			
Liabilities			
Accounts Payable/General Liabilities			
Personal Loan			
Credit Card Debt			
Trust Funds Owed			
Total Liabilities			
Owner's Equity			
ABC Legal Services, Capital			
Total Liabilities and Owner's Equity			

b. Using the worksheet provided, prepare the closing journal entries and post to the general ledger.

ABC Legal Services General Journal					GJ3
Date 20**	Description	PR	Debit	Credit	
	Closing Entries				

PRACTICE

EXCEL

ABC Legal Services
General Ledgers
at December 31, 20

General Bank Account						Account No. 100
Date 20**	Explanation	PR	Debit	Credit	Dr./Cr.	Balance
Dec. 31	Balance Forward	✓			Dr.	15,000

Trust Bank Account						Account No. 115
Date 20**	Explanation	PR	Debit	Credit	Dr./Cr.	Balance
Dec. 31	Balance Forward	✓			Dr.	35,000

Accounts Receivable							Account No. 120
Date 20**		Explanation	PR	Debit	Credit	Dr./Cr.	Balance
Dec.	31	Balance Forward	✓			Dr.	20,250

Prepaid Insurance							Account No. 125
Date 20**		Explanation	PR	Debit	Credit	Dr./Cr.	Balance
Dec.	31	Balance Forward	✓			Dr.	700

Prepaid Expense							Account No. 128
Date 20**		Explanation	PR	Debit	Credit	Dr./Cr.	Balance
Dec.	31	Balance Forward	✓			Dr.	700

Office Supplies							Account No. 130
Date 20**		Explanation	PR	Debit	Credit	Dr./Cr.	Balance
Dec.	31	Balance Forward	✓			Dr.	150

Computer Equipment (Hardware)							Account No. 155
Date 20**		Explanation	PR	Debit	Credit	Dr./Cr.	Balance
Dec.	31	Balance Forward	✓			Dr.	4,750

Depreciation—Computer Equipment							Account No. 156
Date 20**		Explanation	PR	Debit	Credit	Dr./Cr.	Balance
Dec.	31	Balance Forward	GJ3			Cr.	950

Accounts Payable/General Liabilities						Account No. 200	
Date 20**		Explanation	PR	Debit	Credit	Dr./Cr.	Balance
Dec.	31	Balance Forward	✓			Cr.	2,025

PRACTICE

EXCEL

Personal Loan						Account No. 205	
Date 20**		Explanation	PR	Debit	Credit	Dr./Cr.	Balance
Dec.	31	Balance Forward	✓			Cr.	6,000

Credit Card Debt						Account No. 210	
Date 20**		Explanation	PR	Debit	Credit	Dr./Cr.	Balance
Dec.	31	Balance Forward	✓			Cr.	4,500

Trust Funds Owed						Account No. 215	
Date 20**		Explanation	PR	Debit	Credit	Dr./Cr.	Balance
Dec.	31	Balance Forward	✓			Cr.	35,000

ABC Legal Services, Capital						Account No. 300	
Date 20**		Explanation	PR	Debit	Credit	Dr./Cr.	Balance
Dec.	31	Balance Forward	✓			Cr.	17,165

ABC Legal Services, Drawings						Account No. 350	
Date 20**		Explanation	PR	Debit	Credit	Dr./Cr.	Balance
Dec.	31	Balance Forward	✓			Dr.	5,000

Income Summary — Account No. 355

Date 20**		Explanation	PR	Debit	Credit	Dr./Cr.	Balance

Fees Earned — Account No. 400

Date 20**		Explanation	PR	Debit	Credit	Dr./Cr.	Balance
Dec.	31	Balance Forward	✓			Cr.	23,000

Expense Recovery — Account No. 410

Date 20**		Explanation	PR	Debit	Credit	Dr./Cr.	Balance
Dec.	31	Balance Forward	✓			Cr.	750

Salaries Expense — Account No. 511

Date 20**		Explanation	PR	Debit	Credit	Dr./Cr.	Balance
Dec.	31	Opening balance December 1	✓			Dr.	1,700

Depreciation Expense — Account No. 522

Date 20**		Explanation	PR	Debit	Credit	Dr./Cr.	Balance
Dec.	31	Balance Forward	GJ3			Dr.	950

Insurance—Professional Liability							Account No. 527	
Date 20**		Explanation	PR	Debit	Credit	Dr./Cr.	Balance	
Dec.	31	Balance Forward	GJ3			Dr.	2,500	

Membership/Professional Dues							Account No. 534	
Date 20**		Explanation	PR	Debit	Credit	Dr./Cr.	Balance	
Dec.	31	Balance Forward	✓			Dr.	200	

Office Supplies/General Expense							Account No. 535	
Date 20**		Explanation	PR	Debit	Credit	Dr./Cr.	Balance	
Dec.	31	Balance Forward	GJ3			Dr.	500	

Rent Expense							Account No. 538	
Date 20**		Explanation	PR	Debit	Credit	Dr./Cr.	Balance	
Dec.	31	Balance Forward	GJ3			Dr.	1,800	

Telephone Expense							Account No. 565	
Date 20**		Explanation	PR	Debit	Credit	Dr./Cr.	Balance	
Dec.	31	Opening balance December 1	✓			Dr.	190	

c. Prepare the post-closing trial balance.

PRACTICE
EXCEL

ABC Legal Services Post-Closing Trial Balance December 31, 20**		
Account Titles	Dr.	Cr.

9 Banking Procedures and Accounting for Cash

After reading this chapter, you should be able to:

- establish and replenish a petty cash fund
- reconcile a general bank account
- reconcile a trust bank account

Petty Cash

Because paying for small purchases by cheque can be inconvenient and impractical, most businesses establish a fund for payment of incidental expenses. The **petty cash** fund is used to pay for minor expenses, such as postage and office supplies, or to make change if a client is paying with cash. The firm's policy regarding the types of expenditures that are acceptable for petty cash reimbursements should be clear and communicated to all members of the firm.

The petty cash system is one example of **cash controls** that protect against loss, misuse, or fraud in the handling of cash.[1] It ensures that funds from petty cash will not be used inappropriately—for example, to pay for an employee's lunch because he or she was short of money that day.

Establishing a Petty Cash Account

You will need to establish an account called Petty Cash on the chart of accounts in the Current Assets category. Justin Case has given it number 105, so it appears directly below account 100 (General Bank Account), and he will create a ledger sheet in the general ledger called Petty Cash for this purpose.

Use a general journal entry to establish the petty cash fund. Justin has decided it would be reasonable to have a fund of $50. A cheque is issued and cashed for the desired amount and the cash is placed in a safe location, usually a petty cash box with a lock on it. Figure 9.1 shows the general journal entry used to establish a petty cash fund.

Justin Case, Paralegal General Journal					GJ6
Date 20**		Description	PR	Debit	Credit
Jan.	5	Petty Cash	105	50	
		General Bank Account	100		50
		To establish petty cash fund			

FIGURE 9.1   General journal entry to establish fund

---

1 Law Society of Upper Canada, *The Bookkeeping Guide for Paralegals* (Toronto: LSUC, February 2014) at 60–67.

Recording Petty Cash Entries

A system should be established requiring pre-numbered written requests (vouchers) supported by original receipts for items to be paid out of petty cash to any person. The amount on hand in the petty cash box and the sum of the receipts on hand should equal the firm's established petty cash amount.

The information from the vouchers can be transferred to an auxiliary petty cash record, but that is not essential. It is sufficient to attach the store receipt to the petty cash voucher and keep the vouchers in the petty cash box until entries are made in the general journal. Figure 9.2 shows a sample voucher used for withdrawals from petty cash.

PETTY CASH VOUCHER NO.	1
AMOUNT	$4.80
DATE	January 8, 20**
PAID TO	Tom's Office Supply
FOR	Pens
DEBIT ACCT. NAME	Office Supplies/General Expense ACCT. NO. 535
APPROVED BY	Judith Wells, Assistant
PAYMENT RECEIVED BY	Justin Case

FIGURE 9.2   Petty cash voucher

At all times, the amount of cash plus the total amount of the vouchers should equal the total value of the fund, as shown in Figure 9.3.

Total paid out	$4.80
Cash in petty cash box	45.20
Total petty cash fund	$50.00

FIGURE 9.3   Balancing funds in a petty cash box

Replenishing a Petty Cash Account

In order to replenish the fund to bring the amount of petty cash back up to $50, Judith Wells, who as Justin's assistant is responsible for completing the petty cash vouchers, must record the

221

expenses in the general journal and post the entries to the correct account. If she does not keep a record similar to the one in Figure 9.3, she will use the vouchers to create the general journal entries. Once the entries are made, she will write a cheque payable to herself (or to cash) for the total amount that was spent—in this case, $23.50—and summarize the vouchers as shown in Figure 9.4. The cash will be put in the petty cash box, bringing the float up to $50 again.

Date 20**		Description	Account	Receipts	Paid Out	Balance
Jan.	5	Establish Fund	105	50.00		50.00
	9	Office Supplies/General Expense	535		4.80	45.20
	20	Postage Expense	563		6.00	39.20
	23	Maintenance and Repairs (cleaning products)	532		8.20	31.00
	30	Delivery Expense	550		4.50	26.50
		Total Spent $23.50				
	30	Replenish Fund, Cheque #25	105	23.50		50.00

FIGURE 9.4 Petty cash record tracking expenses

If Judith finds that the fund is too small and needs to be replenished too often, she can simply increase it by writing another cheque to increase the amount kept in petty cash. The journal entry would be similar to the entry that was made establishing the fund. The balance in the general ledger for petty cash usually remains constant at the amount at which the fund has been established. Figure 9.5 shows the journal entries that were made to establish the fund and then to replenish it.

Justin Case, Paralegal General Journal					GJ6
Date 20**		Description	PR	Debit	Credit
Jan.	5	Petty Cash	105	50.00	
		General Bank Account	100		50.00
		To establish petty cash fund			
Jan.	30	Office Supplies/General Expense	535	4.80	
		Postage Expense	563	6.00	
		Maintenance and Repairs (cleaning products)	532	8.20	
		Delivery Expense	550	4.50	
		General Bank Account	105		23.50
		To replenish petty cash fund			

FIGURE 9.5 General journal entries to establish and replenish petty cash fund

Cash Short and Over

A firm may use the petty cash or keep a separate float in the office for the purpose of making change if a client pays with cash. This float will consist of coins and small bills, usually totalling between $25 and $200, depending on the size of the firm. If for some reason the cash in the petty cash box does not equal the amount of the vouchers, the amount of cash short or the amount by which the cash is over should be recorded in a general ledger account called **cash short and over**.

Banking Procedures and Handling of Money

In addition to complying with the requirements of the Law Society of Upper Canada (LSUC) for setting up trust accounts and reporting to the Law Foundation of Ontario, certain internal cash controls should be in place to help run your practice more efficiently and to reduce the risk of errors and fraud.[2]

When a bank account is opened with a financial institution, the bank will require that a **signature card** be filled in as a safeguard against forgery of cheques or other instruments. The bank will provide a set of cheques and a deposit book containing deposit slips to be completed for banking transactions. You are required to list each cheque you are depositing, as well as any cash, and indicate the source of the funds on the deposit slip. (See Figure 5.2 for a sample trust account deposit slip.) Deposits to the general bank account will include similar information. When the deposit is made, the person making the deposit and the bank teller will initial the deposit slip, and the teller will stamp the copy of the deposit slip as proof of the transaction. When using an automated teller to make deposits, you should be aware of all the bank's terms and the risks involved in using an ATM. Make sure a receipt of the deposit is attached to the firm's deposit book.

Withdrawals are allowed from an ATM for the general bank account, but not for trust accounts. Ensure that the signature card for the trust account has been encoded for deposits only by your financial institution.

Debit and credit cards can be used to pay for general office expenses. If a debit card is used, the amount will be deducted directly from the firm's bank account. It is important to keep receipts for any credit or debit card payments because the bank or credit card statements are not sufficient evidence of purchases for tax purposes.

Cheque Endorsement

Endorsement refers to the signing or stamping of a cheque prior to depositing it. Cheques must be endorsed or signed by the person to whom the cheque is made payable before they can be deposited. Three common types of endorsement are as follows:

- *Blank endorsement:* Once the back of the cheque is signed by the person to whom it was made payable, it can be further endorsed and cashed by someone else. This type of endorsement can be unsafe because anyone who gets the cheque could sign the back and cash it. Very few banking institutions will allow blank endorsement.

---

2   *Ibid.*

- *Full endorsement:* The person signing the back of the cheque indicates to whom the cheque may be made payable. For example, a cheque made payable to Justin Case could be endorsed by him, "Pay to the order of Judith Wells," at which point Judith would be entitled to cash the cheque. Very few banking institutions will allow full endorsement.
- *Restrictive endorsement:* This type of endorsement is the usual method used in law firms. It specifies that the cheque must be deposited to the firm's bank account. A stamp for endorsement purposes is often provided when a business bank account is first opened. If a stamp is not used, you will be required to endorse the back of the cheque with the account number to which the cheque is being deposited.

> **Deposit to the Credit of**
>
> **JUSTIN CASE**
>
> **R#20552-004 ACC #0216-520634**

FIGURE 9.6
Endorsement using stamp

Cheques

Business cheques often come in a binder with a stub attached, which is used to keep track of the deposits made to the account, the cheques written, and the bank balance. The cheque stubs can be used to create journal entries. Terms you will encounter with regard to cheques include the following:

- **drawer**: The person writing the cheque (sometimes referred to as the **payor**).
- **drawee**: The financial institution on which the cheque is drawn.
- **payee**: The person to whom the cheque is written.

Many firms use accounting software that simultaneously produces cheques when a bill is being paid, records the payment in the proper journal, then posts the amount to the correct ledger account. This type of software is a great time-saver and a useful tool for keeping all records current.

Reconciling a Bank Account

Reconciliation is the process used to compare the bank statement with the balance in the bank shown in the firm's general ledger or on its cheque stubs. Each month the firm will receive a bank statement for each of its bank accounts, setting out the following information:

- The balance at the beginning of the month
- All deposits that have been received on the account
- All cheques that have been cleared through the account (cancelled cheques)
- All bank charges for the account
- The balance at the end of the month

Banks no longer return cancelled cheques with the bank statement. Instead, for a fee, a scanned copy of the front and back of cheques is provided with the bank statement. The scanned copies show the particulars of when and where a cheque was cashed and by whom.

How to Reconcile the General and Trust Bank Balances

Although there is no formal requirement to reconcile a firm's general operating account with the bank statement, it is good business practice to ensure that your bank records and your accounting records agree.

When reconciling a bank balance, you will want to look for the following discrepancies:

- A **deposit in transit** is one that appears on the firm's records but does not appear on the bank statement. This can happen if the deposit was entered in the firm's books but no one got to the bank until the next day (which happened also to be the day after the cut-off date for the bank statement).
- An **outstanding cheque** is one written by the firm that is not shown on the bank statement because it has not been cashed by the payee. Because it was not presented to the bank for payment, the bank does not show it on the statement.
- Bank **service charges** often vary from month to month and need to be recorded in the firm's books once the amount is determined.
- An **NSF cheque** is one that was deposited but did not go through because there were insufficient funds in the account of the drawer (typically a client). When this happens, the bank notifies the firm by sending a debit memorandum indicating that the deposit has been reversed. There are usually service charges associated with any returned cheques. The firm could also have one of its own cheques returned if there were insufficient funds in the bank account to cover it when it was presented for payment. NSF cheques are sometimes referred to as "rubber cheques" because they bounce back. The service charges for writing a bad cheque are substantial.

EXAMPLE 1

The ending bank balance as shown on the general bank statement for Justin's firm at the end of November is $5,414.31. However, the general ledger shows a balance of $5,366.91 at the end of November, a difference of $47.40. The goal is to find out why there is a difference and to make any corrections needed.

Financial institutions have their own format for preparing bank statements, but the information contained is similar for all banks. Figure 9.7 shows the general bank statement received by Justin Case for the month of November.

STEP 1

Complete the form on the back of the bank statement if there is one, or use a form designed by the firm for the purpose of reconciling the bank statements. The completed form used for reconciling a general bank account is shown in Figure 9.8. This form

demonstrates the reconciliation of Justin's general bank balance for the month of November.

STEP 2

Fill in the date of reconciliation at the top of the form, in Justin's case, November 30, 20**.

STEP 3

Insert the bank balance at the end of the month from the bank statement on the "Balance per Bank Statement" line and place the balance from the general ledger account on the "Balance per General Bank Account Ledger" line near the bottom of the form.

STEP 4

Compare all of the cancelled cheques on the bank statement, noting whether there are any discrepancies in the amounts shown on the bank statement and on the cheque images.

ROYAL BANK OF MONEY

P.O. Box 5011, Station A
Montreal, QC H3C 3B8

General Bank Account Statement

Justin Case, Paralegal	November 1, 20** to November 30, 20**
135 Main Street	
Yourtown, Ontario K3P 1G9	Account number: 0216-520634

ACCOUNT SUMMARY FOR THIS PERIOD

Opening Balance on Nov. 1, 20**		$5,600.00
Total Deposits and Credits	+	$1,272.00
Total Cheques and Debits	−	$1,457.69
Closing Balance on Nov. 30, 20**	=	$5,414.31

ACCOUNT ACTIVITY DETAILS

Date	Description	Cheques and Debits	Deposits and Credits	Balance
Nov. 01	Opening Balance			5,600.00
Nov. 02	Chq. #4	339.00 ✔		5,261.00
Nov. 12	Deposit		700.00 ✔	5,961.00
Nov. 14	Chq. #5	303.69 ✔		5,657.31
Nov. 15	Deposit		300.00 ✔	5,957.31
Nov. 15	Bank Charges	15.00 **o/s**		5,942.31
Nov. 22	Deposit		272.00*	6,214.31
Nov. 22	Chq. #6	800.00 ✔		5,414.31
	Closing Balance			5,414.31

Please check this Account Statement without delay and advise us of any error or omission within 45 days of the statement date.

Royal Bank of Money GST Registration Number: R105248I028

* Bank error; should be 272.60.

FIGURE 9.7   General bank statement

Justin Case, Paralegal
GENERAL BANK RECONCILIATION
as at November 30, 20**

GENERAL BANK ACCOUNT

Balance per Bank Statement	5,414.31
Less: Outstanding Cheques (See list below)	−113.00
Plus: Outstanding Deposits	50.00
Plus/Minus Bank Error	0.60
Reconciled General Bank Balance at November 30, 20**	5,351.91

Outstanding Cheques

Cheque Number	Date	Amount
#7	Nov. 6	22.60
#8	Nov. 15	90.40
Total Outstanding Cheques		113.00

BALANCE PER BOOKS

Balance per General Bank Account Ledger	5,366.91
Add: Deposits by Bank Not Shown in Books	
Deduct: Bank Charges	−15.00
Bank Errors	
NSF Cheque	
Adjusted Balance per Books at November 30, 20**	5,351.91

FIGURE 9.8   General bank reconciliation

\multicolumn{7}{l}{**Justin Case, Paralegal** **General Disbursements Journal**}							GDJ1
Date 20**	Method/ Ref. #	Paid To/Particulars Client/RE	PR	General Ledger Acct. Dr.	Client's General Ledger Dr.	HST Paid Dr.	General Bank Account Cr.	
Nov. 1	chq #4	Lucky Landlord, Rent Exp.	538	300.00		39.00	339.00 ✓	
4	chq #5	LSUC re dues Oct. – Dec.	534	268.75		34.94	303.69 ✓	
5	chq #6	J. Case, Drawings	350	800.00			800.00 ✓	
6	chq #7	Quick Courier, Zimmer re Courier Exp.	4		20.00	2.60	22.60	
15	chq #8	Unitel re Telephone Exp.	565	80.00		10.40	90.40	
30		Totals		1,448.75	20.00	86.94	1,555.69	

FIGURE 9.9 General disbursements journal checked off

STEP 5

Prepare a list of outstanding cheques. Compare the cheques shown on the bank statement and those shown in the general disbursements journal. Place a check mark next to the cheque amount on the bank statement and a check mark next to the corresponding amount in the general disbursements journal. Any cheques that are not checked off in the disbursements journal are outstanding. List these amounts on the bank reconciliation form in the "Outstanding Cheques" section. Total the outstanding cheques and place the total on the "Less: Outstanding Cheques" line as shown in Figure 9.8.

STEP 6

Look for any amounts in the Cheques and Debits column of the bank statement that did not appear in the general disbursements journal. Deduct the amount in the "Balance per Books" section of the bank reconciliation. Add lines as required.

STEP 7

Check to see if there were any cheques outstanding from the previous month that have still not cleared the bank. In Justin's case, there are none. If there were any, you would add those cheques to the outstanding list because they are still outstanding. You might also choose to do a follow-up at that point to see why the cheques had not been cashed.

STEP 8

Using the deposit book for the general bank account (see Figure 9.10), compare all deposits on the bank statement with those in the deposit book, checking off each item and noting any discrepancies in the amounts.

STEP 9

Outstanding deposits: Compare the total amount of the deposits on the bank statement to the total deposits shown in the general ledger for the month (Figure 9.11). In Justin's situation, there was a deposit of $50 made using the general journal on November 21 that does not appear on the bank statement. Enter the amount of the outstanding deposits on the "Plus: Outstanding Deposits" line on the bank reconciliation form. Add additional lines if there is more than one deposit outstanding.

STEP 10

Bank errors: These are relatively rare but do occur occasionally. Typical bank errors include an entry being made to another customer's account or incorrectly recording the amount of a deposit or cheque. Notify the bank if it has made an error and the bank will correct it. In Justin's case, you will note a bank error in the deposits entered on the bank statement. The records of the firm show a deposit for $272.60 on November 22 (see Figure 9.10) but the bank recorded the amount as $272.00. The bank account is understated by $0.60, so the bank must add this amount to the bank balance. You should telephone the bank, ask it to make the correction, and request a bank memo confirming the correction. Place the amount on the "Plus/Minus Bank Error" line.

STEP 11

Calculate the reconciled bank balance. In Justin's case, you arrive at a total of $5,351.91.

CURRENT ACCOUNT DEPOSIT SLIP

DATE			INITIALS	
12	☆☆	11	JC	RW
DD	MM	YR	Depositor	Tellers

CASH COUNT

COIN		
X 5		
X 10		
X 20		
X 50		
X 100		
	Cash Subtotal $	

R#20552-004 ACC #216-520634

LIST OF CHEQUES

CHEQUE IDENTIFICATION

	NAME	CHEQUE	REF. #	AMOUNT
1	Howes	Tr. Chq. #4	File No. 1	700.00
2				
3				
4				
5				
			Cheque Subtotal $	700.00

CREDIT ACCOUNT OF JUSTIN CASE, PARALEGAL

DEPOSIT SUMMARY

Visa Vouchers	
Cash Subtotal	
Cheque Subtotal	700.00
Deposit Total $	700.00 ✓

CURRENT ACCOUNT DEPOSIT SLIP

DATE			INITIALS	
15	☆☆	11	JC	RW
DD	MM	YR	Depositor	Tellers

CASH COUNT

COIN		
X 5		
X 10		
X 20		
X 50		
X 100		
	Cash Subtotal $	

R#20552-004 ACC #216-520634

LIST OF CHEQUES

CHEQUE IDENTIFICATION

	NAME	CHEQUE	REF. #	AMOUNT
1	Jones	Tr. Chq. # 5	File No. 2	300.00
2				
3				
4				
5				
			Cheque Subtotal $	300.00

CREDIT ACCOUNT OF JUSTIN CASE, PARALEGAL

DEPOSIT SUMMARY

Visa Vouchers	
Cash Subtotal	
Cheque Subtotal	300.00
Deposit Total $	300.00 ✓

FIGURE 9.10   Deposit slips for general bank account (continued on next page)

CURRENT ACCOUNT DEPOSIT SLIP

DATE			INITIALS	
22	**		JC	RW
DD	MM	YR	Depositor	Tellers

CASH COUNT	COIN	2.60
Zimmer	X 5	
No. 4	7 X 10	70.00
	X 20	
	2 X 50	100.00
	1 X 100	100.00
	Cash Subtotal $	272.60

R#20552-004 ACC #216-520634

LIST OF CHEQUES

CHEQUE IDENTIFICATION

NAME	CHEQUE	REF. #	AMOUNT
1			
2			
3			
4			
5			
		Cheque Subtotal $	

CREDIT ACCOUNT OF JUSTIN CASE, PARALEGAL

DEPOSIT SUMMARY

Visa Vouchers	
Cash Subtotal	272.60
Cheque Subtotal	
Deposit Total $	272.60 ✓

CURRENT ACCOUNT DEPOSIT SLIP

DATE			INITIALS	
21	**		JC	RW
DD	MM	YR	Depositor	Tellers

CASH COUNT	COIN	
Crozier	X 5	
No. 5	1 X 10	10.00
	2 X 20	40.00
	X 50	
	X 100	
	Cash Subtotal $	50.00

R#20552-004 ACC #216-520634

LIST OF CHEQUES

CHEQUE IDENTIFICATION

NAME	CHEQUE	REF. #	AMOUNT
1			
2			
3			
4			
5			
		Cheque Subtotal $	

CREDIT ACCOUNT OF JUSTIN CASE, PARALEGAL

DEPOSIT SUMMARY

Visa Vouchers	
Cash Subtotal	50.00
Cheque Subtotal	
Deposit Total $	50.00 O/S

FIGURE 9.10 Deposit slips for general bank account (concluded)

General Bank Account							Account No. 100
Date 20**		Explanation	PR	Debit	Credit	Dr./Cr.	Balance
Oct.	30		GJ2		500.00	Dr.	5,600.00
Nov.	21		GJ3	50.00		Dr.	5,650.00
	30	Totals from General Receipts Journal	GRJ1	1,272.60		Dr.	6,922.60
	30	Totals from General Disbursements Journal	GDJ1		1,555.69	Dr.	5,366.91

FIGURE 9.11   General bank account ledger sheet

STEP 12

The line indicating the adjusted balance per books at the end of the month must equal the reconciled general bank balance at the end of the month.

STEP 13

. Bank charges or credits: Look at the bank statement to determine whether there are any bank charges that have not been recorded in your records. You will note that there is a bank charge of $15. This amount must be deducted from the balance in the general ledger to arrive at the correct bank balance. Deduct $15 on the bank charges line. Because these bank charges were not

recorded in the books of the firm, you must create a general journal entry and post it to the general ledger. The journal entry you would make is shown in Figure 9.12.

STEP 14

Any credits made to the account by the bank should also be recorded. For example, if the bank had paid interest on the account, you would need to enter it. In Justin's case, there weren't any credits.

STEP 15

Compute the adjusted balance at the bottom of the form per the firm's books. This amount should equal the reconciled general bank balance shown in Figure 9.8.

Justin Case, General Journal					GJ3
Date 20**		Description	PR	Debit	Credit
Nov.	30	Bank Charges and Credit Card Expense	507	15.00	
		General Bank Account	100		15.00
		To record bank charges for November			

FIGURE 9.12   General journal entry to record bank charges

Reconciling the Mixed Trust Bank Account

In Chapter 5 you learned how to enter data into the trust bank journal and post to the client trust and general ledgers. You will need to have the bank statement and these records on hand when preparing the bank reconciliation statement for a mixed trust account.

Bylaw 9, part V, section 18(8) of the Law Society of Upper Canada requires that the monthly bank reconciliation statement be accompanied by a monthly **trust comparison** showing the amount of money held in trust for each client. This is done by preparing

- a reconciliation of the trust bank balance; and
- a detailed listing showing the amount of money held in trust for each client and identifying each client for whom money is held in trust.

Bylaw 9, part V, section 22(2) requires that you complete the trust bank reconciliation and trust comparison by the 25th day of each month for all trust funds held in the previous month. The bank statement for the previous month is usually sent out before the end of the second week of the following month, so the 25th gives you plenty of time to prepare the reconciliation. (See Figure 9.13.) Any discrepancies discovered in the trust account records should be corrected as soon as they are discovered. Any bank or posting errors should be corrected before the month-end.

Bear in mind that you must reconcile each trust bank account operated by the firm, including interest-bearing accounts, GICs, and term deposits, every month—even if there was no activity in the account for a particular month.

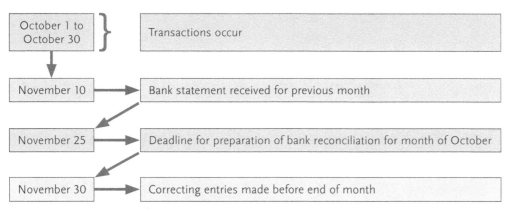

FIGURE 9.13   Timeline for mixed trust bank reconciliation

The process followed to complete the trust bank reconciliation statement is similar to reconciling the general bank account, but with a few added steps.

EXAMPLE 2

STEP 1

Compare the cheque images of the cancelled cheques with the entries shown on the trust bank statement (Figure 9.14) and note any discrepancies in the amounts shown. Verify whether the error was made by the bank or by the firm, and make any necessary corrections.

STEP 2

Outstanding cheques: Compare the cheque entries on the trust bank statement with those in the trust bank journal or deposit book. Check off all cheques that cleared the bank in your records (we have used the trust bank journal; see Figure 9.15) and on the trust bank account statement (Figure 9.14). List any outstanding cheques, including the cheque number, date of issue, and amount on the bank reconciliation, then place the total on the "Less: Outstanding Cheques" line (Figure 9.17).

STEP 3

Outstanding deposits: Compare the entries on the bank statement with the entries in the trust bank journal or the deposit book for the trust bank account. Check off all corresponding deposits on the trust bank statement and trust bank journal, noting any discrepancies in the amounts. Note that in this example, the deposit $1,600 is shown as two entries in the trust bank journal but as one amount on the trust bank account statement. Any deposits for the previous month that are not recorded on the bank statement should be listed by date and amount. Enter the total amount of the outstanding deposits on the "Plus: Outstanding Deposits" line on the trust bank account reconciliation (Figure 9.17).

STEP 4

List any bank errors and/or posting errors individually by date of occurrence, and provide a brief explanation. A copy of any supporting documentation, such as a bank memo, should be attached to your reconciliation.

ROYAL BANK OF MONEY
P.O. Box 5011, Station A
Montreal, QC H3C 3B8

Trust Bank Account Statement

Justin Case, Paralegal, Trust
135 Main Street
Yourtown, Ontario K3P 1G9

October 1, 20** to October 31, 20**

Account number: 0216-520635

ACCOUNT SUMMARY FOR THIS PERIOD

Opening Balance on Oct. 1, 20**		$0.00
Total Deposits and Credits	+	$4,100.00
Total Cheques and Debits	−	$2,820.00
Closing Balance on Oct. 31, 20**	=	$1,280.00

ACCOUNT ACTIVITY DETAILS

Date	Description	Cheques and Debits	Deposits and Credits	Balance
Oct. 03	Deposit		1,600.00 ✓	1,600.00
Oct. 08	Chq. #1	20.00 ✓		1,580.00
Oct. 16	Deposit		2,500.00 ✓	4,080.00
Oct. 30	Chq. #2	2,500.00 ✓		1,580.00
	Closing Balance			1,580.00

Please check this Account Statement without delay and advise us of any error or omission within 45 days of the statement date.
Royal Bank of Money GST Registration Number: R1052481028

FIGURE 9.14 Trust bank account statement

		Justin Case, Paralegal Trust Bank Journal					TJ1
Date 20**		Received From/ Paid To	File No.	Client/Description	Method of Payment	Trust Bank Account	
						Dr.	Cr.
Oct.	2	Rec. Cliff Howes	1	Cliff Howes/Retainer	Money Order	1,000 ✓	
	3	Pd. Deliveries Inc.	1	Cliff Howes/Courier	Chq. #1		20 ✓
	3	Rec. Frank Jones	2	Frank Jones/Retainer	Credit Card $500 Cash $100	600 ✓	
	15	Rec. James Settlor	1	Cliff Howes/Settlement	Bank Draft	2,500 ✓	
	16	Pd. Cliff Howes	1	Cliff Howes/Settlement	Chq. #2		2,500 ✓
	20	Pd. Minister of Finance	2	Jones/Payment of Fine	Chq. #3		300 **o/s**
	31	Totals				4,100	2,820
						(115)	(115)

FIGURE 9.15 Trust bank journal

STEP 5

Calculate the reconciled mixed trust balance on the bank reconciliation form. Enter this amount on the "Reconciled Mixed Trust Balance" line.

STEP 6

Client trust listing:

- Prepare a list of client balances from the client trust ledgers, identifying the clients for whom you held funds in trust at the end of the previous month.
- List the client names with the balance in the trust accounts, including the last activity date, to help you monitor inactive or dormant accounts.
- Total the client trust listing as shown in Figure 9.16. Enter the information from the client trust listing in the "Client Trust Listing" section, as shown in Figure 9.17.

STEP 7

Trust comparison: Compare the reconciled trust bank balance (Figure 9.17) with the client trust listing total (Figure 9.16). The two amounts should be equal. If the amounts are not the same, you must find and correct the discrepancy.

Justin Case, Paralegal
TRUST BANK RECONCILIATION
as at October 31, 20

TRUST BANK ACCOUNT

Balance per Bank Statement	1,580
Less: Outstanding Cheques (See list below)	300
Plus: Outstanding Deposits	
List:	
Plus/Minus Bank Error	
Reconciled Mixed Trust Balance at October 31, 20**	1,280

Outstanding Cheques

Cheque Number	Date	Amount
Chq. #3	Oct. 20, 20**	300
Total Outstanding Cheques		300

CLIENT TRUST LISTING
(from clients' trust ledger balances)
as at October 31, 20

File Name	Last Activity Date	Amount
1. HOWES, Cliff re Small Claims Court	Oct. 15, 20**	980
2. JONES, Frank re *Highway Traffic Act*	Oct. 9, 20**	300
Total Trust Liabilities to Clients at October 31, 20**		1,280

TRUST COMPARISON
as at October 31, 20

Reconciled Trust Bank Balance	1,280
Total of unexpected balances per client's trust ledger	1,280

FIGURE 9.17   Trust bank account reconciliation

Justin Case, Paralegal
List of Balances Owed to Clients
October 31, 20

File No.	Account	Last Activity Date	Balance Owed
1	HOWES, Cliff re Small Claims Court	Oct. 15	980.00
2	JONES, Frank re *Highway Traffic Act*	Oct. 9	300.00
	Total Owed to Clients		1,280.00

FIGURE 9.16   Client trust listing

Reviewing the Trust Bank Reconciliation

When you review the monthly trust comparisons you should:

- Ensure that the bank reconciliations are prepared before the 25th of the month.
- List items that were reconciled, giving a clear explanation that can be traced to the bank statement. You will be required to provide this information to the LSUC when you file your annual report.
- If you notice cheques that have remained uncashed for more than two months, follow up to see why they were not cashed. You might need to put a stop payment on a cheque if it has been lost, and a replacement cheque will then need to be prepared.
- If a cheque is stale-dated (more than six months old), a stop payment should be placed on it. If this is done, a reversing entry will be required placing the funds back in the client's trust ledger account. You will need to inquire as to why it was not cashed and provide a replacement cheque, if necessary.
- Ensure that the balance in each client's trust ledger is correct. If an amount was entered in the wrong client's account, this will not be revealed by the bank reconciliation process. The paralegal reviewing the client listing should notice if an amount shown on a client's trust ledger appears to be incorrect.
- Once work on a file has been finished, an invoice should be sent to the client. If funds remain in trust, a refund should also be sent.
- If the bank is taking bank charges out of the trust account, make sure that the bank is contacted and an arrangement is made for all bank charges to be taken out of the general bank account.

Maintenance and Retention of General and Trust Records

The financial records required to be maintained for general and trust accounts may be entered and posted by hand or by mechanical or electronic means, but if the records are entered and posted by hand, this should be done in ink.[3] If electronic records are maintained, a licensee must ensure that a paper copy of the record can be produced promptly on the LSUC's request.[4] If records are kept electronically, it is important to back them up frequently in case of a computer crash. Bylaw 9 also requires that trust financial records be entered and posted so that they are current at all times.[5]

General Bank Records

The financial records required by the LSUC related to general bank accounts must be kept for at least the six-year period immediately preceding the licensee's most recent fiscal year-end.[6] These records include the fees book, general receipts and disbursements journals, general

---

3 Bylaw 9, part V, s 21(1).

4 Bylaw 9, part V, s 21(2).

5 Bylaw 9, part V, s 22(1).

6 Bylaw 9, part V, s 23(1).

ledgers, and all related bank records such as passbooks, cancelled cheques, and bank reconciliations. If money is received in cash, a book of duplicate receipts must be kept for the most recent six full years plus the current year.

Trust Bank Records

The financial records related to trust accounts required by the LSUC must be kept for 10 years plus the current year.[7] These records include the trust bank journal, trust transfer journal, the monthly trust reconciliation, valuable property record, and all bank passbooks, cashed cheques, signed electronic trust transfer requisitions, and printed confirmations of electronic transfers.

Dormant Accounts

Dormant accounts are funds held in trust on behalf of a client that are unclaimed. Perhaps a client paid a retainer and then disappeared, and you have been unable to contact her over a period of two years. Section 59.6 of the *Law Society Act* permits a licensee to apply for permission to transfer such funds to the LSUC if the client cannot be located despite reasonable efforts after two years, or if the lawyer or licensed paralegal is unable to determine who is entitled to the money. The procedure for transferring such moneys to the LSUC is set out in bylaw 10.

Documentation for a CRA Audit

Regardless of whether your business is organized as a sole proprietorship, partnership, or corporation, there is a high likelihood that it will be audited by the Canada Revenue Agency (CRA) at some point.

The CRA auditor can examine books and records, documents, previous tax returns, and business records including ledgers, journals, invoices, receipts, contracts, and bank statements with bank reconciliations. Your personal records such as bank statements, mortgage documents, and credit card statements, as well as personal or business records of a spouse or family member, may be included. Adjustments made by your bookkeeper or accountant to arrive at income for tax purposes can also be reviewed.

TAX TIP

---

7   Bylaw 9, part V, s 23(2).

CHAPTER SUMMARY

The objective of this chapter has been to outline the obligations of a licensee with respect to reviewing the accounting records at the end of each month to ensure that the requirements of the Law Society of Upper Canada are being met. Reconciling the general bank account promptly each month is part of the month-end process before completing your financial statements. If the duties of operating and maintaining bank accounts are delegated to others, the reconciliation will enable the licensee to evaluate whether tasks are being performed correctly and in compliance with LSUC rules. Any errors or differences identified by the reconciliation may alert you to a need for greater supervision of employees who may need additional training.

KEY TERMS

cash controls, 220
cash short and over, 223
deposit in transit, 225
dormant accounts, 235
drawee, 224
drawer, 224
endorsement, 223
NSF cheque, 225
outstanding cheque, 225
payee, 224
payor, 224
petty cash, 220
reconciliation, 224
service charges, 225
signature card, 223
trust comparison, 230

FURTHER READING

Canadian Bankers Association (CBA), "Cheques—What You Need to Know," online: <http://www.cba.ca/en/consumer-information/40-banking-basics/584-cheques-what-you-need-to-know>. See the section "Cheque Cashed by a Different Individual (Counter-Signed Cheques)." The CBA advises consumers, "Check with your financial institution to find out if counter-signed cheques are accepted."

Law Society of Upper Canada, "Reconciling a Trust Account," online: <http://www.lsuc.on.ca/For-Lawyers/Manage-Your-Practice/Financial-Management/Billing/Collections/Trust-Accounts/Reconciling-a-Trust-Account>.

Law Society of Upper Canada, *The Bookkeeping Guide for Paralegals* (Toronto: LSUC, February 2014) at 71–72 ("Monthly Financial Review Checklist"), online: <http://www.lsuc.on.ca/uploadedFiles/PDC/Practice_Review/Paralegal Bookkeeping Guide - February 2014.pdf>.

PUT IT INTO PRACTICE

Case Example: Trust Bank Account Reconciliation

Ann Litigate compared her trust bank account statement against her trust bank journal and noticed a discrepancy. Review the following trust receipts and disbursements journals, trust bank account ledger, and trust bank statement for Ann Litigate for the month of May 20** and advise her on how to prepare a bank reconciliation by answering the following questions.

a. Are there any outstanding deposits for the period?
b. Are there any outstanding cheques for the period?
c. Are there any withdrawals made from the trust bank account for such items as service and bank charges that do not appear in the journals?
d. What is the bank balance at the end of the month shown on the trust bank statement?
e. What is the bank balance shown in the trust bank account ledger?
f. What needs to be done to reconcile the two amounts?
g. What should the total of the client trust ledgers and the reconciled bank balance be?

Trust Receipts Journal				TRJ1
Date 20**	Received from	Description	Method of Payment	Amount
May 1	S. Bailey	S. Bailey—Retainer	Chq. #058	1,500
12	C. Smythe	C. Smythe—Retainer	Chq. #021	1,000
15	D. Pitt	D. Pitt—Retainer	Chq. #002	1,750
28	R. Park, Defendant	F. Moore—Settlement	Chq. #011	5,000
30	K. Thomas	K. Thomas—Retainer	Chq. #095	2,000
			Total	11,250
				(115)

Trust Disbursements Journal				TDJ1
Date 20**	Paid to	Description	Method of Payment	Amount
May 5	Ann Litigate	F. Moore—Courier charges recoverable	Trust Chq. #0023	40
12	Ann Litigate	B. Daley—Paid invoice #350	Trust Chq. #0024	1,100
30	F. Moore	F. Moore—Settlement	Trust Chq. #0025	5,000
			Total	6,140
				(115)

Trust Bank Account						Account No. 115
Date 20**	Description	PR	Debit	Credit	Dr./Cr.	Balance
May 1	Opening Balance					0
30	Trust Totals for May	TJ1	11,250	6,140	Dr.	5,110

ABC Credit Union
Trust Bank Statement
May 1 to May 30, 20**

Date 20**	Description	Ref.	Debit (Withdrawals)	Credit (Deposits)	Balance
	BALANCE FORWARD				0
May 1	Deposit			$1,500	$1,500
5	Cheque	23	$40		$1,460
12	Deposit			$1,000	$2,460
15	Cheque	24	$1,100		$1,360
15	Deposit			$1,750	$3,110
28	Deposit			$5,000	$8,110
30	Deposit			$2,000	$10,110
	Total Debits (Withdrawals) and Credits (Deposits)		$1,140	$11,250	
	Closing Balance				$10,110

REVIEW QUESTIONS

True or False

_____ 1. Bylaw 9 of the Law Society of Upper Canada requires that the general bank ledger be reconciled by the 25th day of the following month after the date of the bank statement.

_____ 2. The petty cash account balance is changed only when establishing, increasing, or decreasing the petty cash balance limit.

_____ 3. Outstanding cheques are added to the bank statement balance.

_____ 4. "Deposit to the Credit of" is an example of a full endorsement.

_____ 5. Deposits in transit are added to the bank statement balance.

_____ 6. Adjustments to the bank statement balance require an adjustment entry in the general journal.

_____ 7. After preparing the·trust bank reconciliation, any bank or posting errors should be corrected before the end of the month in which the most recent bank statement is received.

_____ 8. The ending balances on the general bank ledger or trust bank ledger must equal the ending bank statement balance in order for the records to be reconciled.

_____ 9. Petty cash is an expense account reflected on the income statement.

_____ 10. The value of the petty cash account is equal to the petty cash voucher total and the remaining cash balance in the petty cash box.

Short Answer

Give a full answer for each question:

1. Discuss the following statement: "It is important to keep receipts for any credit or debit card payments."

2. What are some of the goals of internal controls for a business? What are some key considerations for paralegals? (See Law Society of Upper Canada, *The Bookkeeping Guide for Paralegals*, in Further Reading.)

3. What are the record-keeping requirements for general bank account records and trust bank account records, as set out in bylaw 9? For how long must the records be kept?

4. What are the seven steps involved in reconciling the trust bank account against the trust bank ledger?

PRACTICE EXERCISES

Practice Exercise 9.1

Ann Litigate advises her administrative assistant to establish a petty cash fund with a limit of $150 for minor and day-to-day expenses. Ann also advises the administrative assistant that, as custodian of the petty cash fund, she is to replenish the petty cash on a monthly basis.

a. Prepare the general journal entry to show the establishment of the account (January 1, 20**).

b. Based on the following petty cash expenses for the month, prepare the petty cash record tracking expenses:

Jan. 6   Courier charges, Voucher #1 ($15)

Jan. 10   Postage, Voucher #2 ($10.65)

Jan. 12   Parking, Voucher #3 ($12.75)

Jan. 17   Office supplies, miscellaneous, Voucher #4 ($33.50)

Jan. 23   Courier charges, Voucher #5 ($18)

Jan. 27   Postage, Voucher #6 ($10.65)

Jan. 30   Parking, Voucher #7 ($12.75)

c. Prepare the journal entries showing the expenses from the petty cash record tracking expenses and the replenishment of the petty cash fund (January 31, 20**).

PRACTICE

EXCEL

	Ann Litigate Paralegal Services General Journal				GJ3
Date 20**	Description		PR	Debit	Credit

HINT

Check and Balance Petty Cash Fund
The amount of cash on hand plus the amount of all petty cash vouchers is equal to the total value of the fund.

Total paid out	$113.30
Cash in petty cash box	36.70
Total petty cash fund	$150.00

Practice Exercise 9.2

Review and compare Ann Litigate's general bank account ledger for January 20** and the general bank statement for the month-end January 31.

   a. Record and note any differences and discrepancies.

   b. Prepare the bank reconciliation using the worksheet provided.

   c. Prepare adjusting journal entries in the general journal in respect of any corrections.

General Bank Account						Account No. 100	
Date 20**		Explanation	PR	Debit	Credit	Dr./Cr.	Balance
Jan.	1	Opening Balance	GJ2			Dr.	6,300.00
	1	Cheque #11	GJ2		1,500.00	Dr.	4,800.00
	20	Transfer from Trust re Invoice #14-201	GJ2	800.00		Dr.	5,600.00
	30	Cheque #12	GJ2		1,300.00	Dr.	4,300.00
	31	Cheque #13	GJ2		118.73	Dr.	4,181.27
	31	Cheque #14	GJ2		450.00	Dr.	3,731.27

Bank Statement (General Bank Account)

Ann Litigate Paralegal Services
11 Any Street, Ottawa, ON K1A 0B0

ABC Bank
1000 Front St.
Ottawa, ON

Jan. 1 – Jan. 31, 20

Date	Description	Reference	Debit	Credit		Balance
December 31, 20**	Balance Forward				Cr.	$6,300.00
January 1, 20**	Cheque #11	200	1,500.00		Cr.	$4,800.00
January 3, 20**	Deposit—Cheque	121		1,000.00	Cr.	$5,800.00
January 19, 20**	ATM W/D	004430	11.50		Cr.	$5,788.50
January 20, 20**	TFR FR 10002	JXY01		800.00	Cr.	$6,588.50
January 30, 20**	Cheque #12	203	1,300.00		Cr.	$5,288.50
January 31, 20**	Service Charge		23.00		Cr.	$5,265.50
	Total Debits and Credits		$2,834.50	$1,800.00		
	Closing Balance					$5,265.50

Note re bank statement: Debit (Withdrawal); Credit (Deposit)

Ann Litigate Paralegal Services
GENERAL BANK RECONCILIATION
as at January 31, 20**

GENERAL BANK ACCOUNT

Balance per Bank Statement	
Less: Outstanding Cheques (See list below)	
Plus: Outstanding Deposits	
Plus/Minus Bank Error	
Reconciled General Bank Balance at January 31, 20**	

Outstanding Cheques

Cheque Number	Date	Amount
Total Outstanding Cheques		

BALANCE PER BOOKS

Balance per General Bank Account Ledger	
Add: Deposits by Bank Not Shown in Books	
Deduct: Bank Charges	
ATM Withdrawals	
Bank Errors	
NSF Cheque	
Adjusted Balance per Books at January 31, 20**	

PRACTICE
EXCEL

	Ann Litigate Paralegal Services General Journal				GJ2
Date 20**	Description	PR	Debit	Credit	

Practice Exercise 9.3

Review and compare Ann Litigate's trust bank account ledger for January 20** and the trust bank statement for the month-end January 31.

a. Record and note any differences and discrepancies. Note that an error was made by the bookkeeper when cheque #0138 was entered. The amount should have been entered as $260 instead of $280. Remember that the service charge should not appear in the trust bank account.

b. Prepare the bank reconciliation using the worksheet provided.

c. Compare the reconciled trust bank balance with the client trust listing total.

d. Prepare the adjusting journal entry in the trust bank journal provided in respect of any corrections.

Trust Bank Account							Account No. 115	
Date 20**		Explanation	PR	Debit	Credit	Dr./Cr.	Balance	
Jan.	1	Opening Balance	TJ2			Dr.	10,000.00	
	1	Retainer Received— A. Paulo, Cheque #11225	TJ2	1,500.00		Dr.	11,500.00	
	3	Refund to Client from Trust— B. Saul, Cheque #0138	TJ2		280.00	Dr.	11,220.00	
	20	Transfer from Trust re Invoice #14-201	TJ2		800.00	Dr.	10,420.00	
	30	Retainer Received— C. Charles, Cheque #002	TJ2	2,000.00		Dr.	12,420.00	

Bank Statement (Trust Bank Account)						
Ann Litigate Paralegal Services						
11 Any Street, Ottawa, ON K1A 0B0						
ABC Bank						
1000 Front St.						
Ottawa, ON						
Jan. 1 – Jan. 31, 20**						
Date	Description	Reference	Debit	Credit		Balance
December 31, 20**	Balance Forward				Cr.	$10,000.00
January 1, 20**	Deposit—Cheque	11225		1,500.00	Cr.	$11,500.00
January 3, 20**	Cheque	0138	260.00		Cr.	$11,240.00
January 20, 20**	TFR FR 10002	JXY01	800.00		Cr.	$10,440.00
January 31, 20**	Service Charge		23.00		Cr.	$10,417.00
	Total Debits and Credits		$1,083.00	$1,500.00		
	Closing Balance					$10,417.00

Note re bank statement: Debit (Withdrawal); Credit (Deposit)

Ann Litigate Paralegal Services
TRUST BANK RECONCILIATION
as at January 31, 20**

TRUST BANK ACCOUNT

Balance per Bank Statement

Less: Outstanding Cheques (See list below)

Plus: Outstanding Deposits

Plus/Minus Bank Error

Reconciled Mixed Trust Balance at January 31, 20**

Outstanding Cheques

Cheque Number	Date	Amount

Total Outstanding Cheques

BALANCE PER BOOKS

Balance per Trust Bank Account Ledger

Add: Deposits by Bank Not Shown in Books

Deduct: Bank Charges

             Bank Errors

             NSF Cheque

Adjustments

Chq. #0138   January 3, 20**

Incorrect Entry per Books

Correct Entry per Bank Statement

Add to Trust Bank Ledger

Adjusted Balance per Books at January 31, 20**

Ann Litigate Paralegal Services List of Balances, Trust Funds Owed January 31, 20**		
File No./Account Name	*Last Activity Date*	*Balance Owed*
File No. 101, Moore, C.	Nov. 15, 20**	2,100.00
File No. 102, Abernathy, L.	Dec. 1, 20**	1,700.00
File No. 103, Pasec, S.	Dec. 15, 20**	3,200.00
File No. 104, Smith, A.L.	Dec. 29, 20**	3,000.00
File No. 105, Saul, B.	Jan. 3, 20**	(260.00)
File No. 106, Reuter, D.	Jan. 20, 20**	(800.00)
File No. 107, Charles, C.	Jan. 30, 20**	2,000.00
File No. 108, Paulo, A.	Jan. 1, 20**	1,500.00
Total Trust Funds Owed		$12,440.00

Ann Litigate Paralegal Services Trust Bank Journal						TJ2
Date 20**		Received From/ Paid To	File No.	Client/Description	Method of Payment	Trust Bank Account
						Dr.	Cr.

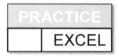

PRACTICE

EXCEL

10 Accounting for GST/HST, Payroll, and Income Tax

After reading this chapter, you should be able to:

- describe different methods for calculating GST/HST and making remittances to the Canada Revenue Agency
- calculate, record, and remit payroll deductions
- explain common income tax considerations

Goods and Services Tax

The goods and services tax is a multi-level, value-added tax that was introduced in Canada on January 1, 1991 by then Prime Minister Brian Mulroney and his finance minister, Michael Wilson. Most Canadians and Canadian companies must pay **GST/HST** on their purchases, including legal fees. Some groups and organizations, such as diplomats, governments, and status Indians, are exempt from paying GST/HST. However, if a false claim for exemption is made by a client, and even if a fake exemption card is presented to avoid paying the tax, you as the business owner still must account for the tax you should have collected.

The provinces of New Brunswick, Nova Scotia, Newfoundland and Labrador, Ontario, and Prince Edward Island, referred to as the participating provinces, harmonized their provincial sales tax with the GST to create the harmonized sales tax (HST). The current rate for HST in Ontario for April 1, 2013 and subsequent years is 13 percent, which includes the 5 percent federal rate and the 8 percent provincial rate.

As mentioned in Chapter 1, as a paralegal you are considered a **small supplier**, exempted from collecting GST/HST if your total annual revenues from all of your businesses are $30,000 or less.

Remitting GST/HST to the Receiver General

To complete a GST/HST return, you need to know the following amounts:

- Your total fees and disbursements or other revenues on which you charge GST/HST.
- The amount of GST/HST you charged (even if it was not collected).
- The amount of GST/HST you paid or is payable on purchases you made for the business. This is referred to as your input tax credit (ITC).
- You might also have to include other amounts on your GST/HST report, such as installments you paid during the year or other adjustments being claimed.

If you are a sole proprietor with a fiscal year-end of December 31, and you have an annual reporting period for GST/HST purposes, your payment is due no later than April 30, although the return is not due until June 15. Payments may be made to the Receiver General using online banking, at a financial institution, or by mail. The Canada Revenue Agency does not accept credit cards. A penalty plus interest is charged on any balance owing if the return is not received by the CRA on time. The penalty is calculated as 1 percent of the amount owing, plus 25 percent of that amount multiplied by the number of months the return is overdue, up to 12 months.

Maintenance of Records

Usually, you have to keep all sales and purchase invoices and other **records** related to your business operations and the GST/HST for six years from the end of the year to which they relate. If you want to destroy your records after six years, the CRA recommends that you send a written request and wait for written approval to do so. As a registrant, you also need correct information on the invoices you get from your suppliers to support your **input tax credit (ITC)** claims. Registered businesses from which you purchase goods or services must provide invoices showing their GST/HST registration number and other required information. You can verify that a supplier provided you with a valid GST/HST number by using the CRA's online GST/HST Registry. The CRA administers an audit program during which auditors may ask to see your records. During an audit, the CRA will make sure that you have charged and reported the GST/HST when required, and that you are entitled to all the ITCs that you claim on your return.

Many rules apply to what can and cannot be claimed as an ITC. As a guideline, claim only those tax-deductible purchases that are authorized under the *Income Tax Act* on which GST/HST is charged. For example, under the *Income Tax Act*, the deduction for meals and entertainment expenses is limited to 50 percent of the cost of the meals and entertainment. Likewise, the ITCs you can claim for this expense are also limited to 50 percent of the amount paid. If you qualify to claim home office expenses for income tax purposes, you can claim the ITCs applicable to the portion of the home expenses you are allowed to deduct from your **income** for calculating your net income for tax purposes. A special calculation is required if you wish to claim GST/HST paid on the purchase of a vehicle. The amount you are allowed for GST/HST is based on what you are entitled to claim based on the permissible capital cost allowance (CCA). You are advised to check the CRA website information on claiming ITCs or speak to a tax professional to ensure the amounts you claim are allowed.

Methods for Calculating GST/HST Remittance

There are three methods used for tracking GST/HST:

- The regular method
- The simplified method
- The quick method

The quick method will not be discussed here because persons who provide legal, accounting, or actuarial services in the course of their professional practice are not permitted to use it.

A paralegal may use either the regular or the simplified method for calculating the amount of GST/HST that must be remitted to the Receiver General.

Regular Method

If you plan to use the regular method for submitting GST/HST remittances, you should ensure that your journals and ledgers are set up with the necessary columns for tracking GST/HST billed to clients and GST/HST paid or payable on purchases by the firm. This will provide you with the data you need for completing the returns. To use the regular method for calculating the amount of GST/HST you need to remit, you will need to know

- the total amount of fees billed to clients on which GST/HST was charged over the reporting period;

GOODS AND SERVICES TAX / HARMONIZED SALES TAX (GST/HST) RETURN WORKING COPY

Do not use this printer-friendly version to file your return or to make payments at your financial institution.

Business Number	Name	
Reporting period From: to:	Due date	**Working copy (for your records)**

▶ Copy your Business Number, the reporting period, and the amounts from the **highlighted** line numbers in this worksheet to the corresponding boxes in your GST/HST return.

Enter your total **sales and other revenue**. Do not include provincial sales tax, GST or HST.
If you are using the Quick Method of accounting, include the GST or HST. **101** |00

NET TAX CALCULATION

Enter the total of all **GST and HST amounts that you collected or that became collectible** by you in the reporting period. **103**

Enter the total amount of **adjustments** to be added to the net tax for the reporting period (for example, GST/HST obtained from the recovery of a bad debt). **104**

Total GST/HST and adjustments for period (add lines 103 and 104) ➡ **105**

Enter the GST/HST you paid or that is payable by you on qualifying expenses **(input tax credits – ITCs)** for the current period and any eligible unclaimed ITCs from a previous period. **106**

Enter the total amount of **adjustments** to be deducted when determining the net tax for the reporting period (for example, GST/HST included in a bad debt). **107**

Total ITCs and adjustments (add lines 106 and 107) ➡ **108**

NET TAX (subtract line 108 from line 105). If the result is negative, enter a minus sign in the separate box next to the line number. **109**

OTHER CREDITS IF APPLICABLE

Do not complete line 111 until you have read the instructions.

Enter any **instalment and other annual filer payments** you made for the reporting period. If the due date of your return is June 15, see the instructions. **110**

Enter the total amount of the GST/HST **rebates**, **only** if the rebate form indicates that you can claim the amount on this line. For filing information, see instructions. **111**

Total other credits (add lines 110 and 111) ➡ **112**

BALANCE (subtract line 112 from line 109). If the result is negative, enter a minus sign in the separate box next to the line number. **113 A**

OTHER DEBITS IF APPLICABLE

Do not complete line 205 or line 405 until you have read the instructions.

Enter the total amount of the **GST/HST due on the acquisition of taxable real property**. **205**

Enter the total amount of other **GST/HST to be self-assessed**. **405**

Total other debits (add lines 205 and 405) ➡ **113 B**

BALANCE (add lines 113 A and 113 B). If the result is negative, enter a minus sign in the separate box next to the line number. **113 C**

Line 114 and line 115: If the result entered on line 113 C is a negative amount, enter the amount of the refund you are claiming on line 114. If the result entered on line 113 C is a positive amount, enter the amount of your payment on line 115.

REFUND CLAIMED	PAYMENT ENCLOSED
114	**115**

Instructions

Line 110
Annual filer with a June 15 due date: If you are an individual with business income for income tax purposes and have a December 31 fiscal year-end, the due date of your return is June 15. However, any GST/HST you owe is payable by April 30. This payment should be reported on line 110 of your GST/HST Tax Return.

Line 111: Some rebates can reduce or offset your amount owing. Those rebate forms contain a question asking you if you want to claim the rebate amount on line 111 of your GST/HST Tax Return. Tick **yes** on the rebate form(s) if you are claiming the rebate(s) on line 111 of your GST/HST Tax Return. If you file your return electronically, send the rebate application by mail to the Summerside Tax Centre.

Line 205: Complete this line **only** if you purchased taxable real property for use or supply primarily (more than 50%) in your commercial activities and you are a GST/HST registrant (other than an individual who purchases a residential complex) or you purchased the property from a non-resident. If you qualify for an input tax credit on the purchase, include this amount on line 108.

Line 405: Complete this line **only** if you are a GST/HST registrant who has to self-assess GST/HST on an imported taxable supply or who has to self-assess the provincial part of HST.

FIGURE 10.1 GST/HST return working copy. Reproduced with permission of the Minister of Public Works and Government Services Canada, 2015.

- the total amount of GST/HST you charged to clients, whether or not it has been collected;
- the total amount you paid or is payable on tax-deductible purchases for GST/HST; and
- the difference between the amount of GST/HST collected from clients and the amount of GST/HST paid or payable for purchases. This is the amount of net tax that either needs to be remitted or for which you are entitled to a refund.

If you are using legal software for accounting purposes, the calculation of these amounts and preparation of a report is usually done automatically. Figure 10.1, above, shows the GST/HST return working copy that is available on the CRA website.[1]

Simplified Method

When you use the simplified method, your bookkeeping records do not need to show the purchase price of goods and GST/HST paid separately. To be eligible to use this method, your annual fees income and your purchases must be $1 million or less. To calculate your GST/HST, add up your ITC-eligible **business expenses**, including the GST/HST paid. You may not include expenses on which no GST/HST is payable, such as salaries, and can claim the GST/HST charged only on purchases deductible as legitimate business expenses under the *Income Tax Act*. For example, if you are living in Ontario, which has a combined GST/HST rate of 13 percent (5 percent federal and 8 percent provincial), the simplified method calculation would be as follows:

Description	Expenses
Rent (includes HST)	$1,070.00
Salaries (HST does not apply)	3,000.00
Insurance (HST does not apply)	50.00
Advertising (HST included)	214.00
Office supplies (HST included)	230.00
Total purchases and expenses	$4,564.00
Step 1	
• Add all purchases and expenses including the HST (GST and PST)	$4,564.00
• Subtract non-taxable items (salaries and insurance)	−3,050.00
Taxable expenses	$1,514.00
Step 2	
• Multiply taxable expenses on which you paid 13 percent HST by 13/113 to calculate the input tax credit	$174.18

FIGURE 10.2 Simplified calculation of GST/HST

---

1 Canada Revenue Agency, "Goods and Services Tax/Harmonized Sales Tax (GST/HST) Return Working Copy," online: <http://www.cra-arc.gc.ca/tx/bsnss/tpcs/gst-tps/bspsbch/rtrns/rtrnwkcpy-eng.pdf>.

Calculate your net tax for each GST/HST reporting period and report this on your GST/HST return. To do so, calculate

- the GST/HST collected or that became collectible by you on the fees billed during the reporting period and
- the GST/HST payable using the simplified calculation above; then
- take the difference between these two amounts, including any adjustments, to arrive at your net tax.

A positive amount must be remitted to the Receiver General. If the GST/HST paid is more than the GST/HST you charged or collected, you can claim a refund for the difference.

Note that the GST/HST rate used above is for Ontario, and the multiplier of 13/113 will vary with the GST/HST rates for your province.

Deciding which method is best for you for calculating GST/HST is complicated. You may wish to speak to an accountant when making a decision.

Remitting GST/HST

Before the end of each GST/HST reporting period, you will receive a form to complete from the CRA that must be filled in and returned along with any payment owing. If you file quarterly, you must send the return along with the amount owing before the end of the following month. That is, a report covering January to March would have to be filed before the end of April. If you file annually, the report must be sent within three months after the end of the one-year period. Remittances may be made by filing online, at a financial institution, or by mail.

Payroll

Salaries can represent a large part of the operating expenses for a firm. Employers are responsible for deducting Canada Pension Plan (CPP) contributions, employment insurance (EI) premiums, and income tax from remuneration paid to employees and for remitting the deductions to the Canada Revenue Agency along with the required reports. If you do not fulfill your obligations or comply with payroll requirements, you may be assessed a penalty with interest, or incur other consequences. On prosecution, a person can be fined from $1,000 to $25,000 or fined and imprisoned for a term of up to 12 months. The CRA can assess a penalty of 10 percent of the amount of CPP, EI, and income tax that was not deducted and will apply a penalty of 20 percent to second or later failures, under certain circumstances.

When you hire an employee, you must:

- obtain your employee's social insurance number (SIN) and
- obtain from your employee a completed Form TD1, Personal Tax Credits Return.[2]

The Payroll Process

Gross pay will be established with the employee at the time of hire. It may be a salary based on various pay periods, usually weekly, biweekly, or monthly. When hiring an employee, you should ensure there is a clear understanding of the rate being paid, the hours of work, and other benefits, such as sick days and vacation time.

---

2 Canada Revenue Agency, "Filing Form TD1, Personal Tax Credits Return," online: <http://www.cra-arc.gc.ca/tx/bsnss/tpcs/pyrll/hwpyrllwrks/stps/hrng/td1/menu-eng.html>.

Suppose Justin Case hires an assistant who will work from 8:30 to 5:00 every day (with one hour off for lunch) at an hourly rate of $20 per hour. That would make for a 7.5-hour day or 37.5 hours a week. At the rate of $20 an hour, this would yield a gross pay of $750 a week. Justin will need to determine how frequently the employee will be paid to determine the gross pay for each pay period before the **payroll deductions** at source can be calculated.

Gross pay	$750 per week x 52 weeks	$39,000
Weekly	$39,000/52 pay periods	$750
Bi-weekly	$39,000/26 pay periods	$1,500
Twice a month	$39,000/24 pay periods	$1,625
Monthly	$39,000/12 pay periods	$3,250

FIGURE 10.3   Calculation of gross pay

TD1 Form

When hiring an employee, you must get your employee's social insurance number and have him or her fill in the TD1 form. This form is used to obtain the employee's claim code to determine the amount of income tax to be deducted from an individual's employment income. There are two forms that must be completed, one federal and one provincial or territorial. Employees complete the forms and give them to their employer, who should keep a completed form with their records.

For the purposes of this chapter, we will assume that Justin's assistant, Judith Wright, has completed the TD1 form and arrived at a claim code 1, because she was previously unemployed and has **personal deductions** she could claim, such as tuition fees and childcare expenses.

Payroll Calculator

The easiest way to calculate source deductions that must be taken from the employee's paycheque and the amounts you will need to remit as employer is to use the Payroll Deductions Online Calculator on the CRA website at <http://www.cra-arc.gc.ca/esrvc-srvce/tx/bsnss/pdoc-eng.html>. The CRA also has tables that can be used manually to look up the amount that must be deducted.

EXAMPLE 1

Justin Case went to the CRA website and used the payroll calculator to find out what deductions had to be taken and how much he would have to remit to the CRA for the pay period. Figure 10.4 shows the report obtained using the payroll calculator.

The report indicates that on a gross paycheque of $1,625.00, the amount of $150.23 must be deducted for federal taxes and $74.82 for provincial taxes, totalling $225.05. The deduction from

gross pay for CPP is $73.22 and for EI is $30.55. The total deductions come to $328.82, and Judith will receive a paycheque of $1,296.18.

Figure 10.5 shows the general journal entries required to record the salaries expense, the employer's payroll contributions, and the employer's remittance to the Receiver General for the salaries paid on December 15. The payroll deductions calculations from Figure 10.4 provide the information you need to make these entries.

Employee's name: Judith Wright Employer's name: Justin Case, Paralegal Pay period frequency: Twice a month (24 pay periods a year) Date the employee is paid: 2014-12-15 Province of employment: Ontario Federal amount from TD1: Minimum—11,138.00 (Claim code 1) Provincial amount from TD1: Minimum—9,670.00 (Claim code 1)			
Salary or wages income (assume $750 gross/week)		1,625.00	
Total cash income			1,625.00
Taxable income for the pay period		1,625.00	
Pensionable earnings for the pay period		1,625.00	
Insurable earnings for the pay period		1,625.00	
Federal tax deduction (Payroll Tax Table, D)	150.23		
Provincial tax deduction (Payroll Tax Table, E)	74.82		
Total tax deductions		225.05	
CPP deductions (Payroll Tax Table, B)		73.22	
EI deductions (Payroll Tax Table, C) *The employer's EI premium is equal to 1.4 times the employee's premium, unless a reduced rate applies.*		30.55	
Total deductions			328.82
Net amount			1,296.18
Employer Remittance Summary			
Employee CPP contributions	73.22		
Employer CPP contributions	73.22		
Subtotal of Canada Pension Plan (CPP)		146.44	
Employee EI contributions	30.55		
Employer EI contributions	42.77		
Subtotal of Employment Insurance (EI)		73.32	
Tax deductions		225.05	
For this calculation, remit this amount		**444.81**	

FIGURE 10.4 **Payroll deductions online calculation**

STEP 1

December 15—This entry reflects that Judith Wright was paid $1,625.00 but received a cheque for $1,296.18 because the source deductions for income tax and her share of CPP and EI were taken off her paycheque. However, the firm is entitled to write off $1,625.00 as a salaries expense because that is its cost.

STEP 2

December 15—The firm contributes the employer's share of EI and CPP for Judith and is entitled to write those expenses off as a tax-deductible expense. Because the remittance is not sent immediately, it is posted to the payroll clearing account as a liability.

STEP 3

December 31—When the firm forwards the source deductions taken from Judith's salary on the 15th plus the employer's share it owes, the liability account Payroll Clearing (#217) is debited, thus reducing it to zero, and a cheque payable to the Receiver General for the amount owing to the Canada Revenue Agency is credited to the general bank account.

Justin Case, Paralegal General Journal				GJ6
Date 20**	*Description*	*PR*	*Debit*	*Credit*
Dec. 15	Salaries Expense	511	1,625.00	
	Payroll Clearing, Income Taxes Payable	217		225.05
	Payroll Clearing, CPP Payable	217		73.22
	Payroll Clearing, EI Payable	217		30.55
	General Bank Account	100		1,296.18
	To record payroll for Dec. 15			
15	CPP Expense	518	73.22	
	EI Expense	517	42.77	
	Payroll Clearing, CPP Payable	217		73.22
	Payroll Clearing, EI Payable	217		42.77
	To record employer's payroll contributions			
31	Payroll Clearing	217	444.81	
	General Bank Account	100		444.81
	To record remittance to Receiver General for December			
	Totals		2,185.80	2,185.80

FIGURE 10.5 General journal entries recording payroll

Vacation Pay and Vacation Time

Employees are entitled to be paid vacation pay after their first full year of employment. Typically in Ontario, an employee is entitled to a minimum payment of 4 percent of gross annual earnings. The employee accrues vacation pay as he or she earns wages regardless of vacation time taken, not taken, or carried over.

Normally, employees take the time off and receive a regular paycheque while they are away. However, if their employment is terminated and vacation pay is owed, this must be paid and will be subject to the source deductions and employer contributions to CPP and EI described above.

The normal minimum vacation time is two weeks in each year that the employee is employed. The employment contract or policy agreement should deal with vacation time that is not taken or is carried over past the prescribed or agreed-upon deadline to take such vacation.[3]

---

3 Ontario Ministry of Labour, "Vacation Time and Vacation Pay," online: <http://www.labour.gov.on.ca/english/es/pubs/guide/vacation.php>.

Taxable Benefits

Some employers provide **taxable benefits** for their employees, such as medical and dental coverage and life insurance premiums. Some of these benefits are deemed to be taxable benefits in the hands of an employee and will be included on the T4 slip issued to the employee at the end of the year.

T4 Information Return

On or before the last day of February in each year, you must file a T4 **information return** with the CRA and provide each of your employees with a T4 slip for income tax purposes. A copy of each T4 slip prepared, as well as a T4 summary of remuneration paid, must be sent to the CRA. These forms can be obtained online on the CRA website.

Income Tax

Legal Requirements for Keeping Records

All records for **income tax** purposes, such as paper documents as well as those stored in an electronic medium (such as on computer disk), must be kept in Canada or made available in Canada at the request of the CRA. The records must be in English or French.

A business is required to keep orderly records of all income received. All receipts, invoices, vouchers, and cancelled cheques indicating outlays of money must also be kept. Such outlays include

- salaries and wages,
- operating expenses such as rent, advertising, and capital expenditures, and
- miscellaneous items such as charitable donations.

Records must be permanent and contain a systematic account of income, deductions, credits, and other information needed to file income tax and GST/HST returns. Incomplete records that use approximates instead of exact amounts are not acceptable. The records must

- allow you to determine how much tax you owe, or the tax, duties, or other amounts to be collected, withheld, or deducted, or any refund or rebate you may claim; and
- be supported by vouchers or other necessary source documents.

If you do not keep your receipts or other vouchers to support your expenses or claims, and there is no other evidence available, the CRA will probably reduce the expenses or claims you have made.

The Six-Year Requirement

If tax returns are filed on time, records must be retained (other than certain documents for which there are special rules) for six years from the end of the last **tax year** to which they relate. You must keep every record necessary for dealing with an objection or appeal until it is resolved and the time for filing any further appeal has expired, or until the six-year period mentioned above has expired, whichever is later.

Types of Operating Expenses

Personal or Living Expenses

In most cases, you cannot deduct personal and living expenses, except for travelling expenses you incur in the course of carrying on a business while away from home. The general rule is that you cannot deduct outlays or expenses that are not related to earning business income.

Prepaid Expenses

A prepaid expense is an expense you pay ahead of time. If you use the accrual method of accounting, claim any expense you prepay in the year or years in which you receive the related benefit.

Accounting and Legal Fees

You can deduct the fees you incurred for external professional advice or services, including consulting fees. You can deduct accounting and legal fees you incur to get advice and help in keeping your records. You can also deduct fees you incur for preparing and filing your income tax and GST/HST returns.

Advertising Expenses

You can deduct expenses for advertising, including advertisements in Canadian newspapers and on Canadian television and radio stations.

Bad Debts

You can deduct an amount for a **bad debt** if

- you had determined that an account receivable is a bad debt in the year, and
- you had already included the receivable in income.

For more information, see Interpretation Bulletin IT-442R, "Bad Debts and Reserves for Doubtful Debts."[4]

Business Tax, Fees, Licences, and Dues

You can deduct your annual licence fees, law association membership dues, and any business taxes you incur to run your business. However, you cannot deduct club membership dues (including initiation fees) if the main purpose of the club is to provide dining, recreational, or sporting facilities for its members.

Insurance Expenses

You can deduct all regular commercial insurance premiums you incur on any buildings, machinery, and equipment that you use for your business. Life insurance premiums are generally not deductible.

---

4   Canada Revenue Agency, "Bad Debts and Reserves for Doubtful Debts," online: <http://www.cra-arc
  .gc.ca/E/pub/tp/it442r/it442r-e.html>.

Interest and Bank Charges

You can deduct the interest you incur on money you borrow to run your business. There is a limit on the interest you can deduct on money you borrow to buy a passenger vehicle.

Maintenance and Repairs Expenses

You can deduct the cost of labour and materials for any minor repairs or maintenance done to property you use to earn income. However, you cannot deduct the value of your own labour. You cannot deduct costs you incur for repairs that are capital in nature, but you may be able to claim CCA on the repaired property. A capital expense generally gives a lasting benefit or advantage. For example, the cost of putting vinyl siding on the exterior walls of a wooden house is a capital expense.

Meals and Entertainment Expenses

The maximum you can claim for food, beverages, and entertainment expenses is 50 percent of either the amount you incur or an amount that is reasonable in the circumstances, whichever is less.

The 50 percent limit also applies to the cost of your meals when you travel or go to a convention, conference, or similar event. However, special rules can affect your claim for meals in these cases. The 50 percent limit does not apply if you incur meal and entertainment expenses to provide a Christmas party or similar event and you invite all your employees from a particular location; however, you are limited to six of these events each year. Also, the 50 percent limit does not apply to meal and entertainment expenses you incur for a fund-raising event that was mainly for the benefit of a registered charity.

Entertainment expenses include tickets and entrance fees to an entertainment or sporting event, gratuities, cover charges, and room rentals such as for hospitality suites. For more information, see Interpretation Bulletin IT-518R, "Food, Beverages and Entertainment Expenses."[5]

Motor Vehicle Expenses

When you are claiming motor vehicle expenses, note that travel from home to the office is not considered travel for business purposes.

You can deduct expenses you incur to run a motor vehicle that you use to earn business income. However, several factors can affect your deduction. The kind of vehicle you own can affect the expenses you deduct. You can deduct motor vehicle expenses only when they are reasonable and you have receipts to support them. The types of expenses you can deduct include the following:

- Fuel and oil
- Maintenance and repairs
- Insurance
- Licence and registration fees
- Capital cost allowance
- Interest you pay on a loan used to buy the motor vehicle
- Leasing costs

---

5 Canada Revenue Agency, "Food, Beverages and Entertainment Expenses," online: <http://www.cra-arc.gc.ca/E/pub/tp/it518r/it518r-e.pdf>.

Figure 10.6 shows the calculation of motor vehicle expenses for Justin Case. The deductible business portion of Justin's vehicle expenses is $4,770. He can also include additional fees he pays for business, such as parking fees of $40 or a supplementary business insurance cost of $100, to increase his deduction to $4,910.

Calculation of Motor Vehicle Expenses	
Kilometres driven to earn business income	27,000
Total kilometres driven in the year	30,000
Percentage for business use: 27,000/30,000 x 100	90%
Expenses:	
Gas and oil	2,400
Insurance	1,900
Interest	800
Maintenance and repairs	200
Total expenses for the car	5,300
Calculation of deduction for tax purposes: $5,300 x 90%	4,770

FIGURE 10.6   Calculating vehicle expenses

To get the full benefit of your claim for a vehicle, you must keep a record of the total kilometres you drive for personal use and the kilometres you drive to earn business income. For each business trip, list the date, destination, purpose, and number of kilometres you drive. Record the odometer reading of your vehicle at the start and end of the **fiscal period**.

You are allowed to claim capital cost allowance on the cost of the vehicle up to a maximum value of $30,000. The rate of depreciation allowed is 30 percent with an adjustment in the year of acquisition, which reduces the amount you are allowed to deduct for CCA by one-half.

Leasing Costs for a Passenger Vehicle

You can deduct amounts you incur to lease a motor vehicle you use to earn income. When you use a passenger vehicle to earn income, there is a limit on the amount of the leasing costs you can deduct. If the lease agreement for your passenger vehicle includes items such as insurance, maintenance, and taxes, include them as part of the lease charges.

Work Space in Home Expenses

If you rent the home in which you have a home office, you can deduct the part of the rent and any expenses you incur that relate to the work space. The amount you can deduct for business-use-of-home expenses cannot be more than your net income from the business before you deduct these expenses. In other words, you cannot use these expenses to increase or create a business loss.

EXAMPLE 2

Justin has space in his home devoted to the sole purpose of running his business. The business uses an area of 35 square metres. The house has 800 square metres, and the annual household expenses are $5,800.

The calculation to determine the tax deduction for use of the space is as follows:

$$35/800 \text{ square metres} \times \$5,800 \text{ expenses} = \$253.75$$

Justin can deduct a total of $253.75 for work space in home expenses. Because capital gain and recapture rules will apply if he deducts CCA on the business-use part of his home and he later sells the home, he should seek professional advice before doing this.

Computer and Other Equipment Expenses

If you lease computers, cellular telephones, fax machines, and other equipment, you can deduct the percentage of the lease costs that reasonably relate to earning your business income. You can also deduct the percentage of airtime expenses for a cellular telephone that reasonably relate to earning your business income. If you buy a computer, cellular telephone, fax machine, or other such equipment, you cannot deduct the actual cost. But you can deduct CCA and interest you paid on money you borrowed to buy this equipment that reasonably relates to earning your business income.

Convention Expenses

You can deduct the cost of going to a maximum of two conventions a year. The conventions must

- relate to your business or professional activity and
- be held by a business or professional organization within the geographical area where the organization normally conducts its business.

This second requirement may not apply if an organization from another country sponsors the convention and the convention relates to your business or professional activity.

Sometimes, convention fees include the cost of food, beverages, or entertainment. However, the convention organizer may not show these amounts separately on your bill. If this is the case, subtract $50 from the total convention fee for each day the organizer provides food, beverages, or entertainment. You can deduct this daily $50 amount as a meal and entertainment expense. However, the 50 percent limit applies to the daily $50 amount.

EXAMPLE 3

Justin attended a two-day convention in May that cost him $600. The organizer did not indicate what part of the $600 fee was for food and entertainment. The CRA allows you to claim the following convention expenses:

Cost of meals and entertainment
Two days at $50/day = $100 allowed at 50% $50
                                                    } Total deduction $550
Cost of convention ($600 − $100 meals) $500

Office Expenses

You can deduct the cost of office expenses, which include small items such as pens, pencils, paper clips, stationery, and stamps. Office expenses do not include larger items such as filing cabinets, chairs, and desks, which are capital items and can be claimed using CCA.

Salaries, Including Employer's Contributions

You can deduct salaries and the employer's share of contributions you pay to employees. You report these salaries by the end of February on a T4 slip (statement of remuneration paid) or T4A slip (statement of pension, retirement, annuity, and other income).

Amounts paid or payable to you or your partners are not deductible and cannot be expensed. They are considered drawings. A drawing is any withdrawal of cash, other assets, or services of a business by the proprietor or partners. This includes such transactions by the proprietor or partners (or family members) as withdrawing cash for non-business use, and using business assets or services for personal use. Professionals must include the cost or value of personal use of business assets or services in their drawings for the year rather than showing them as an expense in their books.

Salaries Paid to Family Members

You can deduct the salary you pay to your child or spouse (including common law partner) as long as you meet all these conditions:

- You actually pay the salary.
- The work your child or spouse does is necessary for earning business or professional income.
- The salary is reasonable when you consider your child's age, and the amount you pay is what you would pay someone else.

Keep documents to support the salary you pay to your child. If you pay your child by cheque, keep the cancelled cheque. If you pay cash, have the child sign a receipt. You can also deduct the salary you pay to a spouse. When you pay your spouse a salary, use the same rules that apply to paying your child. Report the salaries you pay to your children and spouse on T4 slips, the same as you would for other employees. However, you cannot claim as an expense the value of board and lodging you provide to your dependent children or spouse.

Telephone and Utilities Expenses

You can deduct expenses for telephone and utilities, such as gas, oil, electricity, and water, if you incurred the expenses to earn income. You can also claim expenses for utilities that are related to the business use of work space in your home.

Deductions and Remittances

To be able to deduct a business expense, you must have carried on a business in the fiscal period in which the expense was incurred. Because of this, you must be very clear about the date your business started. Determining exactly what you can claim as a start-up expense can be difficult.

Capital Gains

If you sell a property for more than it cost, you may have a capital gain, which is taxable.

TAX TIP

The Canada Revenue Agency has a number of tax information videos for individuals and small businesses on topics such as preparing your income tax and benefit return, and reporting business income and expenses. To watch these videos, go to <http://www.cra.gc.ca/videogallery>. Videos that provide helpful information on filing of HST/GST for new businesses are found at <http://www.cra-arc.gc.ca/vdgllry/bsnss/srs-gsthst-tpstvh-eng.html>.

CHAPTER SUMMARY

Taxes are a fact of life that most of us have come to accept, but who knew that working as a paralegal would turn you into a tax collector? In this chapter we have examined your responsibilities with regard to collection and remittance of GST/HST, collection and remittance of payroll deductions, and payment of income taxes. These tasks are time-consuming, and you must keep yourself informed because tax laws change frequently. Although rates may change, the basic principles remain fairly constant.

Remember that although you are not paid to collect and remit taxes for the government, you will certainly be penalized if you fail to complete these tasks in a correct and timely manner. It is advisable for licensees to consult with an accountant when the time comes to file tax returns each year.

KEY TERMS

bad debt, 257
business expenses, 251
fiscal period, 259
gross pay, 252
GST/HST, 248
income, 249
income tax, 256
information return, 256

input tax credit (ITC), 249
payroll deductions, 253
personal deductions, 253
records, 249
small supplier, 248
tax year, 256
taxable benefits, 256

FURTHER READING

Canada Revenue Agency, Form T2125, "Statement of Business or Professional Activities," online: <http://www.cra-arc.gc.ca/E/pbg/tf/t2125/t2125-14e.pdf>.

Canada Revenue Agency, "GST/HST Videos for Businesses," online: <http://www.cra-arc .gc.ca/tx/bsnss/tpcs/gst-tps/vds-eng.html>. See the following video resources:
- GST/HST Information for a New Small Business
- Payroll Information for a New Small Business
- Preparing T4 and T4A Information Returns—Slips and Summaries

Canada Revenue Agency, Guide T4002(E), "Business and Professional Income," 2014, online: <http://www.cra-arc.gc.ca/E/pub/tg/t4002/t4002-14e.pdf>.

Canada Revenue Agency, "Videos and Recorded Webinars for Businesses," online: <http:// www.cra-arc.gc.ca/vdgllry/bsnss/menu-eng.html>. See the following video resources:
- Series: Reporting Business Income and Expenses
- Series: Payroll Information for a New Small Business

PUT IT INTO PRACTICE

Case Example: Employer, Small Business, and Professional Responsibilities

Review the online CRA resource Checklist for New Small Businesses (<http://www.cra-arc.gc.ca/tx/bsnss/sm/chcklst-eng.html>) and help Ann Litigate create a customized checklist for her CRA filings as an employer and as a small business proprietor and legal professional.

REVIEW QUESTIONS

True or False

_____ 1. GST/HST is remitted on the total amount of GST/HST charged and collected.

_____ 2. The simplified method of calculating GST/HST payable does not need to show the purchase price of goods and GST/HST paid separately but is based on eligible business expenses based on a prescribed formula.

_____ 3. Paralegals have the option of using the quick method to calculate the amount of GST/HST to be paid.

_____ 4. Legal and accounting fees incurred by a business owner for external advice can be deducted as a business expense.

_____ 5. Business records should be maintained for a minimum period of six years from the end of the last tax year to which such records relate.

_____ 6. Payroll calculations include the withdrawals made by the business owner from the business.

_____ 7. Input tax credits can be claimed only on purchases made by the business.

_____ 8. Salaries and the employer's share of contributions paid to employees can be deducted as business expenses.

_____ 9. A small supplier for GST/HST purposes is required to register for GST/HST as soon as it commences operation, regardless of its total annual revenue.

_____ 10. A business can claim only those expenses or portions of such expenses that are related or attributed to earning income for the business.

Short Answer

Give a full answer for each question:

1. What are the record-keeping requirements for business records as stated by the Canada Revenue Agency?

2. What are some examples of ineligible business expenses?

3. What are the steps involved in calculating GST/HST payable using the regular method?

4. What are the steps involved in calculating payroll?

PRACTICE EXERCISES

Practice Exercise 10.1

Based on the entries below in the fees journal and general disbursements journal, prepare a GST/HST worksheet for the month of January 20** according to the regular method. The worksheet is based on the GST/HST return working copy shown in Figure 10.1.

	Fees Journal (Service Revenue)						
Date 20**		Invoice #	Client	Fees Billed	Disbursements Billed	HST Billed (13% ON)	Total Amount Billed
Jan.	1	400	L. Forte	500.00	60.00	72.80	632.80
	3	401	L. Bailey	1,000.00	120.00*	130.00	1,250.00
	5	402	R. Smythe	0.00	120.00*	0.00	120.00
	10	403	C. Schultz	5,000.00	0.00	650.00	5,650.00
	15	405	L. Pepino	1,500.00	0.00	195.00	1,695.00
	18	406	R. Saunders	800.00	300.00	143.00	1,243.00
	25	407	B. Enders	2,400.00	160.00	332.80	2,892.80
Totals:				11,200.00	760.00	1,523.60	13,483.60

* HST not applicable

	General Disbursements Journal						
Date 20**		Paid To	Description	Method of Payment	Amount Paid	HST Paid/ Payable (13% ON)	Total Amount Paid
Jan.	1	Magnum Office Manager	A. Litigate—Paid rent, invoice #1001	Chq. #217	1,000.00	130.00	1,130.00
	7	ATB Web Services	A. Litigate—Paid invoice #A0-111	Chq. #218	120.00	15.60	135.60
	15	A. Booth, secretary	A. Litigate—Paid salary expense*	Chq. #219	1,000.00	0.00	1,000.00
	15	ABC Insurance	A. Litigate—Paid invoice #501	Chq. #220	165.00	21.45	186.45
	25	Centrum Parking	A. Litigate—Paid monthly parking invoice #AA123	Chq. #221	100.00	15.00	115.00
	29	SSI Computers and Electronics	A. Litigate—Paid for computer equipment	Chq. #223	700.00	105.00	805.00
	30	A. Booth, secretary	A. Litigate—Paid salary expense*	Chq. #224	1,000.00	0.00	1,000.00
	31	AAA Advertising	A. Litigate—Paid invoice #A0-112	Chq. #226	85.00	12.75	97.75
Totals:					4,170.00	299.80	4,469.80

* HST not applicable

Net GST/HST Tax Payable	
Total Fees Billed	
Total Disbursements Billed	
Total GST/HST Charged	
Total Purchases (tax-deductible, ITCs)	
Total GST/HST paid or payable on tax-deductible purchases	
Net GST/HST Tax	

GST/HST Worksheet, Net GST/HST Calculation (for the Month of January 20✷✷)				
Total GST/HST Collected or Collectible	Line 103	$		complete
Adjustments	Line 104	$		complete, if applicable
	Line 105		$	add Lines 103 and 104
Total GST/HST Paid or Payable for Eligible Expenses	Line 106	$		complete
Adjustments	Line 107	$		complete, if applicable
Total ITCs	Line 108		$	add Lines 106 and 107
Net GST/HST	Line 109		$	subtract Line 108 from Line 105

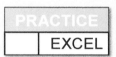

Practice Exercise 10.2

Using the reference sheets supplied, analyze and discuss parts 2, 3, 5, and 6 of a draft Statement of Business or Professional Activities (CRA Form T2125, which is usually prepared by an accountant) based on the following information provided in Chart 1 (Income Statement) and Chart 2 (GST/HST Collected in Respect of Professional Income and Business Expenses). Note: Parts 1 and 4 of this form relate to business income; paralegals should complete the sections relating to professional income.

Chart 1: Income Statement

Ann Litigate Paralegal Services Income Statement for the Period Ended December 31, 20**		
Income		
Fees Earned, Including HST and WIP*		$66,105
Expenses		
Accounting and Bookkeeping	$2,000	
Depreciation Expense	1,360	
Insurance—Professional Liability	2,500	
Membership/Professional Dues	2,000	
Office Supplies/General Expense	4,000	
Rent Expense	12,000	
Salaries Expense	25,000	
Telephone Expense	800	
Motor Vehicle Expense†	4,770	
Total Expenses		54,430
Net Income (Loss)		$11,675

* WIP = work in progress
† From Figure 10.6

Chart 2: GST/HST Collected in Respect of Professional Income and Business Expenses

Period	Sales/ Disbursements	GST/HST	Total Sales
First quarter (January 1 to March 31)	$19,500	$2,535	$22,035
Second quarter (April 1 to June 30)	15,000	1,950	16,950
Third quarter (July 1 to September 30)	10,000	1,300	11,300
Fourth quarter (October 1 to December 31)	14,000	1,820	15,820
Total	$58,500	$7,605	$66,105

Draft Statement of Business or Professional Activities— CRA Form T2125

Part 2—Professional income

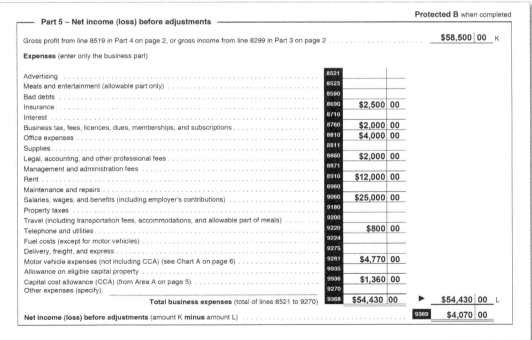

Part 2 – Professional income

☑ If you have professional income, tick this box and complete this part. **Do not complete parts 1 and 2 on the same form**.

Gross professional fees including work-in-progress (WIP) (including GST/HST collected or collectible)	**$66,105** 00 D
Minus any GST/HST, provincial sales tax, returns, allowances, discounts, and GST/HST adjustments (included on line D above) and any WIP at the end of the year you elected to exclude (see Chapter 2 of Guide T4002)	**$7,605** 00 (i)
Subtotal (amount D **minus** amount (i))	**$58,500** 00 E

For those using the quick method – Government assistance calculated as follows:
GST/HST collected or collectible on professional fees eligible for the quick method . . . . _____ (ii)

GST/HST remitted, calculated on (professional fees eligible for the quick method plus GST/HST collected or collectible) multiplied by the applicable quick method remittance rate . . . . _____ (iii)

Subtotal (amount (ii) **minus** amount (iii)) . . . . $0 00 (iv)

Work-in-progress (WIP), start of the year, per election to exclude WIP (see Chapter 2 of Guide T4002) . . . . $0 00 (v)

Adjusted professional fees (Amount E **plus** amounts (iv) and (v)) – Enter this amount on line 8000 in Part 3 below . . . . $58,500 00 F

Part 3—Gross business or professional income

Part 3 – Gross business or professional income

Adjusted gross sales (from amount C in Part 1) or adjusted professional fees (from amount F in Part 2)	8000	**$58,500** 00	G
Plus			
Reserves deducted last year	8290	$0 00	
Other income	8230	$0 00	
Total of the above two lines		$0 00 ▶	$0 00 H
Gross business or professional income (amount G **plus** amount H)	8299	**$58,500** 00	

Enter this amount on the appropriate line of your income tax and benefit return: business on line 162, professional on line 164, or commission on line 166.

Part 5—Net income (loss) before adjustments

Protected B when completed

Part 5 – Net income (loss) before adjustments

Gross profit from line 8519 in Part 4 on page 2, or gross income from line 8299 in Part 3 on page 2 . . . . $58,500 00 K

Expenses (enter only the business part)

	Line	Amount	
Advertising	8521		
Meals and entertainment (allowable part only)	8523		
Bad debts	8590		
Insurance.	8690	$2,500 00	
Interest	8710		
Business tax, fees, licences, dues, memberships, and subscriptions	8760	$2,000 00	
Office expenses	8810	$4,000 00	
Supplies.	8811		
Legal, accounting, and other professional fees	8860	$2,000 00	
Management and administration fees	8871		
Rent	8910	$12,000 00	
Maintenance and repairs	8960		
Salaries, wages, and benefits (including employer's contributions)	9060	$25,000 00	
Property taxes	9180		
Travel (including transportation fees, accommodations, and allowable part of meals)	9200		
Telephone and utilities.	9220	$800 00	
Fuel costs (except for motor vehicles)	9224		
Delivery, freight, and express	9275		
Motor vehicle expenses (not including CCA) (see Chart A on page 6)	9281	$4,770 00	
Allowance on eligible capital property	9935		
Capital cost allowance (CCA) (from Area A on page 5)	9936	$1,360 00	
Other expenses (specify):	9270		
Total business expenses (total of lines 8521 to 9270)	9368	$54,430 00 ▶	$54,430 00 L

Net income (loss) before adjustments (amount K **minus** amount L) 9369 $4,070 00

Part 6—Your net income (loss)

Part 6 – Your net income (loss)

Your share of the amount on line 9369 in Part 5 or the amount from your T5013 slip	$4,070 00	M
Plus: GST/HST rebate for partners received in the year (see Chapter 3 of Guide T4002) **9974**	$0 00	N
Total (amount M **plus** amount N)	$4,070 00 ▶ $4,070 00	O
Minus: Other amounts deductible from your share of the net partnership income (loss) (from the chart in Part 7 below) . . . **9943**		P
Net income (loss) after adjustments (amount O **minus** amount P).	$4,070 00	Q
Minus: Business-use-of-home expenses (your share of amount 3 in part 8). **9945**	$0 00	R
Your net income (loss) (amount Q **minus** amount R) **9946**	$4,070 00	

Enter this amount on the appropriate line of your income tax and benefit return: business on line 135, professional on line 137, or commission on line 139.

11

Computerized Time and Money Management

After reading this chapter, you should be able to:

- use legal software to manage client files
- record time and fees and prepare invoices
- enter general receipts and disbursements
- record trust receipts and disbursements
- recover client costs

Large law firms usually have a centralized accounting department to perform all accounting functions, but smaller firms may use a system in which the licensee and his or her support staff all participate in performing these functions. The systems implemented may range from a manual system, to spreadsheet software, to general or **legal accounting software**. Most legal firms use some sort of accounting software, whether it is generic or a dedicated legal accounting program.

Before purchasing accounting software, you should have a good idea of what tasks you want the software to perform. Are you just looking for **time entry and billing**? Do you need software that will do all journal entries for both trust and general accounts, automatically post them, then prepare reports and financial statements? What kind of reports would be useful in your practice? Do you want productivity reports showing how time is being managed, and reports that prepare GST/HST returns? A major consideration for paralegals starting out will be the cost of the system or software, including the cost of updates, support, and renewal fees. Is the system being investigated easy to use, or does it require extensive training? Do you want to be able to access the software through a mobile device when away from the office? The system you select will be determined by the size of the firm and whether the system needs to be centralized or accessed by various individuals.

A few of the popular software providers for legal services firms are Amicus Attorney, Clio, ESILAW, PCLaw, and Intuit QuickBooks. Some software companies store data on a web server, while others store data on your desktop. We are not recommending the use of any particular accounting software, and this chapter will focus generally on software specifically designed for use in legal practices. The main functions we will review are file management, general and trust accounting, and time and billing.

When starting your own practice, you may find the cost of purchasing specialized legal software daunting. However, keep in mind that the time and effort used to set up a good accounting system will save time and money down the road. It is amazing how a bill generated by a computer can look so much more professional and as a result be less likely to be questioned than one produced by other means.

A good system pays off in other ways. Legal software programs have been developed that keep the requirements of the LSUC in mind and with a view to helping licensees comply with bylaw 9. You should be able to produce the records required by the LSUC seamlessly, practically at the press of a button. However, the old adage "garbage in, garbage out" applies even with the best of software. The information produced by your system will only be as good as the information that is put into it. It is important to establish good bookkeeping practices at the outset.

Getting Started with Legal Accounting Software

Once you have selected the accounting system that meets your needs, take the time to set it up properly. Or, you may be employed by a firm that uses particular software, and you will be expected to learn to use it correctly. Although you may experience some initial frustration, the time and effort required to learn any new software is well spent because you will learn how to gain maximum benefit from its features.

Managing Client Files

Rule 1.02 of the *Paralegal Rules of Conduct* defines **conflict of interest** as the existence of a substantial risk that a paralegal's loyalty to or representation of a client would be materially and adversely affected by the paralegal's own interest or duties to another client, a former client, or a third person. The risk must be more than a mere possibility; there must be a genuine, serious risk to the duty of loyalty or to client representation arising from the **retainer**.

When a new client approaches a firm, it is important to conduct a **conflict search** that checks all of the firm's clients, files, calendars, and vendors to determine if there are any previous contacts with a potential client or file that could lead to a conflict of interest. Nothing is more frustrating, embarrassing, and perhaps expensive to a firm than having to withdraw from a file because a conflict was not discovered in a timely manner. If no conflict is found, the firm may then accept the retainer and open a client file.

The system will usually provide two numbers on file opening: a **client number** and a **client matter** or file number. The client number identifies the name and contact information of the client, whereas the file or matter number describes particulars about the area of law for which the firm has been retained. When new client files are opened on the system, the original client number is used.

Once all the information is entered in the system, print a label for the client file. The label contains information about the file, such as the client name, description, client and file numbers, contact information for the client, responsible lawyer, and date the file was opened.

Type of Law

The system will ask for the type of law that applies to the matter. Classifications of law generally include such topics as provincial offences, litigation, real estate, wills and estates, corporate, or miscellaneous. Selecting this feature allows the firm to track useful information regarding the sources of the firm's income. These classifications are also helpful for collecting statistics for preparation of the licensee's annual report to the Law Society of Upper Canada (LSUC), which asks for a breakdown of the percentage of time spent on various types of law.

Closing Client Files

Archiving files is a job that often suffers the indignity of procrastination. But archiving regularly helps to keep your records accurate. It is important to be vigilant when it comes time to close client files. Your legal accounting software will assign and track a closed file number for archived files to make it easy to retrieve the file if it is ever required. Closing the file when the matter is finished helps to produce client reports that are accurate and reliable. Producing a client listing that contains files that were finished but not closed on the system years ago is frustrating and not helpful. When you want a list of your current clients, you do not want the list to include the names and balances for inactive files. The anticipated date for destruction of a file can be entered when the file is closed.

Files that are to be destroyed should be shredded to protect confidential information contained in them, and a certificate of destruction should be obtained from the company after shredding.

Time Entries and Billing

The time and billing function of accounting software uses explanation codes to indicate the activity that was performed by the licensee. Examples of some commonly used explanation codes are shown in Figure 11.1.

Explanation Codes					
att	attendance at	ct	correspondence to	lr	legal research
cf	correspondence from	dr	drafting	mwc	meeting with client

FIGURE 11.1   Explanation codes

Effort can be saved when entering your time by using an explanation code such as "att" and allowing the system to autofill the phrase to "attendance at." You can then add other information to the explanation such as attendance at "court." In addition to being a time-saving device, explanation codes avoid typographical errors. Codes can be added or deleted when you set up the time and billing system to autofill the description of work you most commonly bill to a file. You are not required to use the codes, but once you become familiar with these shortcuts, you will benefit from the time saved and errors avoided.

Recording Time Entries

There are several different ways software can be used to charge fees to a matter:

- Enter time recorded by hand on a time slip
- Use the time-tracking function of your software to track meetings, telephone calls, and so on
- Charge a **flat rate**
- Convert appointments and phone calls into time entries

Firms usually bill clients based on the amount of time spent working on a file or based on a flat rate or fee. A flat fee is common in files such as traffic court, where the time that will be required is easy to estimate.

When time is being billed by the hour, it is usual to bill in tenths of an hour. Most firms bill time out in six-minute blocks, with each block representing one-tenth of an hour. This makes the calculation of the hourly rate straightforward and has been recognized as reasonable by the profession. It is hard to imagine anyone interrupting what they are doing, taking a phone call, then making a note on the file in less than six minutes. This compromise seems to be acceptable to clients and works for the office. Most time and billing software will round time entries up to the nearest tenth of an hour by default, but this standard can be changed if desired. Figure 11.2 shows a minutes-to-decimal conversion chart to help you calculate blocks of one-tenth of an hour when making time entries. The **billable rate**, which is the hourly rate charged on a file, is multiplied by the time spent working on the file. Each legal professional working in the firm may have a number of hourly rates charged, depending on the type of matter and the client retainer that was entered into.

Minutes	Decimals
1–6	0.1
7–12	0.2
13–18	0.3
19–24	0.4
25–30	0.5
31–36	0.6
37–42	0.7
43–48	0.8
49–54	0.9
55–60	1.0

FIGURE 11.2 Minutes-to-decimal conversion chart

EXAMPLE

If Justin Case worked for 53 minutes on a file at an hourly rate of $80, the software would calculate the amount to bill as follows:

STEP 1

Convert 53 minutes to tenths of an hour, or 0.9, then multiply 0.9 × $80/hour = $72.

STEP 2

To create time entries, you would go to the time entry section in your software, enter the date and file number, select the name of the person who did the work, enter the time and rate if not automatically selected, and let the software calculate the dollar amount to bill.

STEP 3

An explanation of the work that was done is entered using the explanation code and any additional description you wish to use.

STEP 4

Once all the time entries are completed, this information will be used to produce the invoice to the client. It is important to spellcheck your entries before saving to correct any typographical errors, because you do not want any on the final invoice to the client. Remember, when recording time entries, what you type in the explanation section will appear on the bill.

General Receipts and Disbursements

Your software should allow you to write general or trust cheques and make deposits in the program, then print the required cheque or deposit slip. You will need to purchase special cheques to use this function. If the office does not purchase the pre-formatted cheques, cheques can be written by hand and then entered into the system without printing.

The many advantages of a program that records deposits and cheques in journals and simultaneously posts them to the proper general, special, and client ledger accounts include the following:

- Your deposit and cheque balances will always be current.
- Deposits are automatically posted to the individual client's ledger sheet, and the bank account is debited.
- GST/HST is recorded and tracked for preparation of the GST/HST report. The amount of the payment is posted directly to the account to be charged. For example, if Justin Case wrote a $565 cheque for rent, which includes $65 for GST/HST and $500 for payment of rent, the system automatically journalizes the entries and posts $500 to the rent expense account and $65 to the GST/HST input tax credits account, and also credits the general bank account for $565. All this happens when the cheque is written. If explanation codes are used for writing the cheque—for example, "rnt" for rent expense—the system automatically knows the number of the account where rent expense is to be posted. There is no need to look up the account number on the chart of accounts.
- Even if cheques are manually prepared, they can be entered into the system by completing the pro forma cheque on the system, and the cheque is simply not printed.

Recovering Client Costs

Some costs incurred in an office on behalf of clients are not paid for by cheque. Photocopies, faxes, and postage are examples of amounts that get billed to a client without a corresponding bill being received by the firm for that expense. Some photocopiers, facsimile machines, and postage meters are equipped to provide a printout summarizing photocopies and faxes to be charged to a particular client file. In order to recover these expenses from the client, they must be entered into the system, either periodically or at the time of billing.

Because the expense for these items can be substantial, it is worth taking the time to track and bill them. These entries may appear in a special journal called a **client cost recovery journal** and also in the client ledger. Once entered, they will show up on the invoice produced when the client bill is prepared.

Trust Receipts and Disbursements

A trust receipt can be entered as a deposit to the trust bank account in the system. A deposit slip is printed containing all the information required by the LSUC, such as from whom the money was received, the amount of the deposit, and the method of payment (number on the client's cheque). This slip can be taken to the bank and stamped by the teller along with the firm's deposit book. The amount of the deposit is posted as a debit to the trust bank account and credited to the individual client's trust ledger sheet, enabling you to know the current balance of funds held in trust for each client at all times.

Just as with general cheques, trust cheques can also be recorded and printed using legal accounting software. Once a cheque is entered into the system, the trust bank account will be credited and the client trust ledger will be debited. Some software is programmed to safeguard against anyone writing a cheque against a client's trust ledger if there are insufficient funds in that particular client's account. The system produces a warning that there are insufficient funds in the account. When preparing the trust bank reconciliation, which can also be done using the software, the system will produce the client trust listing for comparison with the trust bank balance.

End-of-Period Functions

Legal accounting software can produce the financial statements for any period you request, making it easy to get an income statement and balance sheet showing the results from your practice on a regular basis. The software also provides bank reconciliation features for reconciling your general and trust bank accounts.

Year-End

Once you have reviewed your financial statements, adjustments can be prepared and entered using the general journal. Once the balances have been adjusted, the system is ready to prepare your year-end reports. The system will produce a post-closing trial balance with all the closing entries posted to the individual income, expense, and equity accounts, and you are ready to start the new fiscal year.

Maintaining Electronic Records

If electronic records are kept, be sure to have backups of the system. You may be required to produce printed copies of your information by the LSUC. Having to go back and re-create a set of books because of a computer crash, or even a break-in during which office computers are stolen, is a hardship that is easily avoided. Most insurance companies will not cover the cost of paying someone to re-enter all the data; they cover only the cost of restoring the backup.

The Canada Revenue Agency requires all taxpayers to retain their business records in an electronically readable format. The retained records must provide the information necessary to determine the person's liabilities and obligations, or their entitlement to any refund or rebate under the *Income Tax Act*. The taxpayer is not relieved of this responsibility because of the utilization of a third party, such as an accountant or other service provider. All retained records must be clearly labelled and stored in a secure environment in Canada.

TAX TIP

CHAPTER SUMMARY

Legal software can take care of many functions in a firm, such as tracking calendar appointments, tickler systems, and phone calls, as well as maintaining financial records. Many systems have applications that can be accessed from a mobile device, so entries can be made from any location. Some licensees have found this to be a very convenient feature. Maintaining accurate and up-to-date accounting records is a requirement of the Law Society of Upper Canada. By implementing a good legal accounting system that has billing and accounting features, you will meet the Law Society's requirements as well as be more productive. It is important to be familiar with how legal software works because, at the very least, employees hired by legal firms are usually expected to be familiar with relevant software applications used in the management of a law practice.

KEY TERMS

billable rate, 274
client cost recovery journal, 276
client matter, 273
client number, 273
conflict of interest, 273
conflict search, 273
flat rate, 274
legal accounting software, 272
retainer, 273
time entry and billing, 272

FURTHER READING

Ellen Freedman & Claire Barnes, "Capturing More Time (and Billing It Too!)," online: CBA PracticeLink <http://www.cba.org/cba/practicelink/tayp/capturingtime.aspx>.

Law Society of Upper Canada, "Guide to Opening Your Practice for Paralegals," online: <http://www.lsuc.on.ca/with.aspx?id=2147499334>.

Law Society of Upper Canada, "Practice Management Guidelines," online: <http://www.lsuc.on.ca/with.aspx?id=2147490535>.

PUT IT INTO PRACTICE

Case Example: Simulation Exercises

The following simulation exercises can be used to practise making entries using various types of legal accounting software. The entries should be adapted as needed to correspond with the features of the legal software being used. Although the Law Society of Upper Canada does not require paralegals to learn how to use legal accounting software for licensing purposes, students may find themselves employed in a firm that uses such software, so it is useful to get some practice. Students may wish to inquire about getting a free download from an accounting software provider to try out a system. Your role as a paralegal or law clerk should be entered when setting up the information regarding the firm.

The exercises are designed to demonstrate the following features:

- Preparation of the accounting system by entering accounting, lawyer, paralegal, and law clerk information
- How to open files for new clients
- Preparation of time entries on client files
- Recording receipts and disbursements in general and trust accounts
- Conducting conflict searches for new clients
- Recovering costs for client disbursements such as photocopies and faxes
- Preparation of invoices and transfer of funds from trust to general bank accounts
- Closing a client file
- Preparing financial reports

Simulation Exercise 11.1: Preparing the Accounting System

Set up your system by inserting the name, address, and telephone numbers of the law firm. You should also enter a GST registration number such as RT 112233. Make any other adjustments to the system settings that your instructor thinks are necessary. The names of any paralegals, lawyers, and law clerks working in the firm should be added to the system as well as their billable rates for various files.

Simulation Exercise 11.2: Creating a Matter for a New Client

You should learn the terminology that applies to the software you are using. Help resources are usually available and should be consulted as needed. You must create a file for each new client. New files are often referred to as "matters" and each client matter is given a unique number. Client matters or files are usually numbered consecutively, and the numbers are assigned by the system. Each new client will also have an assigned client number, which is used for all matters related to that particular client. So client no. 1 might have several matters or files, each with a different matter number. It is useful to have a client number because this avoids having to rekey the client's name and address each time a new matter or file is opened for that particular client.

a. Create a new client matter on your system titled "*Karen Fisher v Reveal Cosmetics*." Karen Fisher has come to Justin Case to see about launching a product liability suit against Reveal Cosmetics. Justin feels she has a good case.

The type of law is litigation, and you should select the rate at which the file is to be billed. Fill in the description box for the file by naming the client and the defendant. The description will be the reference line used on the invoice sent to the client; it also appears on the file label. Enter the client's name, address, and telephone number in the areas provided by your system. The system will assign Fisher client no. 1.

Karen Fisher has asked the firm to represent her in a second matter against James King regarding an encroachment on her property. Open a second file for this client, not allowing the system to allocate a new client number. Keep the same client number and allow the system to create a new matter or file number. The firm has quoted a flat rate for this matter of $3,500. Enter this information into your system.

b. Using the information you have learned, create a new client matter for a second client, Robert Crookshank. Title it "Robert Crookshank re Traffic Court." Crookshank will be represented in this matter by a different paralegal in the firm at a different rate. The client's address is 123 York Street, Your Town, Ontario, and his telephone number is (555) 235-2323. The system will automatically assign client no. 2 to Crookshank because no. 1 is taken up by Karen Fisher, and it will allocate file no. 3 to the matter.

Once you have completed this exercise, prepare a list of clients using your software.

Simulation Exercise 11.3: Recording Time and Fees

This exercise describes how to enter hours recorded on a time slip using legal accounting software. When entering time, use the minutes-to-decimal conversion chart provided in this chapter. Use explanation codes, if available, to describe the work done, such as "mwc" for "meeting with client." You can add to the description by including further information such as "to discuss liability suit." You may wish not to charge for the initial interview. The software will allow you to show no charge. It is a good idea to enter this time and show it as not being charged so that the client will be able to appreciate the fact that she received a free consultation.

Enter the following time entries for Justin Case on the *Karen Fisher v Reveal Cosmetics* file using appropriate dates. Remember to convert time to tenths of an hour when recording time entries.

Month	3	Meeting with client to discuss liability suit—½ hour at no charge
	5	Instructing legal staff—20 minutes
	9	Legal research by the law clerk for 1 hour and 15 minutes
	15	Review correspondence from opposite party with offer to settle —15 minutes
	18	Meeting with client to discuss settlement offer—35 minutes

Justin has also provided a time slip setting out the following services performed on the Robert Crookshank file. Record the time entries.

Month	4	Meeting with client to discuss traffic charge—½ hour
	5	Review of HTA sections and legal research—1 hour and 15 minutes
	9	Attendance at traffic court and negotiation of plea—2 hours

Justin also worked on the *Karen Fisher v J King* easement dispute file. Record the time entries.

Month	5	Researching cases on easements—2 hours and 20 minutes
	15	Correspondence with opposite party—½ hour
	20	Response with offer to settle for $3,000—15 minutes
	25	Meeting with client to sign minutes of settlement—20 minutes
	30	Report to client—20 minutes

Produce a report to show the time entries you have made. Your system should allow you to re-enter the system to make corrections to any incorrect time entries.

Simulation Exercise 11.4: Recording Trust Receipts and Retainers

Before a retainer can be entered into a client file or matter, a file must be opened for that client matter on the system. If you do not already have a file for a client, open a file. Then enter the retainers received by depositing the funds to the trust bank account.

The following retainers were received and new files opened by the firm. Conduct a conflict search and create a new client file for the following persons: Susan Silver, David Silver, Angela Finelli, Stephen Bell, and Peter Stubbs. You or your instructor can make up the description, address, and telephone numbers for each client. Use the preferred default rate for all new files.

Date 20**		Transaction Details	Amount	Method	Total
Month	1	*Karen Fisher v J King* re easement—retainer	800	cheque	800
	3	Susan Silver re traffic retainer	900	cr. card	900
	3	Robert Crookshank re traffic court—retainer	700	cert. cheque	700
	3	David Silver re Small Claims Court—retainer	100	cr. card	100
	8	Angela Finelli re traffic —no retainer received	Open client file only		
	10	Stephen Bell, Small Claims Court —no retainer received	Open client file only		
	11	Peter Stubbs re Small Claims Court—retainer	200	cash	200
	30	Received from J. King—settlement on *Karen Fisher v J King* file	3,000	bank draft	3,000

Simulation Exercise 11.5: Recording General and Trust Disbursements

Record the following transactions in your legal software, being careful to use the correct bank account for each transaction. If funds are available in trust for any client, use trust funds; if not, you need to use the general bank account.

Date 20**		Transaction Details	Amount	HST	Total
Month	1	Paid rent to Minto Management (chq. #G198)	1,200	156	1,356
	3	Paid membership dues to the Law Society of Upper Canada (chq. #G199)	600	78	678
	6	Expense recovery: The following charges were recorded for disbursements made in the office, which are to be billed to clients. • Photocopies: (.25 each) – David Silver 20 copies – Stephen Bell 10 copies – Crookshank 30 copies • Faxes: (.30 each) – David Silver 3 pages – Stephen Bell 8 pages – Peter Stubbs 2 pages	Calculate and enter under expense recovery		

(Continued on next page.)

Date 20**		Transaction Details	Amount	HST	Total
	12	Paid traffic ticket to Minister of Finance on behalf of Susan Silver (chq. #T10)	90	0	90
	26	Paid Royal Bank—interest on loan (chq. #G200)	120	0	120
	26	Paid Minister of Finance to file statement of defence re David Silver (chq. #T11)	40	0	40
	27	Paid fine on behalf of Robert Crookshank to Minister of Finance (chq. #T12)	500	0	500
	27	Paid Minister of Finance to issue notice of garnishment on Stubbs file (chq. #T13)	100	0	100
	28	Paid to issue claim re Stephen Bell (chq. #G201) (no retainer)	75	0	75

Simulation Exercise 11.6: Preparing Invoices to Clients

Prepare invoices for the following client files:
- *Karen Fisher v Reveal Cosmetics*
- *Karen Fisher v J King*
- Robert Crookshank re Traffic Court
- Peter Stubbs re Small Claims Court: you have been asked to prepare a quick bill and charge the client $250 for services rendered plus $3.50 for disbursements incurred but not yet recorded. Record the disbursement at the time it is entered on the bill.

Simulation Exercise 11.7: Conducting a Conflict Search and Closing a Client File

John King has called your office to set up an appointment regarding starting an action against Peter Silver. Conduct a conflict search to determine whether there is a potential conflict of interest.

You have completed all work to be done on the *Karen Fisher v J King* file. Close the file on your system.

Simulation Exercise 11.8: Reconciling the Bank Statement and Preparing Reports

Using the bank statement for Justin Case's trust account for the month, reconcile the bank statement with your records.

ROYAL BANK OF MONEY
P.O. Box 5011, Station A
Montreal, QC H3C 3B8

Trust Bank Account Statement

Justin Case, Paralegal
135 Main Street
Yourtown, Ontario K3P 1G9

Month 1, 20** to Month 3*, 20**

Account number: 0216-520635

ACCOUNT SUMMARY FOR THIS PERIOD

Opening Balance at Beginning of Month		$1,000.00
Total Deposits and Credits	+	$5,800.00
Total Cheques and Debits	−	$730.00
Closing Balance at End of Month	=	$6,070.00

ACCOUNT ACTIVITY DETAILS

Date	Description	Cheques and Debits	Deposits and Credits	Balance
Mo. 01	Deposit		800.00	1,800.00
Mo. 03	Deposit		900.00	2,700.00
Mo. 03	Deposit		800.00	3,500.00
Mo. 03	Deposit		100.00	3,600.00
Mo. 12	Deposit		200.00	3,800.00
Mo. 18	Chq. #T10	90.00		3,710.00
Mo. 24	Chq. #T11	40.00		3,670.00
Mo. 27	Chq. #T12	500.00		3,170.00
Mo. 27	Chq. #T13	100.00		3,070.00
Mo. 30	Deposit		3,000.00	6,070.00
	Closing Balance			6,070.00

Please check this Account Statement without delay and advise us of any error or omission within 45 days of the statement date.
Royal Bank of Money GST Registration Number: R1052481028

On your system, prepare a GST/HST report for last month.
Prepare an income statement and a balance sheet for the month.

REVIEW QUESTIONS

Short Answer

Give a full answer for each question:

1. How do you determine what the best legal accounting system or software is for your practice?
2. What are some of the advantages of having a computerized legal accounting system?
3. What are the rules established under bylaw 9 regarding the maintenance of electronic records?
4. What are the key considerations in opening a new client file?
5. Why should you close files in a timely and systematic manner?

APPENDIX

By-Law 9: Financial Transactions and Records

Made: May 1, 2007

Amended: June 28, 2007

          January 24, 2008

          February 21, 2008

          March 20, 2009 (editorial changes)

          September 29, 2009 (editorial changes)

          April 28, 2011

          May 3, 2011 (editorial changes)

Law Society of Upper Canada, *By-Laws* (Toronto: LSUC, 2007–2011),
online: <https://www.lsuc.on.ca/by-laws/>.

PART I
INTERPRETATION

Interpretation

1.   (1)   In this By-Law,

"arm's length" has the same meaning given it in the *Income Tax Act* (Canada);

"cash" means current coin within the meaning of the *Currency Act* (Canada), notes intended for circulation in Canada issued by the Bank of Canada pursuant to the *Bank of Canada Act* and current coin or banks notes of countries other than Canada;

"charge" has the same meaning given it in the *Land Registration Reform Act*;

"client" means a person or group of persons from whom or on whose behalf a licensee receives money or other property;

"firm of licensees" means,

   (a)   a partnership of licensees and all licensees employed by the partnership,

   (b)   a professional corporation established for the purpose of practising law in Ontario and all licensees employed by the professional corporation,

   (c)   a professional corporation established for the purpose of providing legal services in Ontario and all licensees employed by the professional corporation, or

   (d)   a professional corporation established for the purpose of practising law and providing legal services in Ontario and all licensees employed by the professional corporation;

"holiday" means,

   (a)   any Saturday or Sunday;

   (b)   New Year's Day, and where New Year's Day falls on a Saturday or Sunday, the following Monday;

   (c)   Family Day

   (d)   Good Friday;

   (e)   Easter Monday;

   (f)   Victoria Day;

   (g)   Canada Day, and where Canada Day falls on a Saturday or Sunday, the following Monday;

   (h)   Civic Holiday;

   (i)   Labour Day;

   (j)   Thanksgiving Day;

   (k)   Remembrance Day, and where Remembrance Day falls on a Saturday or Sunday, the following Monday;

   (l)   Christmas Day, and where Christmas Day falls on a Saturday or Sunday, the following Monday and Tuesday, and where Christmas Day falls on a Friday, the following Monday;

   (m)   Boxing Day; and

   (n)   any special holiday proclaimed by the Governor General or the Lieutenant Governor;

"lender" means a person who is making a loan that is secured or to be secured by a charge, including a charge to be held in trust directly or indirectly through a related person or corporation;

"licensee" includes a firm of licensees;

"money" includes cash, cheques, drafts, credit card sales slips, post office orders and express and bank money orders;

"related" has the same meaning given it in the *Income Tax Act* (Canada);

"Teranet" means Teranet Inc., a corporation incorporated under the *Business Corporations Act*, acting as agent for the Ministry of Consumer and Business Services.

Time for doing an act expires on a holiday

(2)   Except where a contrary intention appears, if the time for doing an act expires on a holiday, the act may be done on the next day that is not a holiday.

When deemed in trust

(3)   For the purposes of subsections 9(1), (2) and (3) and section 14, cash, cheques negotiable by the licensee, cheques drawn by the licensee on the licensee's trust account and credit card sales slips in the possession and control of the licensee shall be deemed from the time the licensee receives such possession and control to be money held in a trust account if the cash, cheques or credit card sales slips, as the case may be, are deposited in the trust account not later than the following banking day.

PART II
HANDLING OF MONEY BY BANKRUPT LICENSEE

Handling of money by bankrupt licensee

2.   (1)   Subject to subsections (2) and (3), a licensee who is bankrupt within the meaning of the *Bankruptcy and Insolvency Act* (Canada) shall not receive from or on behalf of a person or group of persons any money or other property and shall not otherwise handle money or other property that is held in trust for a person or group of persons.

Exception

(2)   A licensee who is bankrupt within the meaning of the *Bankruptcy and Insolvency Act* (Canada) may receive from or on behalf of a person or group of persons money,

(a)   in payment of fees for services performed by the licensee for the person or group; or

(b)   in reimbursement for money properly expended, or for expenses properly incurred, on behalf of the person or group.

Same

(3)   A licensee who is bankrupt within the meaning of the *Bankruptcy and Insolvency Act* (Canada) may apply in writing to the Society for permission to receive from or on behalf of a person or group of persons any money or other property, other than as permitted under subsection (2), or for permission to handle money or other property that is held in trust for a person or group of persons, and the Society may permit the licensee to do so, subject to such terms and conditions as the Society may impose.

PART II.1
HANDLING OF MONEY BY LICENSEE WHOSE LICENCE IS SUSPENDED

Interpretation

2.1   In this Part,

"suspended licensee" means a licensee who is the subject of a suspension order; "suspension order" means an order made under the Act suspending a licensee's licence to practise law in Ontario as a barrister and solicitor or to provide legal services in Ontario, regardless of whether the suspension begins when the order is made or thereafter.

Handling of money by suspended licensee

2.2   (1)   Subject to subsection (2) and section 2.3, a suspended licensee shall not, during the suspension receive from or on behalf of a person or group of persons any money or other property and shall not otherwise handle money or other property that is held in trust for a person or group of persons.

Exception

(2)   A suspended licensee may receive from or on behalf of a person or group of persons money,

(a)   in payment of fees for services performed by the suspended licensee for the person or group; or

(b)   in reimbursement for money properly expended, or for expenses properly incurred, on behalf of the person or group.

Trust account

2.3   (1)   A suspended licensee shall, within 30 days of the beginning of the suspension,

(a)   withdraw from every trust account kept in the name of the suspended licensee, or in the name of the firm of licensees of which the suspended licensee is a partner or by which the suspended licensee is employed, and, as required, pay to the appropriate person,

(i)   money properly required for payment to a person on behalf of a client,

(ii)   money required to reimburse the suspended licensee for money properly expended, or for expenses properly incurred, on behalf of a client,

(iii)   money required for or toward payment of fees for services performed by the suspended licensee, and

(iv)   all other money that belongs to the suspended licensee or to a person other than a client;

(b)   after complying with clause (a), withdraw from every trust account kept in the name of the suspended licensee, or in the name of the firm of licensees of which the suspended licensee is a partner or by which the suspended licensee is employed, all money belonging to a client and pay the money to,

(i)   the client,

(ii)   another licensee to whom the client has directed the suspended licensee to make payment, or

(iii) another licensee who has agreed with the suspended licensee to accept payment in the event that the suspended licensee is unable to comply with subclause (i) or (ii); and

(c) after complying with clauses (a) and (b),

(i) close every trust account that was kept in the name of the suspended licensee, and

(ii) cancel or cause to be cancelled the suspended licensee's signing authority on every trust account that was kept in the name of the firm of licensees of which the suspended licensee is a partner or by which the suspended licensee is employed.

Compliance with clause (1)(b) not required

(2)   A suspended licensee is not required to comply with clause (1)(b) if the client's file is transferred, in accordance with Part IV of By-Law 7.1, to another licensee in the firm of licensees of which the suspended licensee is a partner or by which the suspended licensee is employed.

Application of sections of Part IV

(3)   Subsection 9(3) and sections 10, 11 and 12 apply to the withdrawal of money from a trust account under this section.

Report to Society on compliance

(4)   A suspended licensee shall, not later than thirty days after the suspension begins, complete and file with the Society, in a form provided by the Society, a report confirming and providing details of the suspended licensee's compliance with this section.

Permission to be exempt from requirement

2.4   A suspended licensee may apply in writing to the Society for an exemption from or a modification of a requirement mentioned in this Part, and the Society may exempt the suspended licensee from or modify the requirement, subject to such terms and conditions as the Society may impose.

PART III
CASH TRANSACTIONS

Definition

3.   In this Part,

"funds" means cash, currency, securities and negotiable instruments or other financial instruments that indicate the person's title or interest in them; "public body" means,

(a) a department or agent of Her Majesty in right of Canada or of a province;

(b) an incorporated city, metropolitan authority, town, township, village, county, district, rural municipality or other incorporated municipal body or an agent of any of them; and

(c) an organization that operates a public hospital and that is designated by the Minister of National Revenue as a hospital under the *Excise Tax Act* (Canada) or agent of the organization.

Cash received

4.   (1)   A licensee shall not receive or accept from a person, in respect of any one client file, cash in an aggregate amount of 7,500 or more Canadian dollars.

Foreign currency

(2)   For the purposes of this section, when a licensee receives or accepts from a person cash in a foreign currency the licensee shall be deemed to have received or accepted the cash converted into Canadian dollars at,

(a)   the official conversion rate of the Bank of Canada for the foreign currency as published in the Bank of Canada's Daily Noon Rates that is in effect at the time the licensee receives or accepts the cash; or

(b)   if the day on which the licensee receives or accepts cash is a holiday, the official conversion rate of the Bank of Canada in effect on the most recent business day preceding the day on which the licensee receives or accepts the cash.

Application

5.   Section 4 applies when, in respect of a client file, a licensee engages in or gives instructions in respect of the following activities:

1.   The licensee receives or pays funds.

2.   The licensee purchases or sells securities, real properties or business assets or entities.

3.   The licensee transfers funds by any means.

Exceptions

6.   Despite section 5, section 4 does not apply when the licensee,

(a)   receives cash from a public body, an authorized foreign bank within the meaning of section 2 of the *Bank Act* (Canada) in respect of its business in Canada or a bank to which the *Bank Act* (Canada) applies, a cooperative credit society, savings and credit union or caisse populaire that is regulated by a provincial Act, an association that is regulated by the *Cooperative Credit Associations Act* (Canada), a company to which the *Trust and Loan Companies Act* (Canada) applies, a trust company or loan company regulated by a provincial Act or a department or agent of Her Majesty in right of Canada or of a province where the department or agent accepts deposit liabilities in the course of providing financial services to the public;

(b)   receives cash from a peace officer, law enforcement agency or other agent of the Crown acting in an official capacity;

(c)   receives cash pursuant to an order of a tribunal;

(d)   receives cash to pay a fine or penalty; or

(e)   receives cash for fees, disbursements, expenses or bail provided that any refund out of such receipts is also made in cash.

PART IV
TRUST ACCOUNT

TRUST ACCOUNT TRANSACTIONS

Money received in trust for client

7.   (1)   Subject to section 8, every licensee who receives money in trust for a client shall immediately pay the money into an account at a chartered bank, provincial savings office, credit union or a league to which the *Credit Unions and Caisses Populaires Act, 1994* applies or registered trust corporation, to be kept in the name of the licensee, or in the name of the firm of licensees of which the licensee is a partner, through which the licensee practises law or provides legal services or by which the licensee is employed, and designated as a trust account.

Interpretation

(2)   For the purposes of subsection (1), a licensee receives money in trust for a client if the licensee receives from a person,

(a)   money that belongs in whole or in part to a client;

(b)   money that is to be held on behalf of a client;

(c)   money that is to be held on a client's direction or order;

(d)   money that is advanced to the licensee on account of fees for services not yet rendered; or

(e)   money that is advanced to the licensee on account of disbursements not yet made.

Money to be paid into trust account

(3)   In addition to the money required under subsection (1) to be paid into a trust account, a licensee shall pay the following money into a trust account:

1.   Money that may by inadvertence have been drawn from a trust account in contravention of section 9.

2.   Money paid to a licensee that belongs in part to a client and in part to the licensee where it is not practical to split the payment of the money.

Money to be paid into trust account: money received before licence issued

(3.1) If a licensee who holds a Class P1 licence receives from a person, prior to being issued the licence, money for services yet to be rendered to a client and the licensee does not perform the services for the client by May 2, 2010, the licensee shall on May 3, 2010 pay the money into a trust account.

Withdrawal of money from trust account

(4)   A licensee who pays into a trust account money described in paragraph 2 of subsection (3) shall as soon as practical withdraw from the trust account the amount of the money that belongs to him or her.

One or more trust accounts

(5)   A licensee may keep one or more trust accounts.

Money not to be paid into trust account

8.   (1)   A licensee is not required to pay into a trust account money which he or she receives in trust for a client if,

(a)   the client requests the licensee in writing not to pay the money into a trust account;

(b)   the licensee pays the money into an account to be kept in the name of the client, a person named by the client or an agent of the client; or

(c)   the licensee pays the money immediately upon receiving it to the client or to a person on behalf of the client in accordance with ordinary business practices.

Same

(2)   A licensee shall not pay into a trust account the following money:

1.   Money that belongs entirely to the licensee or to another licensee of the firm of licensees of which the licensee is a partner, through which the licensee practises law or provides legal services or by which the licensee is employed, including an amount received as a general retainer for which the licensee is not required either to account or to provide services.

2.   Money that is received by the licensee as payment of fees for services for which a billing has been delivered, as payment of fees for services already performed for which a billing will be delivered immediately after the money is received or as reimbursement for disbursements made or expenses incurred by the licensee on behalf of a client.

Record keeping requirements

(3)   A licensee who, in accordance with subsection (1), does not pay into a trust account money which he or she receives in trust for a client shall include all handling of such money in the records required to be maintained under Part V.

Withdrawal of money from trust account

9.   (1)   A licensee may withdraw from a trust account only the following money:

1.   Money properly required for payment to a client or to a person on behalf of a client.

2.   Money required to reimburse the licensee for money properly expended on behalf of a client or for expenses properly incurred on behalf of a client.

3.   Money properly required for or toward payment of fees for services performed by the licensee for which a billing has been delivered.

4.   Money that is directly transferred into another trust account and held on behalf of a client.

5.   Money that under this Part should not have been paid into a trust account but was through inadvertence paid into a trust account.

Permission to withdraw other money

(2)   A licensee may withdraw from a trust account money other than the money mentioned in subsection (1) if he or she has been authorized to do so by the Society.

Limit on amount withdrawn from trust account

(3)   A licensee shall not at any time with respect to a client withdraw from a trust account under this section more money than is held on behalf of that client in that trust account at that time.

Manner in which certain money may be withdrawn from trust account

10.   A licensee shall withdraw money from a trust account under paragraph 2 or 3 of subsection 9(1) only,

    (a)   by a cheque drawn in favour of the licensee;

    (b)   by a transfer to a bank account that is kept in the name of the licensee and is not a trust account; or

    (c)   by electronic transfer.

Withdrawal by cheque

11.   A cheque drawn on a trust account shall not be,

    (a)   made payable either to cash or to bearer; or

    (b)   signed by a person who is not a licensee except in exceptional circumstances and except when the person has signing authority on the trust account on which a cheque will be drawn and is bonded in an amount at least equal to the maximum balance on deposit during the immediately preceding fiscal year of the licensee in all the trust accounts on which signing authority has been delegated to the person.

Withdrawal by electronic transfer

12.   (1)   Money withdrawn from a trust account by electronic transfer shall be withdrawn only in accordance with this section.

When money may be withdrawn

(2)   Money shall not be withdrawn from a trust account by electronic transfer unless the following conditions are met:

    1.   The electronic transfer system used by the licensee must be one that does not permit an electronic transfer of funds unless,

        i.   one person, using a password or access code, enters into the system the data describing the details of the transfer, and

        ii.   another person, using another password or access code, enters into the system the data authorizing the financial institution to carry out the transfer.

    2.   The electronic transfer system used by the licensee must be one that will produce, not later than the close of the banking day immediately after the day on which the electronic transfer of funds is authorized, a confirmation from the financial institution confirming that the data describing the details of the transfer and authorizing the financial institution to carry out the transfer were received.

3.   The confirmation required by paragraph 2 must contain,

    i.   the number of the trust account from which money is drawn,

    ii.   the name, branch name and address of the financial institution where the account to which money is transferred is kept,

    iii.   the name of the person or entity in whose name the account to which money is transferred is kept,

    iv.   the number of the account to which money is transferred,

    v.   the time and date that the data describing the details of the transfer and authorizing the financial institution to carry out the transfer are received by the financial institution, and

    vi.   the time and date that the confirmation from the financial institution is sent to the licensee.

4.   Before any data describing the details of the transfer or authorizing the financial institution to carry out the transfer is entered into the electronic trust transfer system, an electronic trust transfer requisition must be signed by,

    i.   a licensee, or

    ii.   in exceptional circumstances, a person who is not a licensee if the person has signing authority on the trust account from which the money will be drawn and is bonded in an amount at least equal to the maximum balance on deposit during the immediately preceding fiscal year of the licensee in all trust accounts on which signing authority has been delegated to the person.

5.   The data entered into the electronic trust transfer system describing the details of the transfer and authorizing the financial institution to carry out the transfer must be as specified in the electronic trust transfer requisition.

Application of para. 1 of subs. (2) to sole practitioner

(3)   Paragraph 1 of subsection (2) does not apply to a licensee who practises law or provides legal services without another licensee as a partner, if the licensee practises law or provides legal services through a professional corporation, without another licensee practising law or providing legal services through the professional corporation and without another licensee or person as an employee, if the licensee himself or herself enters into the electronic trust transfer system both the data describing the details of the transfer and the data authorizing the financial institution to carry out the transfer.

Same

(4)   In exceptional circumstances, the data referred to in subsection (3) may be entered by a person other than the licensee, if the person has signing authority on the trust account from which the money will be drawn and is bonded in an amount at least equal to the maximum balance on deposit during the immediately preceding fiscal year of the licensee in all trust accounts on which signing authority has been delegated to the person.

Additional requirements relating to confirmation

(5)   Not later than the close of the banking day immediately after the day on which the confirmation required by paragraph 2 of subsection (2) is sent to a licensee, the licensee shall,

(a)   produce a printed copy of the confirmation;

(b)   compare the printed copy of the confirmation and the signed electronic trust transfer requisition relating to the transfer to verify whether the money was drawn from the trust account as specified in the signed requisition;

(c)   indicate on the printed copy of the confirmation the name of the client, the subject matter of the file and any file number in respect of which money was drawn from the trust account; and

(d)   after complying with clauses (a) to (c), sign and date the printed copy of the confirmation.

Same

(6)   In exceptional circumstances, the tasks required by subsection (5) may be performed by a person other than the licensee, if the person has signing authority on the trust account from which the money will be drawn and is bonded in an amount at least equal to the maximum balance on deposit during the immediately preceding fiscal year of the licensee in all trust accounts on which signing authority has been delegated to the person.

Electronic trust transfer requisition

(7)   The electronic trust transfer requisition required under paragraph 4 of subsection (2) shall be in Form 9A.

Definitions

13.   (1)   In this section,

"closing funds" means the money necessary to complete or close a transaction in real estate; "transaction in real estate" means,

(a)   a charge on land given for the purpose of securing the payment of a debt or the performance of an obligation, including a charge under the *Land Titles Act* and a mortgage, but excluding a rent charge, or

(b)   a conveyance of freehold or leasehold land, including a deed and a transfer under the *Land Titles Act*, but excluding a lease.

Withdrawal by electronic transfer: closing funds

(2)   Despite section 12, closing funds may be withdrawn from a trust account by electronic transfer in accordance with this section.

When closing funds may be withdrawn

(3)   Closing funds shall not be withdrawn from a trust account by electronic transfer unless the following conditions are met:

1.   The electronic transfer system used by the licensee must be one to which access is restricted by the use of at least one password or access code.

2.   The electronic transfer system used by the licensee must be one that will produce immediately after the electronic transfer of funds a confirmation of the transfer.

3.   The confirmation required by paragraph 2 must contain,

    i.   the name of the person or entity in whose name the account from which money is drawn is kept,

    ii.   the number of the trust account from which money is drawn,

    iii.   the name of the person or entity in whose name the account to which money is transferred is kept,

    iv.   the number of the account to which money is transferred, and

    v.   the date the transfer is carried out.

4.   Before the electronic transfer system used by the licensee is accessed to carry out an electronic transfer of funds, an electronic trust transfer requisition must be signed by,

    i.   the licensee, or

    ii.   in exceptional circumstances, a person who is not the licensee if the person has signing authority on the trust account from which the money will be drawn and is bonded in an amount at least equal to the maximum balance on deposit during the immediately preceding fiscal year of the licensee in all trust accounts on which signing authority has been delegated to the person.

5.   The data entered into the electronic transfer system describing the details of the electronic transfer of funds must be as specified in the electronic trust transfer requisition.

Additional requirements relating to confirmation

(4)   Not later than 5 p.m. on the day immediately after the day on which the electronic transfer of funds is carried out, the licensee shall,

(a)   produce a printed copy of the confirmation required by paragraph 2 of subsection (3);

(b)   compare the printed copy of the confirmation and the signed electronic trust transfer requisition relating to the transfer to verify whether the money was drawn from the trust account as specified in the signed requisition;

(c)   indicate on the printed copy of the confirmation the name of the client, the subject matter of the file and any file number in respect of which money was drawn from the trust account; and

(d)   after complying with clauses (a) to (c), sign and date the printed copy of the confirmation.

Same

(5)   In exceptional circumstances, the tasks required by subsection (4) may be performed by a person other than the licensee, if the person has signing authority on the trust account from which the money will be drawn and is bonded in an amount at least equal to the maximum balance on deposit during the immediately preceding fiscal year of the licensee in all trust accounts on which signing authority has been delegated to the person.

Electronic trust transfer requisition: closing funds

(6)   The electronic trust transfer requisition required under paragraph 4 of subsection (3) shall be in Form 9C.

Requirement to maintain sufficient balance in trust account

14.   Despite any other provision in this Part, a licensee shall at all times maintain sufficient balances on deposit in his or her trust accounts to meet all his or her obligations with respect to money held in trust for clients.

AUTOMATIC WITHDRAWALS FROM TRUST ACCOUNTS

Authorizing Teranet to withdraw money from trust account

15.   (1)   Subject to subsection (2), a licensee may authorize Teranet to withdraw from a trust account described in subsection 16(1) money required to pay the document registration fees and the land transfer tax, if any, related to a client's real estate transaction.

Conditions

(2)   A licensee shall not authorize Teranet to withdraw from a trust account described in subsection 16(1) money required to pay the document registration fees and the land transfer tax, if any, related to a client's real estate transaction unless Teranet agrees to provide to the licensee in accordance with subsection (3) a confirmation of the withdrawal that contains the information mentioned in subsection (4).

Time of receipt of confirmation

(3)   The confirmation required under subsection (2) must be received by the licensee not later than 5 p.m. on the day immediately after the day on which the withdrawal is authorized by the licensee.

Contents of confirmation

(4)   The confirmation required under subsection (2) must contain,

(a)   the amount of money withdrawn from the trust account;

(b)   the time and date that the authorization to withdraw money is received by Teranet; and

(c)   the time and date that the confirmation from Teranet is sent to the licensee.

Written record of authorization

(5)   A licensee who authorizes Teranet to withdraw from a trust account described in subsection 16(1) money required to pay the document registration fees and the land transfer tax, if any, related to a client's real estate transaction shall record the authorization in writing.

Same

(6)   The written record of the authorization required under subsection (5) shall be in Form 9B and shall be completed by the licensee before he or she authorizes Teranet to withdraw from a trust account described in subsection 16(1) money required to pay the document registration fees and the land transfer tax, if any, related to a client's real estate transaction.

Additional requirements relating to confirmation

(7)   Not later than 5 p.m. on the day immediately after the day on which the confirmation required under subsection (2) is sent to a licensee, the licensee shall,

(a)   produce a paper copy of the confirmation, if the confirmation is sent to the licensee by electronic means;

(b)   compare the paper copy of the confirmation and the written record of the authorization relating to the withdrawal to verify whether money was withdrawn from the trust account by Teranet as authorized by the licensee;

(c)   indicate on the paper copy of the confirmation the name of the client and any file number in respect of which money was withdrawn from the trust account, if the confirmation does not already contain such information; and

(d)   after complying with clauses (a) to (c), sign and date the paper copy of the confirmation.

Special trust account

16.   (1)   The trust account from which Teranet may be authorized by a licensee to withdraw money shall be,

(a)   an account at a chartered bank, provincial savings office, credit union or league to which the *Credit Unions and Caisses Populaires Act, 1994* applies or a registered trust corporation kept in the name of the licensee or in the name of the firm of licensees of which the licensee is a partner, through which the licensee practises law or by which the licensee is employed, and designated as a trust account; and

(b)   an account into which a licensee shall pay only,

(i)   money received in trust for a client for the purposes of paying the document registration fees and the land transfer tax, if any, related to the client's real estate transaction; and

(ii)   money properly withdrawn from another trust account for the purposes of paying the document registration fees and the land transfer tax, if any, related to the client's real estate transaction.

One or more special trust accounts

(2)   A licensee may keep one or more trust accounts of the kind described in subsection (1).

Payment of money into special trust account

(3)   A licensee shall not pay into a trust account described in subsection (1) more money than is required to pay the document registration fees and the land transfer tax, if any, related to a client's real estate transaction, and if more money is, through inadvertence, paid into the trust account, the licensee shall transfer from the trust account described in subsection (1) into another trust account that is not a trust account described in subsection (1) the excess money.

Time limit on holding money in special trust account

(4)   A licensee who pays money into a trust account described in subsection (1) shall not keep the money in that account for more than five days, and if the money is not properly withdrawn from that account by Teranet within five days after the day on which it is paid into that account, the licensee shall transfer the money from that account into another trust account that is not a trust account described in subsection (1).

Interpretation: counting days

(5)   In subsection 16(4), holidays shall not be counted in determining if money has been kept in a trust account described in subsection 16(1) for more than five days.

Application of ss. 9, 11, 12 and 14

17.   Sections 9, 11, 12 and 14 apply, with necessary modifications, to a trust account described in subsection 16(1).

PART V
RECORD KEEPING REQUIREMENTS

REQUIREMENTS

Requirement to maintain financial records

18.   Every licensee shall maintain financial records to record all money and other property received and disbursed in connection with the licensee's professional business, and, as a minimum requirement, every licensee shall maintain, in accordance with sections 21, 22 and 23, the following records:

1.   A book of original entry identifying each date on which money is received in trust for a client, the method by which money is received, the person from whom money is received, the amount of money received, the purpose for which money is received and the client for whom money is received in trust.

2.   A book of original entry showing all disbursements out of money held in trust for a client and identifying each date on which money is disbursed, the method by which money is disbursed, including the number or a similar identifier of any document used to disburse money, the person to whom money is disbursed, the amount of money which is disbursed, the purpose for which money is disbursed and the client on whose behalf money is disbursed.

3.   A clients' trust ledger showing separately for each client for whom money is received in trust all money received and disbursed and any unexpended balance.

4. A record showing all transfers of money between clients' trust ledger accounts and explaining the purpose for which each transfer is made.

5. A book of original entry showing all money received, other than money received in trust for a client, and identifying each date on which money is received, the method by which money is received, the amount of money which is received and the person from whom money is received.

6. A book of original entry showing all disbursements of money, other than money held in trust for a client, and identifying each date on which money is disbursed, the method by which money is disbursed, including the number or a similar identifier of any document used to disburse money, the amount of money which is disbursed and the person to whom money is disbursed.

7. A fees book or a chronological file of copies of billings, showing all fees charged and other billings made to clients and the dates on which fees are charged and other billings are made to clients and identifying the clients charged and billed.

8. A record showing a comparison made monthly of the total of balances held in the trust account or accounts and the total of all unexpended balances of funds held in trust for clients as they appear from the financial records together with the reasons for any differences between the totals, and the following records to support the monthly comparisons:

    i.   A detailed listing made monthly showing the amount of money held in trust for each client and identifying each client for whom money is held in trust.

    ii. A detailed reconciliation made monthly of each trust bank account.

9. A record showing all property, other than money, held in trust for clients, and describing each property and identifying the date on which the licensee took possession of each property, the person who had possession of each property immediately before the licensee took possession of the property, the value of each property, the client for whom each property is held in trust, the date on which possession of each property is given away and the person to whom possession of each property is given.

10. Bank statements or pass books, cashed cheques and detailed duplicate deposit slips for all trust and general accounts.

11. Signed electronic trust transfer requisitions and signed printed confirmations of electronic transfers of trust funds.

12. Signed authorizations of withdrawals by Teranet and signed paper copies of confirmations of withdrawals by Teranet.

Record keeping requirements if cash received

19. (1) Every licensee who receives cash shall maintain financial records in addition to those required under section 18 and, as a minimum additional requirement, shall maintain, in accordance with sections 21, 22 and 23, a book of duplicate receipts, with each receipt identifying the date on which cash is received, the person from whom cash is received, the amount of cash received, the client for whom cash is received and any file number in respect of which cash is received and containing the signature of the licensee or the person authorized by the licensee to receive cash and of the person from whom cash is received.

No breach

(2)   A licensee does not breach subsection (1) if a receipt does not contain the signature of the person from whom cash is received provided that the licensee has made reasonable efforts to obtain the signature of the person from whom cash is received.

Record keeping requirements if mortgages and other charges held in trust for clients

20.   Every licensee who holds in trust mortgages or other charges on real property, either directly or indirectly through a related person or corporation, shall maintain financial records in addition to those required under section 18 and, as a minimum additional requirement, shall maintain, in accordance with sections 21, 22 and 23, the following records:

    1.   A mortgage asset ledger showing separately for each mortgage or charge,

        i.   all funds received and disbursed on account of the mortgage or charge,

        ii.   the balance of the principal amount outstanding for each mortgage or charge,

        iii.   an abbreviated legal description or the municipal address of the real property, and

        iv.   the particulars of registration of the mortgage or charge.

    2.   A mortgage liability ledger showing separately for each person on whose behalf a mortgage or charge is held in trust,

        i.   all funds received and disbursed on account of each mortgage or charge held in trust for the person,

        ii.   the balance of the principal amount invested in each mortgage or charge,

        iii.   an abbreviated legal description or the municipal address for each mortgaged or charged real property, and

        iv.   the particulars of registration of each mortgage or charge.

    3.   A record showing a comparison made monthly of the total of the principal balances outstanding on the mortgages or charges held in trust and the total of all principal balances held on behalf of the investors as they appear from the financial records together with the reasons for any differences between the totals, and the following records to support the monthly comparison:

        i.   A detailed listing made monthly identifying each mortgage or charge and showing for each the balance of the principal amount outstanding.

        ii.   A detailed listing made monthly identifying each investor and showing the balance of the principal invested in each mortgage or charge.

Financial records to be permanent

21.   (1)   The financial records required to be maintained under sections 18, 19 and 20 may be entered and posted by hand or by mechanical or electronic means, but if the records are entered and posted by hand, they shall be entered and posted in ink.

Paper copies of financial records

(2)   If a financial record is entered and posted by mechanical or electronic means, a licensee shall ensure that a paper copy of the record may be produced promptly on the Society's request.

Financial records to be current

22.   (1)   Subject to subsection (2), the financial records required to be maintained under sections 18, 19 and 20 shall be entered and posted so as to be current at all times.

Exceptions

(2)   The record required under paragraph 8 of section 18 and the record required under paragraph 3 of section 20 shall be created within twenty-five days after the last day of the month in respect of which the record is being created.

Preservation of financial records required under ss. 18 and 19

23.   (1)   Subject to subsection (2), a licensee shall keep the financial records required to be maintained under sections 18 and 19 for at least the six year period immediately preceding the licensee's most recent fiscal year end.

Same

(2)   A licensee shall keep the financial records required to be maintained under paragraphs 1, 2, 3, 8, 9, 10 and 11 of section 18 for at least the ten year period immediately preceding the licensee's most recent fiscal year end.

Preservation of financial records required under s. 20

(3)   A licensee shall keep the financial records required to be maintained under section 20 for at least the ten year period immediately preceding the licensee's most recent fiscal year end.

Record keeping requirements when acting for lender

24.   (1)   Every licensee who acts for or receives money from a lender shall, in addition to maintaining the financial records required under sections 18 and 20, maintain a file for each charge, containing,

(a)   a completed investment authority, signed by each lender before the first advance of money to or on behalf of the borrower;

(b)   a copy of a completed report on the investment;

(c)   if the charge is not held in the name of all the lenders, an original declaration of trust;

(d)   a copy of the registered charge; and

(e)   any supporting documents supplied by the lender.

Exceptions

(2)   Clauses (1)(a) and (b) do not apply with respect to a lender if,

(a)   the lender,

    (i)   is a bank listed in Schedule I or II to the *Bank Act* (Canada), a licensed insurer, a registered loan or trust corporation, a subsidiary of any of them, a pension fund, or any other entity that lends money in the ordinary course of its business,

    (ii)   has entered a loan agreement with the borrower and has signed a written commitment setting out the terms of the prospective charge, and

    (iii)   has given the licensee a copy of the written commitment before the advance of money to or on behalf of the borrower;

(b)   the lender and borrower are not at arm's length;

(c)   the borrower is an employee of the lender or of a corporate entity related to the lender;

(d)   the lender has executed the Investor/Lender Disclosure Statement for Brokered Transactions, approved by the Superintendent under subsection 54(1) of the *Mortgage Brokerages, Lenders and Administrators Act, 2006*, and has given the licensee written instructions, relating to the particular transaction, to accept the executed disclosure statement as proof of the loan agreement;

(e)   the total amount advanced by the lender does not exceed $6,000; or

(f)   the lender is selling real property to the borrower and the charge represents part of the purchase price.

Requirement to provide documents to lender

(3)   Forthwith after the first advance of money to or on behalf of the borrower, the licensee shall deliver to each lender,

(a)   if clause (1)(b) applies, an original of the report referred to therein; and

(b)   if clause (1)(c) applies, a copy of the declaration of trust.

Requirement to add to file maintained under subs. (1)

(4)   Each time the licensee or any licensee of the same firm of licensees does an act described in subsection (5), the licensee shall add to the file maintained for the charge the investment authority referred to in clause (1)(a), completed anew and signed by each lender before the act is done, and a copy of the report on the investment referred to in clause (1)(b), also completed anew.

Application of subs. (4)

(5)   Subsection (4) applies in respect of the following acts:

1.   Making a change in the priority of the charge that results in a reduction of the amount of security available to it.

2.   Making a change to another charge of higher priority that results in a reduction of the amount of security available to the lender's charge.

3.   Releasing collateral or other security held for the loan.

4.   Releasing a person who is liable under a covenant with respect to an obligation in connection with the loan.

New requirement to provide documents to lender

(6)   Forthwith after completing anew the report on the investment under subsection (4), the licensee shall deliver an original of it to each lender.

Requirement to add to file maintained under subs. (1): substitution

(7)   Each time the licensee or any other licensee of the same firm of licensees substitutes for the charge another security or a financial instrument that is an acknowledgment of indebtedness, the licensee shall add to the file maintained for the charge the lender's written consent to the substitution, obtained before the substitution is made.

Exceptions

(8)   The licensee need not comply with subsection (4) or (7) with respect to a lender if clause (2)(a), (b), (c), (e) or (f) applied to the lender in the original loan transaction.

Investment authority: Form 9D

(9)   The investment authority required under clause (1)(a) shall be in Form 9D.

Report on investment: Form 9E

(10)   Subject to subsection (11), the report on the investment required under clause (1)(b) shall be in Form 9E.

Report on investment: alternative to Form 9E

(11)   The report on the investment required under clause (1)(b) may be contained in a reporting letter addressed to the lender or lenders which answers every question on Form 9E.

GLOSSARY

accountant professional who maintains, inspects, or interprets financial accounts. The accountant prepares the various reporting and financial statements required for the business.

accounting cycle process of recording the accounting events of a company. The cycle begins when a transaction occurs and ends with its inclusion in the financial statements. The eight steps of the accounting cycle are: (1) journalize the transaction; (2) post entries; (3) prepare the trial balance; (4) prepare the worksheet; (5) prepare the adjusted trial balance; (6) prepare the financial statements; (7) prepare the closing entries; and (8) calculate the post-closing trial balance. See Figure 3.1.

accounting equation an equation based on the balance sheet accounts (assets, liabilities, and owner's equity) in which the left-hand side of the balance sheet must equal the right-hand side (debits = credits), as follows:

$$\text{Assets} \ = \ \text{Liabilities} \ + \ \text{Owner's Equity}$$

accounting period any monthly, quarterly, or annual period that marks the beginning and end of financial reporting.

accounting standards a set of principles that govern the reporting of financial information in a consistent, ethical, and accurate manner. Accounting standards vary by jurisdiction, but in an increasingly global economy, they are becoming more and more uniform in their application. In Canada, accounting standards include generally accepted accounting principles (GAAP); International Financial Reporting Standards (IFRS); accounting standards for private enterprises (ASPE); accounting standards for public sector entities (PSAS); and accounting standards for not-for-profits (NFPO).

accounting standards for private enterprises (ASPE) *See* **accounting standards**.

accrual basis of accounting the principle that revenue is recorded when it is earned regardless of whether or not payment has been received, and expenses are recorded when incurred. This is the approach used by paralegals as required under the *Income Tax Act*; compare *cash basis of accounting*.

accrued interest expense   interest expense on a loan or other debt that has not yet been paid.

accrued interest revenue   interest revenue earned because of an outstanding debt owed to the business owner by way of an accounts receivable.

accrued revenues   revenues that are earned in a period but not yet billed or paid.

accrued salaries expense   salary expenses that occur after the pay period end but before the end of the reporting period.

accumulated depreciation   the total amount that has been written off as an expense against a particular asset over time. Depreciation is calculated in the contra-asset account.

adjusted trial balance   the balance that shows the updated income statement and balance sheet entries on the worksheet.

adjusting entries   updates to accounts made as a result of changes to the account balance from the last reporting period. For example, when payment is made on accrued expense or revenue accounts, an adjustment is made to reflect the change to the balance sheet account, the income statement account, or both. However, the cash or bank account would not be adjusted; instead, the appropriate account would be adjusted on the opposite balance of that account. Typical adjustments are prepaid accounts and depreciation.

adjustment   a change made to the journal entries and general ledger at the end of an accounting period after the initial trial balance is prepared. Often, these adjustments have been accruing over the accounting period because it is more efficient to recognize the change at the end of the period.

amortization   the calculation of the decline in value of an asset from its original value to its residual or remaining value.

assets   all the cash, property, and other valuable items that a business or a person owns or is entitled to.

bad debt   money owed to a company that has not been successfully collected. Also known as a write-off because it is "written off" as a loss.

balance sheet   a financial statement showing the assets, liabilities, and capital of a business at a particular date.

balance sheet account   one of two types of general ledger accounts. (Income statement accounts are the other type.) Balance sheet accounts are used to sort and store transactions involving assets, liabilities, and owner's equity.

barter transaction   an exchange of goods or services that does not involve money. The goods or services received could be considered proceeds from a business operation and must be included in income. Barter transactions may also have GST/HST implications.

billable rate   the rate at which a professional charges a client; for paralegals, this is typically based on the amount of time spent working on a file at an hourly rate (e.g., $80/h). The time billed must be time spent working on the file to move the matter forward, providing legal advice, researching, drafting, and conducting meetings with clients and third parties (including telephone calls). If the hourly billable rate changes during the retainer, the client must be notified or a new retainer agreement should be negotiated.

billable work   work performed on a file that will be billed to a client, such as court attendances, legal document preparation, correspondence, and telephone calls.

book value   the historical cost of an asset minus accumulated depreciation.

bookkeeper   person who records the day-to-day transactions of the accounting process. A bookkeeper is not an accountant, but an accountant may perform some of the tasks associated with bookkeeping. Having a bookkeeper enter and track data is typically more cost-effective than having an accountant do so.

bookkeeping   the system and tools used to analyze and record the day-to-day and cyclical financial transactions specific to a business.

business expenses   costs that are considered reasonable for a particular type of business and that are incurred for the purpose of earning income; also known as operating expenses. Business expenses can be deducted for tax purposes. Non-business-related expenses, which are either personal in nature or not related to earning business income, are not tax-deductible.

business number (BN)   a number that identifies a business to the government for all business purposes, including remittances of GST/HST, corporate income tax, and payroll.

capital account   the investment by the owner in a business. Capital is not always cash; it can be assets that the owner chooses to invest in the company. The capital account includes the owner's beginning investment plus or minus the profits or losses earned by the firm.

capital cost allowance (CCA)   the means by which Canadian businesses may claim depreciation expense for calculating taxable income under the *Income Tax Act*.

cash basis of accounting   the principle that recognizes revenue only when the revenue is actually received and expenses only when payment has actually been made; compare *accrual basis of accounting*.

cash controls   internal systems to protect against the loss, misuse, or fraud of cash, including cash payment and receipt systems. Petty cash is an example of a cash payment and receipt system that has rules and procedures to safeguard against internal abuse.

cash receipts   a book of duplicate receipts maintained as proof of financial transactions; a requirement for paralegals in accordance with bylaw 9, part V, section 19(1) of the Law Society of Upper Canada. Cash receipts in this context should not be confused with the cash received and documented on a general receipts journal, which is a special journal.

cash short and over   cash short is an income statement account that records shortages and overages in petty cash on hand and petty cash disbursements. When cash is short, debit this account to show the increase in expenses as a result of the shortage. When cash is over, credit this account to show the increase in income as a result of the overage. *Example:*

20**		Dr.	Cr.
Jan. 1	Expense Accounts	X	
Jan. 31	Cash Short and Over	X (short)	X (over)
Jan. 31	General Bank Account		X
	To replenish the petty cash fund ($100 limit)		

chart of accounts   a customized, detailed chart that creates a unique identification number for each business account, typically used in a firm's operation over the accounting cycle. This helps to reduce the number of entries and posting descriptions. New accounts can be added to the chart, but the chart should be ordered in a logical sequence similar to the balance sheet, the statement of owner's equity, and the income statement.

class   assets included in a particular account. For example, the account for office furniture will include desks, chairs, and other types of furniture.

client cost recovery journal   journal in which are entered expenses on behalf of clients that are recoverable from them. Such costs are typically recorded as a disbursements recoverable journal entry and are included as disbursements on the client invoice and in the fees book. Also, funds can be transferred from the trust account provided that the expense has been incurred and the client agrees to the expense (by way of the client's written authorization or a written retainer agreement).

client general ledger. *See* **client ledgers**.

client ledgers   the records of a firm's ongoing transactions, organized by client matter or file number, in respect of all receipts and disbursements made on behalf of or in regard to the firm's clients. The *client trust ledger* records payments taken by the firm for invoices sent to the client; disbursements paid from the trust account on behalf of the client; and the balance remaining in trust. The *client general ledger* records fees and disbursements received from the client; balance owing; and disbursements paid by the firm on behalf of the client when no trust funds are available. This ledger is especially useful if you need to report to a client the amounts that have been received by the firm as payments and those that remain outstanding in respect of funds that are not held in trust.

client matter   the descriptor for each client file, indicating the area of law and the particulars of the subject matter. *Example:* Client—Ann Smith, Matter re Small Claims (Smith ats Brown) File No. 101-0001.

client number   identifies the client by assigning a unique number associated with the client's name and contact information. *Example:* Client number 101 (Ann Smith, 123 Avenue Road, Toronto, ON).

client trust ledger. *See* **client ledgers**.

close the books   to "zero out" the income, expense, and withdrawal accounts by transferring the net amounts to the capital account and starting these accounts at a $0 balance in the new accounting period. *See* **closing entries**.

closing balance   the total balance for each account at the end of an accounting period, which becomes the opening balance for the next period.

closing entries   journal entries that record temporary account balances at the end of a reporting period (revenue, expenses, withdrawals, and income summary accounts) and the transfer of such balances to the capital account.

compound entry   a situation in which there are more than two entries for each transaction, such as when there are two debit entries and only one credit entry, or vice versa.

conflict of interest   an interest, financial or otherwise, that might adversely affect a licensee's judgment or loyalty with regard to a client or prospective client, or that would cause a licensee to prefer a third party's interests over those of a client or prospective client. (See rule 1.02 of the *Paralegal Rules of Conduct* of the Law Society of Upper Canada.)

conflict search   a search of a firm's client database or manual list that checks all of the firm's current and former clients, files, and vendors against related or opposing parties and former clients of former firm affiliations to determine whether there are any previous contacts with a potential client or file that could lead to a conflict of interest.

contra-asset account   an account linked to a long-term asset account that tracks and records the decrease in value of the asset without affecting its original value. It is called "contra" because although it is shown on the balance sheet as an asset account, and it represents an "opposite" normal balance for an asset account.

credit (Cr.)   an account entry that is found on the right side of a financial statement, journal, or ledger.

current assets   cash, or assets that will be converted into cash within one year. *Examples:* cash in bank accounts, accounts receivable, prepaid insurance.

DEAD CLIC   a memory device for determining which accounts show a normal debit balance and which have a normal credit balance—that is, **D**ebit **E**xpenses **A**ssets **D**rawings; **C**redit **L**iabilities **I**ncome **C**apital.

debit (Dr.)   an account entry that is found on the left side of a financial statement, journal, or ledger.

deposit in transit   a deposit made by the firm but not reflected on the bank statement by the statement cut-off date. To balance the internal records with the bank statement, this deposit amount (typically an outstanding cheque) would have to be added to the bank balance on the bank reconciliation statement.

depreciation   the calculation of the cost or expense of a long-term asset (such as property, plant, equipment, or intangibles) over the course of its useful life, representing the asset's decline in value.

dormant account   funds remaining in trust that are unclaimed by a client for more than two years. When this occurs, the paralegal can apply to the Law Society of Upper Canada for permission to transfer such funds to the LSUC. (See section 59.6 of the *Law Society Act* and bylaw 10.)

double-entry bookkeeping   an essential component of the accounting system, requiring that there be a check and balance of debits and credits. Every transaction must have at least two entries—a debit entry and a credit entry.

drawee   the financial institution on which a cheque is drawn.

drawer   the person who writes a cheque.

endorsement   the signing or stamping of a cheque by the payee (the person to whom a cheque is made payable), thereby transferring the rights of the cheque to the payee from the payor. See Figure 9.6.

expanded accounting equation   an equation that correlates the balance sheet assets with the income statement accounts (income and expenses) and the statement of owner's equity (increases and decreases to the capital account), as follows:

$$\text{Assets} = \text{Liabilities} + \text{Capital} - \text{Withdrawals} + (\text{Income} - \text{Expenses})$$

See Figure 2.3.

expense   day-to-day, regularly occurring costs, charges, and items that are consumed or used up; the costs of doing business.

expense account   all the expense accounts on the income statement that have a normal debit balance.

expense recovery   reimbursement for expenses incurred on behalf of clients in furtherance of their legal matters. Such expenses (e.g., photocopy, printing, faxing, courier, and court filing costs) should be described and disclosed in a retainer agreement. Some expenses are not subject to GST/HST and some have tax already included. Paralegals should be sure to apply HST only where required.

external users   stakeholders that are interested in a firm's financial accounting.

fees book   the record of a firm's billings for all clients, including fees for legal services, disbursements, and GST/HST.

fees journal   *See* **fees book**.

financial statements   a point-in-time reporting of the financial position of a business for each accounting period (monthly, quarterly, or annually), including the income statement, the statement of owner's equity, and the balance sheet.

fiscal period   the accounting period over which a firm reports its business or professional income.

fiscal year   any 12-month period selected by a firm to mark the beginning and the end of its financial reporting and tax reporting year (e.g., January 1 – December 31). For a sole proprietorship or partnership, the fiscal period is based on the calendar year; for a corporation, it may be any 12-month period (that coincides with the cycle of its business operation). The firm usually establishes its fiscal period when it files its first income tax return or when it registers a business account with the Canada Revenue Agency.

fixed or capital assets   assets that have a long life. They may be purchased with cash or on credit. *Examples:* land, buildings, equipment, vehicles.

flat rate   a charge that is the same in all cases. Paralegals can bill on a flat-fee basis when the time that will be required is easy to estimate (such as traffic court fines and certain routine or easy-to-resolve matters). The flat rate is established at the discretion of the paralegal but should reflect the industry standard in order to be competitive.

general bank account   a business bank account used by a firm for general business purposes, including depositing receipts and paying bills.

general disbursements journal   a record of payments from the general bank account by the firm to a third party. Such expenses may be incurred by the paralegal for the legal services practice or on behalf of a client, or for any other payment made by the firm to another party.

general journal   a record that tracks the day-to-day financial transactions of a firm chronologically, without any special categorization of the accounts.

general ledger   a record that posts journal entries by category in the order shown on the chart of accounts. The general ledger provides an ending balance after calculating the debits and credits for each account; this ending balance is used to prepare the trial balance.

general monetary retainer   an amount paid to a lawyer by a client to secure the availability of the lawyer for a specific period of time. The legal professional who receives a "general retainer" is not required to account for or to provide services. However, section 8(2)(2) of bylaw 9 must be reviewed with caution in order to ensure that the conditions required by the Law Society of Upper Canada are satisfied.

general receipts journal   a record of payments received into a firm's general bank account. These may include amounts received from the paralegal, a third party, or a client.

generally accepted accounting principles (GAAP)   the common set of accounting principles and procedures that companies use to compile their financial statements. GAAP is a combination of authoritative standards set by policy boards and the commonly accepted ways of recording and reporting accounting information.

government users   government users are interested in tax accounting, and businesses are required to submit income tax returns annually.

gross pay   the total amount of salary received before taxes or other deductions (such as health insurance) are deducted from it.

GST/HST   a tax that is added to most goods and services purchased in Canada. Each province has its own rate of tax. The HST (harmonized sales tax) is used in provinces where both the federal GST (goods and services tax) and the PST (provincial sales tax) have been combined into a single value-added sales tax. In Ontario, the HST is 13 percent.

historical cost   the original price paid for an item.

income   the amount received by a firm in the sale of its goods or services. Income is reported for income tax purposes and will also be used to determine the amount of deductions or credits that apply to the business or the individual; income is sometimes referred to as "revenue."

income statement   a financial statement showing the revenues and expenses for a particular accounting period; a temporary record that starts at a "zero" balance each new accounting period.

income statement account   one of two types of general ledger accounts. (Balance sheet accounts are the other type.) Income statement accounts are used to sort and store transactions involving revenues, expenses, gains, and losses. Debit all credit balances on the income account (i.e., bringing the balance to $0) and credit it to the income summary account.

income summary account   a transitional account into which all income statement revenue and expense accounts are transferred at the end of an accounting period. The net amount transferred into the income summary account equals the net profit (a credit balance) or loss (a debit balance) that the business incurred during the period. The income summary is a temporary record that must be closed (i.e., bringing the balance to $0).

income tax   a federal program that provides the government with revenue collected from all residents who are required to pay income tax. Income tax revenues are used for various programs and initiatives of the federal government. The Department of Finance sets the prescribed basic income tax rates, which vary progressively with the amount of taxable income. There are rates of tax at both the federal and the provincial levels.

information return   a form filed by employers, trusts, and businesses to report to the Canada Revenue Agency about their income, source deductions, credits, and other relevant information. Each form has a number identifying its purpose. *Example:* Employers prepare a T4 slip for each employee, who in turn files it with his or her personal income tax form.

input tax credit (ITC)   the amount that GST/HST registrants can recover for GST/HST paid (or payable) or owed on their purchases and expenses related to their business activities.

internal controls   internal checks and balances used to create efficiency, to protect and safeguard the assets of the business, and to prevent fraud and theft. Such controls are customized for each business and process but typically follow industry standards and best practices. *Example:* having at least two signatories on any negotiable instrument, such as a cheque.

internal users   a company's own stakeholders who are interested in accounting for purposes of making management decisions, such as those related to profitability or expansion.

International Financial Reporting Standards (IFRS)   a set of international accounting rules imposed on publicly accountable enterprises—for example, corporations whose shares are listed on a stock exchange, banks, etc.

journal entries   a means of tracking and chronologically recording the day-to-day financial transactions of a firm, without any special categorization of the accounts. Journals document the source of the transaction and are called books of original entry. Where there is a need to specify and categorize a journal by account, this is known as a special journal.

Law Foundation of Ontario   a non-profit organization, created by statute in 1974, governed by a five-person volunteer board of trustees and supported by a staff team, which funds legal programs and initiatives geared toward improving access to justice. The interest collected from the mixed trust accounts of licensees is used to fund many of these initiatives.

legal accounting software   special software designed for general business and trust accounting. It provides automatic calculations, posts automatically to ledgers, and produces financial and other reports.

liabilities   all the legal debts and obligations that a firm or a person owes to its creditors or customers.

licensee   paralegals and lawyers who are licensed to practise by the Law Society of Upper Canada (LSUC).

limited liability partnership   a form of partnership established by professionals who are self-governed (e.g., doctors, lawyers, accountants, dentists). An LLP is not a corporation, but liability can be minimized through professional and other general liability insurance.

loss   the situation in which expenses exceed income.

matching principle   a basic underlying guideline in accounting that directs a firm to report an expense on its income statement in the same period as the related revenues.

mixed or pooled trust bank account   an account that holds funds for the benefit of more than one client and may be disbursed only by the rendering of an account for services or upon the authorization and direction of the client. The funds belong to the client and can be refunded or recovered by the client in the event of termination of the file or services, or where there are unused funds. (See bylaw 9, section 7.)

monetary retainer   an advance payment made by a client, held in trust by a lawyer or paralegal for future services. In contrast, where services have already been rendered or billed, or disbursements already incurred on behalf of a client, the payment is not deposited in trust but is instead deposited into the general bank account. (See bylaw 9, sections 7 and 8.) Monetary retainers are sometimes referred to as "unearned revenue" or "prepaid services."

multi-discipline practice (MDP) or affiliation   an arrangement among licensed legal professionals and non-licensed professionals who seek to work together through an association or partnership. MDPs are usually considered where the licensee and the non-licensee have overlapping practices or disciplines or where there is the prospect of mutual referrals. An "affiliation" is a more loosely held form of organization and may involve a larger group of professionals seeking to maximize marketing and professional support. (See bylaw 7, part III.)

net income   as reported on the income statement, the situation in which income exceeds expenses, which will cause an increase in a company's equity.

net loss   as reported on the income statement, the situation in which expenses exceed income, which will cause a decrease in a company's equity.

non-billable work   work performed in relation to a file that is not billed to the client, such as a free consultation.

normal balance   the debit or credit sides of a financial statement, journal, or ledger where increases are recorded. Some accounts (such as assets) have a normal debit balance, so an entry on the debit side increases the balance in the account. Other accounts (such as liabilities) have a normal credit balance, so an entry on the credit side increases the balance in the account.

normal credit balance. *See* **normal balance**.

normal debit balance. *See* **normal balance**.

NSF cheque   a cheque that is cashed by the payee where there are insufficient funds in the payor's account to cover it. An NSF cheque is returned with a service charge. In preparing the bank reconciliation statement, the payor would credit (subtract from) the internal records the amount of the NSF cheque and the amount of the related service charge.

office supplies inventory   an asset account that reflects the value of the supplies that the firm has on hand; as office supplies are used up or consumed, this is recognized as an office supplies expense.

opening balance   the total balance for each account at the beginning of the accounting period. The total is taken from the ending or closing balance of that account from the last period.

outstanding cheque   a cheque issued by the payor that has not been cashed by the payee and therefore appears on the payor's internal records but not on the bank statement. To prepare the bank reconciliation, the payor would credit (subtract from) the bank balance the amount of the outstanding cheque (as if the transaction had been completed and the cheque paid from the payor's bank account).

owner's equity   the value of assets remaining after all liabilities have been deducted; this residual value is what is received by the owner or shared by the shareholders or partners. Also called capital.

partnership   a firm managed by two or more persons who share in the profit, loss, and risk of the business. At least one partner must be a general partner, whose duty it is to manage the business; the other partners may be passive investors or take a less active role. Liability is unlimited but shared. (See bylaw 7, part I.)

payee   a person to whom money, such as a cheque, is paid or is to be paid.

payor   a person who pays, especially in the case of a bill or cheque.

payroll deductions   source tax deductions, such as income tax deductions, Canada Pension Plan (CPP) contributions, and employment insurance (EI) premiums, that are deducted from an employee's income and sent regularly to the Canada Revenue Agency. Employers also contribute to some deductions and make their own CPP and EI contributions.

permanent accounts   balance sheet accounts; called "permanent" because their balances carry over from one fiscal period to the next.

personal deductions   income tax deductions that reduce tax for some taxpayers and promote certain activities considered to be beneficial, such as tuition fees and childcare expenses.

petty cash   cash on hand for a business to pay for "petty" or small expenditures such as postage, office supplies, parking, and other similar expenses. Petty cash is controlled internally by the establishment of a petty cash fund.

petty cash account   an asset account on the balance sheet, established by issuing a cheque to the custodian of the petty cash account. Each payment from the petty cash account is represented by a voucher. (See Figure 9.2.) When the petty cash account is reduced or has a zero balance, the petty cash fund is replenished to bring it back to the petty cash limit originally established, as follows:

20**		Dr.	Cr.
Jan. 1	Petty Cash	$100	
	General Bank Account		$100
	To establish (or increase) the petty cash fund ($100 limit)		

20**		Dr.	Cr.
Jan. 31	Expense Accounts (Postage, Office Supplies, Parking)	$72.50	
	General Bank Account		$72.50
	To replenish the petty cash fund ($100 limit)		

post, posting   the process of transferring information from a journal to a ledger.

post-closing trial balance   the listing of the balance sheet accounts (assets, liabilities, and owner's equity) after all adjustment and closing balances have been reduced to zero from the temporary accounts and have been transferred to update the capital account (owner's equity).

post reference (PR)   the numerical identifier for each account referenced on a chart of accounts. The PR makes it easy to cross-reference and identify journal entries.

prepaid expenses   expenses for a good or service that are paid in advance of the payment due date or before the use or consumption of the good or service. *Examples:* prepaid rent, prepaid insurance.

professional corporation   lawyers or licensed paralegals who carry on the practice of law or the provision of legal services through an incorporated entity. (See bylaw 7, part II.)

profit   the situation in which income exceeds expenses.

reconciliation   the comparison of transactions recorded in a firm's internal records (the general ledger or bank account ledger) against the transactions reported on the bank statement (e.g., deposits, cheques issued, interest, bank charges) and the preparation of a bank reconciliation statement to confirm that the ending balances for the internal records and the bank statement are balanced. If the records are not balanced, the bookkeeper/accountant will need to investigate possible errors either in the firm's internal records or on the bank's part. It is good practice to reconcile both the general bank account ledger, and the trust bank account ledger, against the general bank account and the trust bank account statements.

records   documents that must be maintained by businesses and individuals to verify the information that is filed with the Canada Revenue Agency, such as account books, sales and purchase invoices, contracts, bank statements, and cancelled cheques. You must keep records at your business or residence in Canada for at least six years from the end of the last tax year to which the records relate, and the CRA must have access to these records if requested.

residual value   the estimated value of the asset at the end of its useful life.

retainer   an agreement between a client and a legal services provider for the engagement of legal services, describing the scope of services to be provided, the billing rate, and the billing practices.

revenue recognition principle   a basic guideline in the accrual approach to accounting that requires revenues to be shown on the income statement in the period in which they are earned, not in the period when the cash is collected.

separate interest-bearing trust account   a bank account that is held for each individual client who requests it, and who has large sums of money that are to be held for an extended period of time. The licensee has a duty to account for the interest on the funds in the separate interest-bearing account; interest accrues to the client. (See paragraph 2(b), "Separate Interest Bearing Trust Account," in *The Bookkeeping Guide for Paralegals* of the Law Society of Upper Canada.)

service charges   fees charged by a bank to manage customers' bank accounts. These fees may be regular monthly charges or charges per transaction. Service fees are expenses on the income statement and reduce the cash account.

shareholder's equity   the equity account in an incorporated company.

signature card   a card signed by anyone opening an account at a financial institution. It is kept on file to confirm the person's identity.

slide   an error resulting from incorrect placement of a decimal point in writing numbers.

small supplier   a supplier whose annual revenues from taxable supplies (before expenses) from all businesses total $30,000 or less. Once annual revenues exceed $30,000, the business must be registered and must start collecting GST/HST.

sole proprietorship   a business managed by a sole owner and operator, in his or her own name or under another, as authorized by a business name licence; liability is unlimited.

special journal   a specific journal, used instead of the general journal, to identify specific transactions by special categories. A general journal can be used but may not be helpful or efficient for reporting purposes. Special journals include trust receipts journals, general receipts journals, trust disbursements journals, general disbursements journals, and fees journals.

stakeholders   internal and external parties who rely on the information provided by a business in making decisions; these may include employees and customers.

statement of owner's equity   a financial statement used to calculate owner's equity in the firm after taking into account any profits or losses of the firm less money withdrawn by the owner; a permanent record that uses the ending balance of the last accounting period as the opening balance of the new period.

straight-line amortization method   a calculation of depreciation cost or expense at an equal amount over the life of the asset, so that the allocated monthly, quarterly, or annual costs are of equal value over time. *Example:* An asset with an original value of $3,000, a residual value of $500, and an estimated shelf life of 3 years would have an annual depreciation cost of $833 ($2,500/3 years). See Figure 7.4.

T-account   a tool used to show a particular account according to the debits and credits. *Example of a T-account for an asset account:*

Account Name

Debit	Credit
(+) increase	(−) decrease

tax year   the period for which income tax is to be paid, based on either the calendar year or the elected or designated fiscal period.

taxable benefits   benefits—such as money, or the value of goods or services—that an employer pays or provides to an employee in addition to salary or wages. *Examples:* employer contributions to a provincial health insurance plan, life insurance premiums, dental and medical benefits.

temporary accounts   income, expense, and withdrawal accounts; called "temporary" at year-end because a fresh start is needed each year.

time entry and billing   a method of tracking the time spent on billable client matters, whether manually or through the use of a computerized system. For each activity, the time and description are entered. *Best practice:* Enter the actual time (in hours and minutes, 00:00) for appointments, meetings, and telephone calls or matters where a significant amount of time is spent on an activity together with the calculated time in tenths of an hour. This approach avoids client complaints and disagreements about billing. Entering time on a daily basis, or as an activity is completed, is the best way to ensure accuracy.

transposition   the accidental reversal of digits in making a journal or ledger entry.

trial balance   A list of the closing balances of the general ledger accounts that are arranged according to the chart of account listings and categorized as either debits or credits. If the debit entries equal the credit entries, the trial balance is balanced.

trust bank account   a bank account in which a law professional (acting as an authorized custodian) holds money that belongs to clients, not to the firm. Trust funds are used for specific purposes—for example, to pay court filing fees on behalf of a client.

trust bank journal   a record of deposits to and withdrawals from a trust bank account, representing money belonging to clients and held in trust until services are rendered. Instead of using a general trust bank journal, a paralegal may wish to set up special journals for reporting purposes, called the trust receipts journal (records receipts into trust) and the trust disbursements journal (records disbursements from trust).

trust bank reconciliation   a comparison of the trust bank balance with the trust journal and trust listing balances. To obtain a reconciled balance, take the ending balance of the trust bank statement and subtract the amount of the outstanding cheques, then add any outstanding deposits.

trust comparison   a comparison of the reconciled trust bank balance with the client trust listing total. The two amounts should be equal.

trust control accounts   accounts that provide the total of the moneys received in trust from all clients and the total of moneys owed to clients. The balance sheet includes the trust bank account (e.g., funds received; an asset account) and trust funds owed (e.g., money owed to clients; a liability account). The totals in the two accounts should be equal.

undepreciated capital cost (UCC)   the balance of the capital cost left for further depreciation at any given time. The amount of CCA claimed each year will lower the UCC of the property.

valuable property record   a record of any property, other than cash, belonging to clients that is being held in trust or for safekeeping.

withdrawals   money taken out of the firm by the owner without regard to the sale of goods or services, thus reducing the equity value in the business. Money taken out of the business does not go back into the business but is used for the personal benefit of the owner. Shareholder withdrawals are known as *dividend payments*.

work in progress (WIP)   an account of work that has not been completed or services that have been performed in part but are still in progress and, therefore, not yet included as earned income or revenue. (1) The account WIP Accrued (an asset account) has a debit balance; WIP Professional Fees (an income account) has a credit balance. (2) When a bill is prepared, the journal entry would be: Accounts Receivable (Asset)—Dr.; Fees Earned—Cr. (3) In order to clear WIP Accrued (as a result of preparing an invoice and billing the client) for a particular period and bring it to $0 or to a value corresponding to the amount billed, the journal entry would be a reversing entry: WIP Professional Fees (Income)—Dr.; WIP Accrued (Asset)—Cr.:

Asset Accounts

WIP Accrued		Accounts Receivable	
500 (1)		500 (2)	
	500 (3)		
Balance 0			

Income Accounts

Fees Earned		WIP Professional Fees	
	500 (2)		500 (1)
		500 (3)	
			Balance 0

worksheet a form of internal reporting of the trial balance, specific adjustment entries, and adjusted trial balance showing the updated income statement and balance sheet entries. Additional columns can be used specifically for the income statement and the balance sheet. The worksheet is usually prepared in columns similar to a spreadsheet. *Example:*

Account Titles	Trial Balance		Adjustments			Adjusted Trial Balance		Income Statement		Balance Sheet	
	Dr.	Cr.	Dr.		Cr.	Dr.	Cr.	Dr.	Cr.	Dr.	Cr.
Office Supplies	50		35			85					
Trust Funds Owed		1,000			500		1,500				

INDEX

O

office expenses, 261
office supplies inventory, 157
opening balance, 23, 26, 66
operating expenses, *see* expenses
outstanding cheque, 225
owner's equity
    calculation of, 22
    defined, 21
    statement of
        defined, 76–77
        format, 95
        interpretation, 186
        preparation, 185–186

P

partnership, 3
payee, 224
payor, 224
payroll
    gross pay, 252–253
    overview, 252
    Payroll Deductions Online Calculator, 253–255
    T4 information return, 256
    taxable benefits, 256
    TD1 form, 253
    vacation pay/time, 255
payroll deductions, 253
permanent accounts, 189
personal deductions, 253
personal expenses, 257
petty cash, 220–223
petty cash voucher, 221
post-closing trial balance, 39, 193
post reference (PR), 54, 66
posting, 40, 67–71
prepaid expenses, 159, 257
professional corporation, 4
profit, 24
    see also net income

R

receipts, 44
reconciliation, 224
records, maintenance of, 249
    see also books and records
residual value, 159
retainer
    conflict of interest and, 273
    defined, 6
    general monetary retainer, 7
    monetary retainer, 7
revenue, *see* income
revenue recognition principle, 162

S

separate interest-bearing trust account, 9
service charges, 225
shareholder's equity, 21
signature card, 223
six-year requirement, 198, 256
slide, 73
small supplier, 10, 248
sole proprietorship, 3
special journals
    accounts receivable journal, 125
    client billing, and, 120–121
    defined, 108, 120
    expense recovery, 121–122
    fees book, 123–124
    general disbursements journal, 129–130
    general receipts journal, 127–129
    invoice payment, 124–125
    invoice preparation, 121
    posting from, 131, 134–140
    transactions
        analysis, 132–134
        recording, 126–131
    utility, 125
spot audits, 110
stakeholders, 18
statement of owner's equity, *see*
    owner's equity, statement of
straight-line amortization method, 160